What business leaders had to say about the original *Building Wealth*:

"*Building Wealth* is a commonsense, down-to-earth, no-nonsense guide to how anyone with real commitment can achieve financial independence." —Anthony Robbins, bestselling author of *Awaken the Giant Within* and *Unlimited Power*

"Russ Whitney is wealthy now, but he started with a lot less than the average person reading this book. He can—and will—show you how to create a fortune out of virtually nothing. In this fast-reading, easy-to-understand book, you'll learn a wealth-building system that you can start using tomorrow." —Jimmy Calano, CEO, CareerTrack

"No fluff—just the specifics and inspiration needed on every page to help anyone achieve financial independence. Besides, while reading an advance copy it gave me an idea which made me $15,000 (no joke, Russ)." —Verne C. Harnish, Founder, Young Entrepreneurs Organizations (YEO)

"*Building Wealth* is a real winner. I have read dozens of 'how to' books, and even coauthored one, but this is one of the few books that, within weeks of purchasing it, shows you how to put cash back in your pocket." —Kevin Harrington, coauthor, *The Best 100 Spare Time Business Opportunities Today*

"*Building Wealth* is great! Russ's principles for financial independence really excited me! This is not only interesting reading but valuable information to improve your life!"
—Art Williams, Founder, A. L. Williams Insurance Corporation

"Russ Whitney is a terrific writer and a captivating speaker, but best of all he has experienced wealth-building for himself. For aspiring entrepreneurs and anyone trying to maximize their personal profitability potential, Russ Whitney delivers the insights right here in *Building Wealth*." —Greg Renker, Television Producer and Cofounder, Guthy-Renker Corporation

BUILDING WEALTH

Achieving Personal and Financial Success
in Real Estate and Business Without
Money, Credit, or Luck

RUSS WHITNEY

A Fireside Book
Published by Simon & Schuster
New York   London   Toronto   Sydney

FIRESIDE
Rockefeller Center
1230 Avenue of the Americas
New York, NY 10020

This Fireside Edition 2006

FIRESIDE and colophon are registered trademarks
of Simon & Schuster, Inc.

For information regarding special discounts for bulk purchases,
please contact Simon & Schuster Special Sales at 1-800-456-6798
or business@simonandschuster.com.

Designed by William Ruoto

Manufactured in the United States of America

10   9   8   7   6   5   4   3

Library of Congress Cataloging-in-Publication Data

Whitney, Russ.
    Building wealth : achieving personal and financial success in real estate and
business without money, credit, or luck / Russ Whitney.
        p.   cm.
    "Second edition"—Introd.
    Includes index.
    1. Finance, Personal.   2. Investments.   3. Real estate investment.
I. Title.

HG179.W5254   2006
332.024'01—dc22   2006045046

ISBN-13: 978-0-671-86617-4
ISBN-10: 0-671-86617-6
ISBN-13: 978-0-7432-9161-3 (pbk.)
ISBN-10: 0-7432-9161-1 (pbk.)

CONTENTS

ACKNOWLEDGMENTS

To note everyone who in some way made a contribution to this book would be a book in itself and an impossible list to compile. There are, however, some special people who deserve recognition:

Ingrid, my wife of thirty years, who has worked tirelessly as my personal and professional partner in our various endeavors, cared for our children, and been patient and supportive with my whims.

Thea, Russell, and Michael, my children and true legacy, who help me see the world through a fresh perspective.

The late Russell Walter Whitney (1931–1970), my father, who was my foundation.

The staff at Whitney Information Network Inc., and its subsidiaries, who share my commitment to helping others improve their lives.

The great people who contributed to the initial creation of this book in 1993 and who supported the project to revise it. In particular, I appreciate the efforts of Steve Champa, Marie Code, Kent Densley, Tim Lin, Kevin Shriner, Anil Singh, Marian Van Dyke, and Erika Villamizar.

Our hundreds of thousands of students, many of whom have been the source of the stories and illustrations in this book; they provide daily affirmation of my efforts.

My literary agent, Michael Baybak, for his support and faith in this effort.

Jacquelyn Lynn, who provided valuable editorial assistance and insight, and who was so patient when the writing turned to rewriting, both with the first version of this book and with this revision.

Finally, all of those people who told me all of these years that it cannot be done. You have pushed me to give you hope.

My thanks to all of you.

INTRODUCTION TO
the Second Edition

―――⟩⟨⟨⟩―――

When I wrote *Building Wealth*—a project that began in 1992—I wanted to create a book that would tell people exactly how I became a millionaire and how they could do the same thing. I'd already written one book and a number of training manuals, but I wanted to reach a broader audience.

At the time, the content was leading-edge. It combined practical real estate investing strategies, business advice, and motivation—and while most of the information it contains is still useful today, our world has changed so much that *Building Wealth* is no longer complete. Consider this: in the early 1990s, the Internet was still something only geeks and nerds understood, most property records were maintained on paper or microfilm, and phrases like "send me an e-mail," "surfing the net," and "check their Web site for information" had not yet entered our vocabulary.

The specific strategies I explained will still work, but you need to know how to use them in today's investing environment with today's technology and resources. Also, I want to share with you the many things I've learned since *Building Wealth* was first published.

If you read the original *Building Wealth,* you'll find plenty of new material here as well as some familiar information that you'll be able to use to achieve your financial goals. I learn more about real estate investing and wealth-building strategies every day, and I'm honored to have the opportunity to share that with you in *Building Wealth,* second edition.

ORIGINAL INTRODUCTION

⸺ ⸙ ⸺

You're tired of being in debt. You're tired of watching a fortunate few live the good life while you're buried under a mountain of bills. You're tired of grinding away at your job with nothing to show for it.

Most people are looking for vehicles to provide them with more money, more freedom, and more quality time to spend with their families and friends. Yet most people are not financial geniuses, and very few of us have any significant amount of capital to begin building wealth with. That's why you need this book; in it you'll find a variety of conventional and unconventional methods to make money that no one but a street-smart, self-taught millionaire *could* teach you.

I wrote this book from my heart, and I made sure it was loaded with nuts-and-bolts information derived from my real-life experiences. I not only share my own personal story of how I became a millionaire, but I also tell you about dozens of regular, everyday people who have used my techniques successfully. You'll learn how we did it, and you'll learn how you can do it for yourself.

This book is so practical that you can read it quickly, immediately begin putting my strategies into action, and see instant results. These are not pie-in-the-sky ideas that work only in an ideal environment. You're not likely to find these strategies taught in any college course. Not one of them requires anything more than common sense and a basic knowledge of simple arithmetic to implement.

After reading this book, you can begin working toward financial independence right away, regardless of your circumstances. You will have enough information to enable you to move quickly toward a new and brighter future. You will know how to find capital, how to create part-time income and make it grow into financial independence, how to establish and repair credit, how banks really operate, how the government can help you become wealthy, and exactly what you have to do to build your personal fortune.

My motivation is simple. I became wealthy in part by reading and studying hundreds of self-help books. Though some of these books are quite good, the majority of them depend on capital, credit, or luck—or a combination of all three—for their methods to work: in short, an ideal world. The problem is, we don't live in an ideal world. I wanted to create a book with methods that have been proven in the real world, with practical advice you can always trust and believe in, and that will work for you regardless of your present position.

CHAPTER 1

LIGHT YOUR INTERNAL FIRE

Destiny is not a matter of chance; it's a matter of choice.
—UNKNOWN

When I was twenty, I got the best job I thought I'd ever have: I was making $5 an hour killing hogs.

I worked in a slaughterhouse where, on a good day, fourteen hundred hogs were butchered. The process was systematic. The four-hundred-pound hogs were herded up a chute. At the top of the chute, they were stunned by an electric shock to the back of the neck, causing them to fall onto a conveyor belt. At that point, we could shackle their hind legs (that was my job) and they were flipped upside down so the man next to me could cut their jugular vein. Then they would bleed to death.

It was messy, disgusting work, and I believed I would be doing it for the rest of my life.

Then I noticed a magazine ad for a "get-rich" program. I was wary and didn't respond to that ad; in fact, I studied a number of ads before I answered any of them. But just reading the first one set my thoughts in motion, and it wasn't long before I realized that I didn't want "a job"—and certainly not a job in a slaughter-house.

I wanted to be wealthy.

It was quite an ambition for a high school dropout with a bad attitude. And even though I knew what I wanted, I didn't know how to go about getting it. So I started answering some of the ads that ran in the back of magazines. I got replies about how to make mail order millions, how to make $300,000 a year stuffing envelopes, the lazy way to riches, various franchises, and dozens of other responses that were probably a mix of legitimate opportunities and outright scams.

You can still find these ads in magazines. They're also all over the Internet. If you've ever responded to any of them, you've got a good idea of the kind of stuff that filled my mailbox. If you haven't, I'm going to save you a lot of disappointment, time, and money. I'm going to tell you how to find the real road to more money and security.

But first, it's important that you know how I did it. As I said, when I decided I wanted to become wealthy, I was a twenty-year-old high school dropout working at a dead-end job. I could easily have used my lousy childhood as an excuse for never achieving anything significant. Also, I had to consider that I was married and my wife was expecting our first child. I had obligations and bills, and I needed a steady income. I didn't have much, but I couldn't afford to risk what I had.

So there I was, accumulating a drawerful of moneymaking ideas—some scams, some legitimate. But even the legitimate ones wouldn't work for me, primarily because they required large up-front investments. Then I saw an ad for a book on building wealth that did not claim you could be an overnight success but promised long-term, sustainable results. I discussed it at length with my wife, because the book (long since out of print) was $10—twice my hourly wage and a significant amount of money for us at the time. We debated, and since the publisher offered a money-back satisfaction guarantee, we finally decided to give it a try. I mailed in the order, and when the book came, I started to read it.

I literally stayed up all night reading, taking notes, and making plans. I was young and naive, but I wasn't stupid. I immediately realized there was no magic to building wealth. It was definitely something I could do.

Three weeks later, I made $11,000.

Now, that's not a tremendous amount of money, but it was

more than I made in a year at the slaughterhouse—and I did it on a part-time basis. I thought, if I could make that much money that quickly after reading one little book, imagine what I could do if I read a few more! I began building a library of these types of books, focusing on the fundamental principles, and selectively following the advice that sounded realistic and sensible.

By the time I turned twenty-three, I was able to quit my job because I had become financially independent. By the time I was twenty-seven, I was one of the youngest self-made millionaires in the United States.

The methods I used were not complicated. I've refined them slightly over the years, and they are still working for me today. They can be used by virtually anyone, anywhere, on a full- or part-time basis, and they don't necessarily require a lot of capital or credit. They do, however, require that you redirect your thinking and develop a game plan.

I've taken the fundamental principles—the ones that work—and figured out how anyone, regardless of experience or education level, can use them to become wealthy, too. Basically I have cut out the pie-in-the-sky stuff, the empty promises, and put together a program that I *know* works—and I know it works because I've done it, and I've already taught countless others how to do it.

I can't tell you how wealthy you will eventually become, but I can tell you this: if you will follow the steps outlined in this book, you will see a rapid improvement in your financial circumstances, and you will be on your way to building your own personal fortune.

THINK LIKE A HIGH SCHOOL DROPOUT

At the age of twenty, it seemed as if my life had been just one hardship after another. My mother left my father and me when I was three, and then he died when I was fourteen. Not only was I emotionally devastated, but I had to get a job to support myself and wound up quitting school in the eleventh grade. I was naive, and I was desperate for something or someone to believe in. Everywhere I turned, I hit a wall.

But I kept on looking. I found my wife and knew almost from the minute we were introduced that this was the woman I would spend the rest of my life with. We both came from working-class backgrounds where the accepted life pattern was to work at a job, save up enough to make a down payment on a house, have children, work until you were sixty-five, retire with a gold watch and a meager pension, and die a few years later. After we were married, we realized we wanted more for ourselves and our children. I began my search for financial security, and Ingrid provided the much needed moral support. It wasn't easy, but we knew that America was full of rags-to-riches stories, and if it could happen for someone else, it could happen for us.

All we had to do was figure out a way.

In my own case, I went out and applied one idea—and made $11,000 in three weeks. I had faith in a system. Had I been a little more sophisticated, a little more educated, I might have questioned it, and I might not have tried it. But I was thinking like the high school dropout I was, and it worked.

When I was traveling around the country giving lectures, I would frequently ask audiences for a show of hands of those who had gone to college. The usual response was about 90 percent. Even today at the conferences and trainings where I speak, the response is similar. This means the vast majority of the people who want to hear what I have to say about wealth building have a college education—and they're coming to hear a high school dropout tell them how to make more money. And the real irony is that their education may well be the reason why they don't have more money than they do.

Let me be clear on this: a college education does have value, but formal schooling will not teach you how to make money. You probably know some well-educated people who are living a life of financial failure, or at least economic mediocrity. You may be one of them. If you are, take heart: you can overcome your education.

THE PARALYSIS OF ANALYSIS

I once had a business partner who held an MBA along with degrees in engineering and accounting. Every time I came up with a new idea, he would sit at his large, polished oak desk, making notes on a legal pad, and coming at the idea from every angle possible to try to figure out why it wouldn't work. While he was doing that, I would be at the bank trying to get it financed.

Of course, there is merit to evaluating an idea carefully for the risk-and-reward ratio. But if you constantly focus on what could go wrong, you'll bury yourself under so much fear that you'll never accomplish anything. And the problem with most colleges is that they teach what I call the paralysis of analysis. They teach students how to figure out all the reasons why something won't work, instead of teaching them to go to work.

While I'm sure there are exceptions, it has generally been my experience that the more educated an individual is, the less likely it is that he or she will demonstrate the characteristics that lead to true financial independence. Business schools teach people how to get along in the corporate environment and do the nuts-and-bolts work of managing a company. Engineering schools teach people how to be engineers. Journalism schools turn out reporters. Medical schools produce doctors. These are all fine professions, but the people doing them are doing jobs—and if your primary source of income is from a job, it will be difficult for you to ever achieve true financial independence.

Most schools, whether at the primary, secondary, or postsecondary level, typically teach students how to perform at a job. That's okay if all you want out of life is a job, if you'll be content to go to work every day, struggling to put a little money aside so you can take a vacation every year, and hoping to have enough left over to support yourself in retirement. But if you want more, you must study the methods of wealthy people and learn how the rags-to-riches (or even middle-income-to-very-wealthy) stories truly happened.

I talk to thousands and thousands of college graduates every year who tell me they bought into the "go to college, get a good job, and life will be rosy" idea, but today they're stuck in jobs they don't like and are worried about losing. They're struggling to pay bills, and they're searching for a way to get more out of life. These people and countless others have changed their lives by using just a few of the strategies you will learn in the following pages.

A point of clarification here: I am not advocating that we shut down our colleges and universities. Certainly when I'm sick, I want a doctor who is highly trained in his specialty. I want an attorney who knows and understands the law. The executives who run Whitney Information Network Inc. and Whitney Education Group Inc. all have undergraduate and graduate degrees. I believe all education has value. However, I have taught my children to think like high school dropouts, and I encourage all of my students to do the same, because I know that's the only way they will achieve their own financial security.

Remember, high school dropouts lack formal education, but they do not necessarily lack intelligence and common sense. I am a high school dropout, but I am an internationally recognized expert in wealth building, I can articulately converse on a variety of subjects other than business and investing, I've written a number of books, and I am routinely called on by business and civic leaders when they need advice. Oh, yes, and I'm a multimillionaire.

THERE'S A BIGGER REASON FOR WEALTH THAN THE MONEY

I don't worship at the altar of the almighty dollar, and I'm not suggesting that you should, either. But having money makes your life easier, and having lots of money makes your life a lot easier.

As I look back, I can clearly see how I built the desire and be-lief that I should and could become wealthy. I can almost hear you groan, because most how-to books do the desire bit to death. You must have a *burning* desire, they say, a wrenching feeling in your gut that drives you to acquire wealth. It sounds as if you could eat a bowl of spicy chili and be on your way to your first million in a few hours.

Of course, we all want money and the niceties and freedoms having money provides. But just fantasizing about a bigger house, a sleeker car, and a membership at the country club won't get you those things. There's got to be a reason for the wealth that's bigger—much bigger—than the money itself.

Let me share how, for me, the desire for wealth grew from a tiny spark of an idea to a powerhouse of energy, determination, and the guts to get it done.

I've already mentioned that my mother left my father and me when I was three years old. My father remarried, but unfortu-nately, the woman he chose turned out to be the stereotypical wicked stepmother. She was sweet and loving until they were married, then her attitude toward my father became one of grudging accommodation. To me, she was negative and abusive. She told me repeatedly that I was no good, that I would never amount to anything, and that I would probably wind up spend-ing most of my life in jail. She also physically abused me. I re-member clearly how she held my hands over the flame of a gas stove to discipline me.

This type of treatment is more than difficult for a child to deal with, it's overwhelming. When you hear over and over that you are a bad person, you come to believe it. I tried to take my prob-lems to my father, but my stepmother convinced him that I was either exaggerating or lying. And he worked long, exhausting hours as an elevator mechanic. I was miserable, but I didn't feel I could burden him when he would come home tired and dirty from his dead-end job. So I bottled up my frustration, anger, and confusion and focused on surviving.

My father was thirty-nine when he died of heart disease. I

lived with an aunt for about a year, then ran away from her home and moved in with my eighteen-year-old half sister. She couldn't afford to support me, so I quit school and went to work. I lied about my age to get a job as a short-order cook from five o'clock in the morning to three in the afternoon. I'd clean up from the restaurant and dash across the street to put in a few hours as a minimum-wage telemarketer. Then, using a fake driver's license, I drove a taxi until one or two in the morning. Now, I don't recommend that any youngster lie about his or her age to get a job or drive with a fake license; I'm telling you what I did because I want you to know where I came from. I needed all three jobs because none by itself would pay enough to cover my share of our living expenses.

My half sister did her best, but she was barely more than a child herself, and she wasn't equipped to deal with a troubled teenage brother. And in spite of all the hours I spent working, I still found the time to get in with the wrong crowd and get into serious trouble. I got arrested and went to jail for two years.

And that was probably the best thing that could have happened to me at the time.

While I was in jail, I was protected and disciplined. I had time to think about what had happened to me and what I wanted in life—and I wanted to be a success. I earned my GED and tutored other inmates. When I got out, I got the job in the slaughterhouse and was determined to build a decent life for myself.

I was working at the slaughterhouse when I met and married my wife, and she became my partner in our wealth-building strategies. Today, Whitney Information Network is a publicly traded international company that employs hundreds of people and helps its students change their lives in a positive, productive way. I am also an owner, partner, or investor in a wide range of other companies, and I continue to actively invest in real estate. I have made millions of dollars and helped others do the same. But I was never really motivated by the money.

Sure, I wanted to be wealthy. I wanted to be a millionaire. But it wasn't for the Rolex watch, although today I have one. It wasn't for the nice homes or expensive cars, although I have those, too. It took me years to understand what was driving me—and it wasn't positive thinking. For me, it was simply this: if I could become a millionaire, it would make all the pain from the past go away. I would be *somebody*. I could show all those people, like my stepmother, who said I would never amount to anything that they were wrong. Most important, I could give my family all the security and safety that I had never had and I so badly wanted them to have.

To build the desire necessary to achieve wealth, you must unleash the energy of your own pain. Maybe your pain comes from someone telling you that you wouldn't ever succeed. Maybe your pain comes from imagining your children in a mediocre, financially deprived life. Whatever its source, you must find that pain, crystallize it, and understand what will make it go away.

Fortunately, somewhere along the way, my pain and animosity faded. I never gloated about my success to my stepmother. By the time I began achieving my financial goals, it wasn't necessary. And gradually the need to escape the pain of my unhappy childhood was replaced with the need to repeat the pleasure my achievements generated. The challenges and rewards of building wealth became my motivators.

MAKING MONEY SHOULDN'T HURT

I am absolutely fascinated by wealthy people. I want to know how they got that way and what keeps them going. Years ago, I found a study that tracked the fortunes and misfortunes of twelve thousand wealthy people from across the United States. This study pointed out one significant common characteristic among people who are wealth builders: *they love what they do!*

Have you ever wondered why wealthy people keep on working? Why did Sam Walton continue to be actively involved in the running of Wal-Mart Stores Inc. until his death—long after he had made more money than he would ever spend? Don't you think that Michael Eisner, former chairman and CEO of the Walt Disney Company, made enough money while still in his forties so that he could retire with a lifestyle most of us only dream about? He did, but he continued to work. Bill Gates could stop working today and never spend all the money he has—so why doesn't he? Why did Bill Cosby keep doing television shows and Madonna keep recording music after they became two of the richest entertainers in the world? Why does J. K. Rowling keep writing Harry Potter books?

The answer is simple: they love what they do. Work is not a chore for them. They're eager to get up in the morning, to tackle new projects, to reach new goals. And because they love what they do, they are willing to do what it takes to succeed.

When I speak at conferences, I frequently ask how many people do not like what they do to earn money. Some people find their jobs tolerable, but the vast majority do not like what they do to make a living. Most people have a job for which they're paid just enough not to quit, and they work just hard enough not to get fired. Only a few really love the work they do. That being true, we have unwittingly associated the process of making money with something that's painful or, at best, not pleasurable.

Think about this. If you have for years associated making money with pain, your brain has built a wall between yourself and the pleasure wealth and prosperity bring. When you think about money, deep down you may be focusing on ideas like "not fun," "boring," "no future," "wasting time"—all things that are painful. And when you think about big money, your idea is "big pain." It's entirely possible that this thought process has caused you to unknowingly sabotage your dreams in the past.

But it doesn't have to be that way in the future. Making money can—and should—be fun. Becoming wealthy does not have to be all trials and tribulations. Once you find the right vehicle—one that will make money and be enjoyable at the same time—you'll see how this process works and how it will keep on working for the rest of your life.

A friend of mine makes this point quite clearly. He's successful and likes what he does, but he doesn't *love* it, and here's how I know that: He usually comes into his office around nine or ten in the morning. He claims he's not a "morning person," so he chooses to come in late, then stay late if necessary. But this guy loves to fish. Fishing is a passion with him. If I were to call him at any time and suggest we go fishing the following morning, he'd be up at 4:30 a.m. and have coffee brewed, sandwiches made, and the boat ready to go by 5:00 a.m. Interesting behavior from someone who claims he's not a "morning person."

Business and making money can be extremely pleasurable, as pleasurable as fishing is for my friend. I love what I do. Simply put, it's fun for me. I love everything about the process of investing in and developing real estate. I love the education side of my business because I get to teach people how to do what I've done and watch them change their lives.

When the stories of wealthy people are told, over and over the common thread of loving what they do clearly shows through. It doesn't matter if they are Bill Gates of Microsoft, a computer whiz kid who became one of the world's richest men; or Wally "Famous" Amos, a black man from a Harlem ghetto who made a fortune selling chocolate chip cookies; or Mary Kay Ash, who built her own empire and helped others become wealthy with Mary Kay Cosmetics; or any of the many others who have achieved their financial goals. They all loved what they were doing.

When making money becomes your hobby, getting up early is no longer a chore. Staying late doesn't matter because you're enjoying yourself. In fact, you'll be having so much fun that you'll toss out the time clock. You won't need it. And when you find the right vehicle that lets making money become your hobby, you'll find yourself generating significantly more dollars in much less time than you're spending on your job right now. What's more, as you'll see in the pages of this book, locating that ideal wealth-building vehicle isn't difficult.

WHAT MOTIVATION CAN'T DO

I have attended countless motivational lectures over the years, including the one that concludes with the drama and excitement of a fire walk. At one such event, I was preparing to leave when I struck up a conversation with a young fellow who was all pumped up. He was pacing back and forth, breathing hard, his eyes flashing, and on an incredible adrenaline high created by the session we had attended. I commented that it was great to see someone so excited, then I asked what he was going to do.

"I don't know," he replied, "but, by God, when I find it, I'm going to really get going."

Obviously he was truly motivated. His problem was that he didn't have a clue as to what path he would follow to reach the goal he hadn't yet defined. He was excited, but just being excited and bursting with positive energy isn't enough to make you wealthy. That excitement, that adrenaline high, is only temporary, and without a plan, all the enthusiasm in the world is worthless. You need to know how you will acquire your money.

This book will provide you with a workable, step-by-step plan to build wealth that includes a variety of proven techniques. Some will appeal to you, others won't, but you will have plenty of choices. My point is this: Motivation alone isn't enough. Method alone isn't enough. But the combination of true motivation and proven method is a guaranteed winner.

CHAPTER 2

THE 95 PERCENT RULE WILL MAKE YOU WEALTHY—OR KEEP YOU BROKE

Things may come to those who wait, but only those things left by those who hustle.
—ABRAHAM LINCOLN

The first major milestone on the road to wealth is financial independence, and it's time to figure out how *you* are going to get there—and to understand why so many people never do. I call it the 95 Percent Rule, and it will either make you wealthy or keep you broke.

Most people are more negative than positive in their thinking and their perception of life. But if you ask successful people whether they believed their success was possible before it happened, they'll tell you they did. They believed it, they planned for it, they worked for it, and they achieved it.

Ask unsuccessful people whether they believe they will be successful, and they'll likely tell you no. They may not be so blunt about it, they may have excuses—"if I had more education," "if I hadn't married so young," "if I didn't have all these responsibilities," "if I could just get a break," etc.—but essentially their answer will be that they don't believe they will be successful. In other words, they have a negative attitude about themselves and their future. They may even convince themselves that they enjoy their failure.

I saw this clearly back when my company offered only one basic real estate program. In the average crowd of a thousand people, a few would take the principles I taught, put them into action, and make big money. A slightly larger group would use my ideas to achieve some moderate success. The rest would listen attentively, take copious notes, purchase some of the more detailed home-study materials—and do absolutely nothing at all. Even more fascinating is this: if, during the seminar, I asked the audience if they believed these percentages applied to their group, they unanimously agreed.

The structure of our training programs has changed significantly, but unfortunately, human nature has not. We still see too many students who listen attentively, who recognize that what they are being taught works and can take them to financial freedom and serious wealth, and yet they will not take any action to achieve their dreams.

What's the message here? These people are telling me that most people are negative, that they themselves are probably negative, and that they can't or won't do anything about it.

These people are victims of the 95 Percent Rule. They are the 95 percent of the population who will plod along, living their lives one day at a time, barely getting by, and unable to plan for the future. Their dreams will never even come close to reality. They'll make wishes, but they'll never set goals or make plans to change their circumstances.

Their primary contact with success is secondary—that is, they're content to watch it happen to other people, either acquaintances or characters in movies, on television, or in books. But they know it will never happen to them. And because their belief is so strong, they are right.

What's different about the 5 percent who do achieve financial security and wealth?

Is it intelligence? No. I've known some extraordinarily brilliant people who can't seem to raise their income above the poverty level. I've also known some people with average IQs who enjoy extremely above-average incomes.

Is it timing? No. We all live—physically, at least—in the present. Timing is a common denominator that can't be changed. At any moment, someone is getting wealthy, and a lot of other people are staying poor.

Is it location? Not really. Certainly your opportunities will differ with your geography, but in any given community, small or large, at any place on the globe, you will find people who are successful and people who are not.

Is it the 95 Percent Rule? You bet!

WHY THINGS ARE ALWAYS GREAT

When you greet your coworkers in the morning, what kind of things do you hear? My guess is that when you say, "How are you today?" the responses you get are in the vein of "I'm getting by" or "Can't complain," spoken in a dull monotone. Sometimes the answers will be more articulate, as in "I've got a touch of the flu" or "My car wouldn't start this morning, and the mechanic is estimating $1,800 for repairs." Sometimes they'll even say, "Just fine," in a tone that lets you know they're anything but fine. Then there's always the guy who sets the tone for the day by responding to your "Good morning" with a snarled "What's good about it?"

How often do you ask someone how they are and hear, "Great, absolutely great!"—and you know it's a sincere answer?

Could it be, just maybe, about 5 percent of the time?

Could the 95 Percent Rule be at work here?

And when someone responds to you with something like "Great!" doesn't it lift you up just a bit? Of course it does. And I'll tell you something else: *it lifts them up, too.*

We believe what we say. When we respond to greetings with a

mumbled "I'm doing okay" or "I can't complain," we will build a life that fits that description. And if all you want is a life where you're getting along without anything to gripe about, just keep on talking this way. If you want to make yourself sicker, talk about your aches and pains. If you want to have a bad day, talk about the negatives.

Are you getting the picture?

So make the word *great* an integral part of your vocabulary and use it when anyone asks how you are. When things are going exactly as you planned, that's great. If an important business deal just fell through, that's okay, *you* are still great. If you just broke your leg, make it the greatest broken leg you've ever had.

You can't control everything that happens, but you *can* control your attitude about it. If you give negativity control over your attitude, it will take control over your circumstances. Force positivity to control your attitude, and you will enrich not only your own life but the lives of people around you.

If you do nothing else as a result of reading this book but change the way you respond to inquiries about your health and status, you will have made a major improvement in your life. And if you do that much, you'll find the remaining steps toward personal and financial wealth will come more simply than you ever thought possible.

Before you decide that I'm just another motivational preacher, let me stress that positive thinking alone won't make you wealthy. You won't make a fortune just by being enthusiastic and visualizing piles of cash. You need strategies, plans, and methods, and you're going to learn them in later chapters. But your attitude is a critical component of success.

You wouldn't want to enter into a business deal with someone whose outlook was consistently gloomy. A banker isn't going to lend you money for a project when your attitude is pessimistic. And who wants to be around someone who wears a consistently sour expression on his face?

Dr. Walter Doyle Staples said it best in his book *Think Like a Winner:*

When you change your thinking,
you change your beliefs;
When you change your beliefs,
you change your expectations;
When you change your expectations,
you change your attitude;
When you change your attitude,
you change your behavior;
When you change your behavior,
you change your performance;
When you change your performance,
you change your life!

Once you start telling other people that you and your life are *great*, you'll start to believe it yourself. You'll begin to see changes in your aura. You'll see changes in the way others respond to you. Most important, you'll constantly be reminding yourself of the new "moneymaking you" we are about to build.

WHY YOU'VE BEEN FOOLED INTO THINKING WEALTH IS BEYOND YOU

If 95 percent of the population is more negative than positive, it's safe to say that's because we've spent our lives being exposed to more negatives than positives. That means we've heard over and over why we can't achieve certain things, why we shouldn't expect too much out of life, why we should just go to work every day, pay our bills, and raise our children to do the same.

Years ago, I saw a bumper sticker that read "I owe, I owe, it's off to work I go." That isn't funny, it's a tragedy! And it's worse than depressing, it's devastating. The dream destroyers are everywhere, spreading their negativity like a cancer—even when they have no idea that's what they're doing.

I routinely ask the people who attend my wealth-building training programs if they've told anyone what they were planning on doing. Then I ask if anyone they told tried to discourage them from coming. Without fail, more than half of the people who shared their plans with others (and a substantial number didn't for this very reason) had to deal with negativity.

Even more frightening is that people who don't know me, who don't have any idea what my programs are about, are not only passing judgment on what I do but are also trying to kill someone else's dream of a better life. Why do people do that? Primarily because misery really does love company. For the most part, people who are unhappy with their lives don't really want to see anyone else do well. Rather than boost you up, they prefer to drag you down. I know that sounds harsh, and I genuinely don't believe they do it on purpose. But it's the reason that, whether you realize it or not, you have always believed wealth was beyond you and that "getting wealthy" was something other people did.

That's not true!

Wealth is available to anyone who is willing to go after it using sound, tested wealth-building techniques. That means wealth is possible for you, for the clerk at the convenience store, for anyone—even all the negative people who would try to stop you. And now you have a weapon to use against those dream destroyers: a simple, one-syllable word that's been in your vocabulary almost all your life: *Great!* It's like having a can of bug spray handy when a roach scampers across your kitchen floor. You'll get rid of the negativity that surrounds you either by chasing it away or killing it completely.

PEOPLE ARE HAPPY TO HELP YOU FAIL

Because there is no way to make money without interacting with others to varying degrees, you need a basic understanding of human nature. You already know that people are motivated by the need to experience pleasure and avoid pain. What you also need to know is that people love to talk about their problems, but they don't want to hear about yours. They might sound sympathetic as you talk, but they don't really want to hear it. More important, they probably don't care about your problems, so why bother telling them? And if they are willing to listen, it's usually with a smirk of internal satisfaction that somebody is worse off than they are. Or they might try to top your tale of woe with that age-old phrase "You think you've got problems? Wait until you hear mine!"

We all have problems, but wallowing in them won't make them go away. Of course, you can't ignore them, either. So resolve not to talk about them unless you are in a situation set up for problem-solving.

You must come to terms with this reality: when you walk into the office in the morning and coworkers say, "How are you today?" they don't want a health report or a financial statement. So don't give them one. Instead, say, "Great!"—no matter how things really are. They will be pleasantly surprised and may even allow some of your positive energy to rub off on them.

You might feel a little uncomfortable when you first start saying "Great!" That's understandable, because it probably goes strongly against the grain of the habits you've acquired over a lifetime. But no one ever got anywhere without great (there's that word again!) enthusiasm. This small word can literally change your life. If you keep saying "Great!" even when you don't quite mean it, you will come to believe it, and in less time than you might imagine, it will become true.

HOW TO REVERSE LIFELONG PATTERNS

After I started my first business and had to hire people to work for me, I realized that my negativity affected my employees' productivity. I'd stop by the job site, scowling and snarling, and they'd slow down. Finally I decided that since I had found books that told me how to make money, maybe I could find some on how to have a better attitude. I bought one of those rah-rah positive-attitude books, and I hated every page of it. I thought it was the stupidest thing I'd ever read. Why? Because the author said that to become positive, you have to go around saying things like *super* and *fantastic*—words that were not in my everyday vocabulary. Not only did the technique seem phony, but I wasn't about to embarrass myself or put my oversize young ego on the line doing something I thought was silly.

But my desire to become a millionaire soon overcame my ego. I had to make the pain of my early years go away, and I knew reaching that million-dollar mark would do it. I had to make sure that my wife and children would never want for anything. And if being positive and saying dumb things would help me reach my goal, then I'd give it a try.

It was one of the hardest things I've ever done.

I began meeting with my employees and pumping them up by telling them how well things were going, what a great job they were doing, and how they were going to benefit when we had the project complete. I used words like "Great!" I smiled and put plenty of positive energy in my voice and gestures. In short, I put on a terrific show. And when I was finished, I'd scurry around the corner, out of their sight, and breathe a deep sigh of relief that my performance was over. I could go back to scowling and being negative until it was time to talk to my employees again.

Two interesting things happened. First, worker productivity increased significantly. I was delighted, because that meant more profits. Second, and even more important, I began liking myself when I was wearing my positive mask. Some of my own medicine was working on me.

The more I pretended to be positive, the more I liked how I felt when I was doing it. The more I liked how I felt, the more I did it. Pretty soon, it wasn't uncomfortable anymore, and it wasn't long before I realized I had experienced a metamorphosis. I had unwittingly transformed myself from someone who was totally committed to negativity to someone who was positive, happy, and on a continuous search for bright things and the overall good in life.

People saw the change and thought it wouldn't last. In fact, my wife will tell you that I did a complete attitude turnaround in just a few days, and she sometimes found my new optimism irritating. But eventually it grew on her. Today, being positive is an integral part of both our natures. Being positive has enriched our lives in more ways than we can count. And being positive has helped us build our personal fortune.

THE MAGIC OF CONSCIOUS CHANGE

People are not born either positive or negative. A positive attitude is not a magic ingredient some of us have and some of us don't. It's something we either develop—or we don't. We are shaped by our environment, and we tend to follow the path of least resistance. That means if we are exposed more to negative attitudes than positive ones, we will tend to be negative.

If you're thinking that it's easy to have a positive attitude once you've got a lot of money, you're right. But it's not easy to get wealthy without a positive attitude. I'm sure there are some wealthy negative people out there, but I've never met one of them—and I'd be willing to bet that their wealth was inherited, not earned. Let me also point out that money doesn't change people, it just makes you more of what you are. If you're a jerk when you're poor, you'll just be a bigger jerk if you become rich.

So what comes first—the attitude or the money?

There's no definitive rule that one has to come before the other. I was already well on my way to financial independence when I discovered how important it was to my ultimate success that I be more positive about life. And I was positive, all right—I was positive that I wanted to be wealthy. Today, I can wholeheartedly agree with Sophie Tucker, who is credited with saying, "I have been poor and I have been rich. Rich is better."

You'll find acquiring wealth is much easier once you've developed a wealthy attitude, and you do that through *conscious change*. To the casual observer, the results of your conscious change may look like magic, but there's nothing at all magical about the process. Conscious change is simply the tool you use to adjust your attitude so you feel deserving of wealth. Here's how it works:

When you do something—anything from scratching your ear to making a million-dollar business decision—you are acting either by design or from reflex. Most of our day-to-day activities are automatic; our actions and reactions are fairly predictable based on our life conditioning.

Picture this: You're relaxing in a chair, minding your own business, and you don't know me. All of a sudden, I burst into the room and throw a basketball at your chest. Within a split second, you'll throw up your hands to block the ball. Why? For the same reason you allow people to dump their negativity on you day in and day out. For the same reason you have convinced yourself you can't get wealthy. For the same reason you believe you'll be stuck in a workaday rut for the rest of your life.

You block the ball because your reflexes tell you to. In that split second it takes for your hands to go up, you will recall that if a large object strikes you, it will hurt. That reflex was plugged into your brain when you were a small child, it has steadily been reinforced over the years, and it works without any active thought on your part.

Let's change the scenario a little bit. You're still relaxing in a chair, but this time I enter a bit more slowly, and you know me and trust me. I tell you the basketball I'm carrying is made of foam, not rubber, and weighs only a few ounces. I say I'm going to toss it gently so it will bounce off your chest and drop into your lap, and that when I do this, I want you to leave your hands at your sides. You don't need to block the ball because you're not going to be hurt by it.

I toss the ball. It hits your chest and softly falls into your lap. Your arms don't move. Mission accomplished. We have just altered the way you think—for the moment, anyway.

If you try this experiment with friends, you'll find the people sitting down will tense as they wait for the ball's impact. They know what's really happening, but they are rapidly searching their past for an appropriate response, one that is based on their life experiences. And their life experiences will tell them they must block the ball. But we have just proven that your ingrained responses can be changed. We were able to change years of programming simply by being aware of that programming and by believing the change wouldn't hurt.

HOW TO FEED YOUR MIND

How do you purge the negativity from your mind? The answer is a process called Mindfeed. I learned it by accident and confirmed it during a period when I was working on understanding just exactly how I managed to overcome my negative upbringing and become a millionaire. I needed to know how my attitude changed, how I kept my marriage together, how I learned enough about business without much formal education to make huge fortunes in several totally unrelated fields.

Why me? Because I learned to feed my mind with positive material. And why not you? There's absolutely no reason why you, too, cannot enjoy a life full of personal satisfaction and material comfort. You can begin by applying the process that will create the most dramatic change in the shortest time, and that process is Mindfeed.

We feed our bodies with liquid and solid foods every day. If we didn't, we would dehydrate and starve. Our minds operate on the same principle, but they need food of a different type. Just as a plant stretches toward light, our minds seek nourishment—and if that nourishment isn't healthy and positive, the only alternative is unhealthy and negative.

What do you get from reading most newspapers, watching television, even scanning the news on the Internet? Primarily rape, murder, car crashes, unpleasant economic news, and similar mental junk food. It's the mental equivalent of high-fat, high-calorie snacks—they may taste good on your tongue, but they are ultimately harmful to your body. I'm not suggesting that you cancel your newspaper subscription, sell your television, and toss your computer. What I am suggesting is that you become as care-ful—or even more careful—about what you feed your mind as you are about what you feed your body.

When I bought my first get-rich book, I was searching for a new message. I didn't know about positive attitudes. I didn't know about success. All I knew was that I wanted to get rich. For me, rich was happy, because I didn't know any better. And I real-ized that if I wanted to get rich, I needed to listen to people who were rich. I needed to listen to people who were positive. I needed people to tell me it could be done and I could do it.

Belief is a powerful tool, and after I'd read a few books and listened to a few cassette tapes with good messages, I became a believer. But I didn't stop reading and listening. I continued to feed my mind with positive, productive information.

This is how Mindfeed works. It's the process of continually searching for good written and audio materials (books, articles, CDs, DVDs, etc.) with quality messages from people who have accomplished what we desire. It's the ability to sort and reject negativity, whether it comes from an individual or the media. It's the ammunition you need to offset the negatives you can't avoid. Amazingly easy and remarkably effective, Mindfeed is simply feeding your mind daily with nourishing material that will make you healthy, happy—and wealthy.

A HOBBY THAT WILL MAKE YOU A FORTUNE

Ninety-five Percenters are often scornful of Mindfeed. Many have shelves full of books and audio recordings that didn't work for them. You may even have some of them in your own home or office. This is your opportunity to revive that past investment and finally make it pay off. Books and recordings are nothing more than inanimate objects. They may hold valuable information, but results require action, and the action must come from you.

My personal library includes hundreds of books, cassette

tapes, CDs, DVDs, and home-study courses. I've bought just about every self-help product that's come along in the past twenty-five years, from inexpensive paperbacks to audio and video sets costing hundreds of dollars. And I'm still buying them, because they have ideas that I can use to become a better person, to strengthen my relationships with family and friends, and to make more money.

My first financial success came from a technique I discovered in a "how to get rich" book. It came from feeding my mind. It just made sense to me that if I could get one idea and make $11,000 in three weeks, then feeding my mind with more ideas would help me make more money. But had I not *tried* that first technique, it wouldn't have been the technique's fault. And if I wasn't willing to try, all the books and recordings in the world would be worthless to me.

Essentially, I have made self-help my hobby, and it's a hobby that has made me wealthy. I look for information on how to improve myself, and I want to learn how other people have done so. Then I take what I consider to be the best ideas and apply them in my own life and businesses. And I'm not alone in the practice. Ask any self-made wealthy person if they routinely study a variety of self-help and self-improvement methods. I think you'll find that they all have extensive libraries and enjoy learning how to make themselves better and wealthier. Virtually all of them share my passion for Mindfeed in one form or another. They all understand that being wealthy is a way of life, not just the balance in your bankbook.

This is not just a lot of psychological claptrap—it's common sense. And common sense existed a long time before psychology ever did. So make self-help *your* hobby. Uses these five simple steps:

1. Haul down all the books, tapes, CDs, and DVDs you already have and dust them off. Take inventory; you need to know what you have so you know where to look when you need information.

2. Look for an idea you can apply today that will help you make money or improve some other area of your life. (By the way, you'll find plenty of them in this book.)
3. Put the idea into play, and watch what happens.
4. Do step number three again—and again.
5. Continue feeding your mind and building your library until self-help becomes a way of life for you.

CHAPTER 3

You Can Get Wealthy Only If You Know What Wealth Is

Genius is the ability to simplify those things we perceive as complicated.
—C. W. Gran

Picture this scenario: You've found a method of generating $4,000 to $6,000 of steady, reliable monthly income. It's a fairly simply method, something you could put into action within the next 90 to 120 days. And the income is passive, which means you don't have to spend eight hours a day at the plant or the office to earn it.

Would you quit your job?

I hope you saw yourself handing in your resignation.

Of course, $4,000 to $6,000 a month is not a fortune, but for most people it's enough to cover basic living expenses, allow for reasonable recreation and entertainment, and provide the freedom to begin building wealth. This is what financial independence is. It's the first step in becoming wealthy; it's the ability to break free of the shackles of a workaday job; it's the recognition that money rarely comes in windfalls but rather in steady, planned, increasingly larger increments.

When most of us think about becoming millionaires, our minds automatically reject the picture. Why? First, because we associate making money with pain. Second, because the idea of a million dollars is so far outside the realm of our day-to-day experience that we feel it is unattainable. And third, because becoming wealthy means a lot of work and responsibility, and it's definitely something that only happens to other people.

The result is almost guaranteed failure.

So what should you do to change the pattern?

First, as we've already discussed, do what other wealthy people have done and find something you love, so that making money is not painful. In later chapters, we'll take a look at various ways you can accomplish this.

Second, you need to learn how to set up short-term and midrange goals and make them work for you. It's not necessary to start with a goal of $1 million; you just have to start with enough income to allow you to quit your job. Then you move on to $250,000, then $500,000, and then $1 million. Once you are financially independent, you can build on the momentum to reach true wealth.

Third, take action and don't let anything deter you.

If you're doing something you enjoy, the work and responsibility are easy to accept, and the idea of being wealthy is even more natural than being poor ever was.

WHAT *NOT* TO DO WITH FINANCIAL INDEPENDENCE

When I tell people I was financially independent at age twenty-three, their reaction is usually one of awe. They make comments about my good fortune or my "Midas touch." They tell me I must be a genius, or that I have incredible luck.

That's all totally absurd. I don't have a Midas touch, I'm not a genius, and there wasn't much luck involved in what I did.

What was financial independence for me was still poverty or at best a modest income for most people. After three years at the slaughterhouse, I was earning $6 an hour, or about $1,000 a month. Granted, $1,000 went a lot further then (in the late

1970s) than it does now, but it didn't fund a luxurious lifestyle. I was able to meet all my personal bills with that salary, which meant that if I had $1,000 a month from another source, I could safely quit my job.

Financial independence for me was only $1,000 a month. When I had created a net income of $1,400 a month from my real estate investments, I knew I could leave the slaughterhouse and concentrate all my efforts on becoming wealthy. I'll explain how I did that, but the point here is not that I had managed to build an income independent of my job—an income that actually paid more than my job—but how I used that income.

Here's what I did *not* do. I did not use any of that extra money on consumable items, such as cars, jewelry, or clothing that would depreciate in value and create debt. While I was still working at the slaughterhouse, I plowed every dollar I made in real estate back into my hobby of moneymaking to get the income up to a level that would cover my basic monthly bills: my mortgage, my car payment, and necessities for my family. Once I had enough money coming in to do that, I quit my job and invested all of my time in my hobby.

And this is the most pleasurable hobby I've ever had: the hobby of accumulating wealth and security for myself and my family. My success at this hobby has given me the freedom to pursue other interests, such as boating, fishing, tennis, and enjoying time with my wife, children, and friends. And because I was willing to forgo luxuries early on, I can now afford expensive cars, elegant jewelry, and clothes for myself and my family, and an assortment of other consumer items that were once only dreams.

You see, the first step toward financial independence is a small one. It's creating just enough regular income to allow you to quit your job so you can focus your energies on the various vehicles that can and will make you a millionaire. When you look at financial independence from this angle, it's not overwhelming; in fact, it's quite manageable. And you'll never again fall victim to the idea that success is beyond you.

WHAT YOU MUST HAVE IN COMMON WITH THE WEALTHY AND THE SUPERWEALTHY

The business of getting wealthy in America has changed over the past quarter century or so, and successful wealth seekers have adjusted their strategies accordingly. One of the fastest-growing methods of making money in America today is being in business for yourself.

Small business are truly the backbone of the American economy. More than a half million small businesses with employees open every year in the United States—and that doesn't count the part-time and full-time operations that don't have employees. This spirit of entrepreneurship is not exclusive to America—it's thriving around the world. Even traditionally socialist countries are seeing the wisdom of private enterprise. Individuals across the globe are seizing the opportunity to be in business for themselves and to control their own destinies.

There is, however, a difference between people who start a business just to make a living and people who start a business to become wealthy. The people in the second category all have something in common with one another and with high-dollar-earning corporations: with few exceptions, they all own real estate. Certainly, they all make money in a variety of ways, but their portfolios have a solid foundation of real estate investments. In many cases, the superwealthy receive a high percentage of their long-range money—that is, steady yields from assets that regularly increase in value—from real estate.

I have always believed that intelligence means you can learn from your mistakes, but true genius means you also learn from the mistakes and experiences of others. So if there is a clear pattern of wealthy individuals investing in real estate, and you want to become wealthy, does it make sense for you to follow their example? Of course it does.

Consider Arnold Schwarzenegger. Before being elected governor of California, he made millions in movies, but he was also an extremely savvy real estate investor. He was buying and fixing up run-down properties in California while he was still an obscure bodybuilder. In fact, that's what he did while he was training for the competitions that would ultimately make him famous. For Schwarzenegger, real estate was the initial stepping-stone toward financial independence and the freedom it would provide him to pursue his acting career, other wealth-building opportunities, and eventually politics.

Bob Hope will be remembered as a gifted entertainer, but he was also a savvy California real estate investor who earned the nickname Mr. Real Estate because he owned so much land. His pal Bing Crosby also invested in real estate. Actress Jane Seymour is a multimillionaire, and she didn't earn it all from television miniseries. A major portion of Seymour's fortune came from buying California real estate, restoring houses, and reselling them for a considerable profit. Cable news pioneer Ted Turner is Time Warner's largest individual shareholder and has a number of other business interests—but since he is the largest private landowner in the United States (some 1.8 million acres in ten states), it's probably safe to say that he receives a substantial portion of his income from real estate. German billionaire Josef Schorghuber bought a sheep pasture in 1954 and turned it into the first of thousands of office and housing developments in Munich. He later diversified into other businesses, including breweries and travel agencies, but real estate remained a strong portion of his wealth portfolio.

When Taikichiro Mori died in January 1993, at the age of eighty-eight, he was known as the richest private citizen in the world. He made his $13 billion fortune in Tokyo real estate. The Hunt family of Texas is best known for oil money, but their real estate holdings are major. When billionaire Ross Perot disclosed his financial holdings during the 1992 presidential campaign, his portfolio included a significant amount of real estate in addition to tax-free state and municipal bonds and other relatively risk-free investments.

Because these wealthy individuals recognize the value of real estate, it naturally follows that the corporations they influence also invest in real estate. If you check the holdings of the world's major corporations, you'll find they include real estate.

Let's bring the idea of real estate investment closer to home: the largest single purchase most people will ever make will be their home, and the largest single sum of money they will ever receive will come from the sale of that house. For that reason alone, you need a solid understanding of the various ways real estate can contribute to your bottom line.

SIMPLE BUT NOT EASY

Are you ready for a simple plan to reach financial independence? Great!

But first, note that I used the word *simple,* but I didn't use the word *easy.* Becoming financially independent is simple, but it's not necessarily easy.

Simple means anyone can do it.

Simple means it does not take complex formulas to figure it out.

Simple means anyone with common sense can go out and do it if he or she has any initiative at all.

Not easy, on the other hand, means you may have to make some phone calls. You might have to get up early. You might even have to do some paperwork.

Not easy means that anything worthwhile in life is not going to be tossed in your lap because you just happen to be a nice person.

What *simple but not easy* does mean, though, is that you can achieve financial independence if you want it badly enough. My wife and I have done it. The millionaires and billionaires I just told you about did it. Thousands of my students have done it. I have friends who started out as construction workers and are millionaires today. I offer these examples to prove that no matter who you are, no matter what your present circumstances are, no matter what your background is, financial independence is within your grasp.

REACHING FINANCIAL INDEPENDENCE
IN 180 DAYS OR LESS

Imagine a typical house in Any City, USA. In places like Detroit or St. Louis, this house might sell for $150,000. In Los Angeles or even Florida, the price might be $300,000. For the purpose of explanation, the actual price doesn't matter, but we will assume that every house in the neighborhood sells for a comparable amount.

The problem with purchasing such a house to rent as an investment is that in most cases the rent won't cover the mortgage payment.

Or could it?

If you take the conventional viewpoint, the answer is no. But by changing your perception you'll see that buying a house like this one is just one of many ways you can put yourself on the fast track toward financial independence. Here's one technique I used.

After I moved to Florida, I found a house listed in the real estate classifieds of the local paper in Fort Myers. The owner was very motivated to sell the property because she wanted to move closer to her children, who lived in another city. She was more interested in a steady income than in a large, lump-sum payment that would have cost her thousands in capital gains taxes, so she agreed to take a small down payment and hold the mortgage. This was perfect for me, because it meant that I didn't have to go through the hassle of getting a bank loan or the expense of paying points.

The house had five bedrooms upstairs. Downstairs there was a living room, a dining room, and another large room. I left the living room alone but hired a carpenter to turn the other large room and the dining room into four rooms. It cost me $500 and the price of plywood and prehung doors from the local building supply store. Then I put the following ad in the newspaper:

Cozy rooms for rent—$55 per week.

Now, $55 was about $10 below what other rooms in the area were renting for, but everything else was comparable—size, furnishings, the number of bathrooms (this house had three the tenants shared), etc.—so it took me less than two weeks to achieve 100 percent occupancy. I had ten rooms to rent out, which meant each week I was bringing in almost as much as I would have in a month if I had rented the house to a single family.

Here's how the numbers stacked up (remember, this was back in the early 1980s; real estate prices, rents, and materials were lower then, but the arithmetic works the same):

RENTAL INCOME

---

10 rooms @ $55 each per week = $550 per week
$550 per week x 4.3 weeks = $2,365 per month
$2,365 per month x 12 = $28,380 per year

MONTHLY EXPENSES

Mortgage = $676.81
Other expenses* = $322.00
* Insurance, taxes, utilities, garbage collection

SUMMARY

Total rents = $2,365
Less mortgage = $676.81
Less expenses = $322.00
Net monthly profit = $1,366.19

My profit, or net positive cash flow on this house, was more than $16,000 per year. Even after subtracting my initial costs, this is a tidy sum to earn by doing little more than making bank deposits.

So I did it again. My next property was a larger house that I was able to convert into thirteen rooms. Of course, my expenses were higher—about $1,500 per month—but that still left me with a net positive cash flow of $1,500 per month. In a short time, with some creative thinking, those two little rooming houses were earning me $2,800 a month. That's over $33,000 a year net income—more money than most people earned at their job, working eight or more hours a day doing something they hated.

If you had a little more information on the details and put a little pressure on yourself, could you make one small rooming house deal in the next 90 to 120 days? Sure you could. You might even stretch it to two deals, because that will give you your first taste of financial independence—and believe me, nothing tastes sweeter.

Does this mean your destiny is running rooming houses? No, not unless you want to do so. But consider this: Conrad Hilton, who founded the Hilton hotel chain, got his start by renting rooms in his family's New Mexico home. In chapter 8, I'll explain rooming houses in complete detail, so you'll have the information you need to use this wealth-building vehicle.

Are rooming houses the only way to gain financial independence? Of course not. Rooming houses are a possible, simple, manageable first step, and they will buy you the freedom to pursue your dreams. However, they are just one way, not the only way.

Since buying my first two rooming houses, I have owned or been involved in dozens of other businesses that have earned varying amounts of money and increased my wealth. More than half of these were started with little or no money. The point is, I was able to get involved in these other businesses because I had financial independence, not necessarily a lot of capital, and because I had taught myself to see things other people didn't.

CHAPTER 4

How to Turn $1,000 into $4.7 Million in Eighteen Months

People are always blaming their circumstances for what they are. I don't believe in circumstances. The people who get on in this world are the people who get up and look for the circumstances they want, and, if they can't find them, make them.
—George Bernard Shaw

Once you know how great it feels to have your own personal fortune, you'll never again be satisfied with just getting by. When a series of circumstances tied up most of my money and resources for an extended period, I had to figure out how to rebuild my fortune—and do it quickly. This is how I took $1,000 and turned it into $4.7 million in just eighteen months, and how you can do it, too.

But first, a brief history.

I made my first fortune in real estate in upstate New York. I bought run-down properties, fixed them up, and turned them into steady moneymakers. By the time I was twenty-five, I owned well over $1 million in real estate and was an owner or a partner in several other businesses. I was financially independent because of the income my properties and businesses generated, so I decided it was time to investigate investment opportunities in other parts of the country. I chose Florida for a number of reasons.

The most obvious was the climate. I was tired of six months a year of freezing temperatures and snow. It's harder to do exterior maintenance in the winter in the North, and the heating bills were an expense I thought it would be nice to get rid of. Properties in a more attractive climate should be easier to maintain and therefore more profitable, I reasoned.

Another important consideration was that New York was losing population at the rate of about 4 percent per year at the time, but Florida was growing by leaps and bounds. Property values in New York were fairly stagnant, but they were rapidly increasing in Florida. Though I could have continued to increase my personal wealth in New York, I decided that if I was going to continue investing in real estate, I wanted to do it in a growing area.

Before I tell you what happened when I moved, let me emphasize that just because you live in a Northern climate, you aren't automatically excluded from using my methods to make money with real estate or other businesses. Every geographic region has its advantages and disadvantages, and I'll explain more about how to recognize and capitalize on various circumstances as we go along. For now, let me reassure you that older Northern and Midwestern cities are great places to begin investing in real estate because the properties are usually affordable and they generate decent cash flow. In addition, older cities have a variety of government programs that offer incentives to people who are willing to invest in disadvantaged areas.

I have used those programs and made money while I provided a valuable service to the community. But I was ready to move on, so I took a trip to Florida. I had been there before on vacations, but now I was looking with an eye to investing. I had to find an established city with distressed and older properties that I could rehabilitate, but I also wanted a vibrant and growing area for other business opportunities. I found the ideal situation in southwest Florida with two neighboring communities, Fort Myers and Cape Coral.

Fort Myers is an older city. It was the site of Thomas Edison's winter home and laboratory, and Henry Ford had a home there for many years. I knew I would have no trouble finding older properties to fix up. The adjacent city, Cape Coral, began as a hundred square miles of scrubland on the Gulf of Mexico in 1958. The second-largest city in land area in the state (the largest is Jacksonville), it is an excellent example of foresight on the part of its developers. They dug more than four hundred miles of navigable canals that will take a boater from his backyard right out to the Gulf of Mexico. Thanks to those canals, waterfront property—which almost always goes for a premium price—is plentiful in Cape Coral. The town was planned for an eventual population of 500,000. When I first saw it, only 37,000 people made their homes there; today the population has grown to approximately 250,000 and the city is one of the hottest real estate markets in the country. Talk about an embryo opportunity!

A Realtor I met with had been working in the area for about sixteen years, and he had long since achieved millionaire status thanks to Cape Coral real estate. He had a deal on twelve lots for $24,000 that sounded good, so I gave him a deposit and listened attentively as he tried to sell me on the idea of moving to Cape Coral.

I investigated a few more cities before heading back to New York. I was still debating the idea of moving as I drove through North Carolina and had to turn the heat on in the car because it was getting colder outside. That clinched it: I wanted to move. All I had to do was convince my wife to give up the familiarity and security of the family, friends, and community she had lived with all her life and move fifteen hundred miles away to a place where she didn't know a soul. I thought it would take every ounce of persuasion I could find.

WRONG DECISIONS GIVE YOU RIGHT EXPERIENCES

The temperature was below freezing and it was snowing when I got home. I presented my idea to Ingrid, and to my surprise, she was immediately enthusiastic. We decided our best strategy would be to dissolve our New York holdings. We thought we could do that in six months, so we set a goal of moving the following September.

I put our properties on the market. Because of our circumstances, I was now a motivated seller. This is good from a buyer's point of view, and I'll explain more about it in chapter 6, but for now suffice it to say that I was at a definite disadvantage, particularly in a stagnant market. I received several ridiculously low offers, but I had already decided on my bottom line, and I was determined to get it.

Though I was charging forward at full speed with our plans to move, I decided to back out of the lot purchase in Cape Coral. Up until that point, all of my successes had occurred when I controlled my own investment—that is, when I saw the property, knew the market, and negotiated the deal either by myself or with a real estate agent. Even though the Realtor in Cape Coral had been introduced to me with a strong referral from a close friend, the fact was that I barely knew him, and I was getting ready to send him a sizable down payment on lots I had never seen that were far away. Another factor was that although I had plenty of cash flow, I didn't have much ready cash at the moment to use as working capital; my assets were tied up in the real estate I was trying to sell.

I decided that the Cape Coral lots were just too risky, so I forfeited my deposit and canceled the deal. It turned out to be an expensive mistake, because the broker found another investor for those lots, who sold them again nine months later for $60,000—a $36,000 profit. I may have made a bad decision, but obviously there was plenty of money to be made in Florida. Notice what I just said. I missed a $36,000 opportunity and thought it was great because now I knew for sure there was plenty of money to be made in Florida.

I'm telling you this part of my story so you know that successful people make mistakes, too. The difference is that they don't quit because they make a mistake; they learn and keep going, and that's what you have to do. I have studied the life stories of many successful people, and they've all made their share of mistakes. They are proof that making a mistake doesn't mean you've failed; it just means you have to find another way, take a different action, and produce a different result. Mistakes give you the experience you need to make better decisions the next time. Never let the possibility of making a mistake keep you from pursuing your dreams.

Gail Borden's first attempts to concentrate foods resulted in a "meat biscuit" that consumers denounced as an inedible failure. When he later tried to condense milk, he was happily unaware that scientists of the day said the process was impossible. Early efforts at condensing milk produced burned, foul-tasting broths, but Borden finally found a technique that worked. His first condensed-milk company failed when consumers were slow to buy the product. His second company was better financed and also benefited from a growing public awareness of the need for food cleanliness and quality standards. That plant grew into one of the world's food giants. Gail Borden died in 1874 and is buried in New York's Woodlawn Cemetery. On his tombstone are the words "I tried and failed; I tried again and again, and succeeded."

Fred Smith came from a moneyed background and was a student at Yale when he presented a then unique concept for an air freight operation in a business term paper. One can only imagine the chagrin of the professor who gave the paper a C, because Smith would make the concept it outlined into one of the greatest entrepreneurial success stories of our time: Federal Express Corporation, now known as FedEx.

Missing that Florida deal wasn't the only error I made during this period. I was working hard at marketing my properties, but I couldn't find anyone who was willing to pay my asking price. We had to push our moving goal from September to January. But we were still determined to go, and Ingrid and I made a trip to Cape Coral together in November. We bought a six-unit apartment building there with about $4,000 cash by assuming three existing mortgages and arranging for seller financing on a fourth mortgage. (I'll explain how to use these and other creative financing techniques in later chapters.) We planned to live in one unit and rent the others while we built up our real estate portfolio in Florida.

On the surface, moving from a nice house in New York to a much smaller apartment in Florida might look like a step backward, but we didn't think so. It was what we had to do to reach our ultimate goal, and we were willing to make what some people might think of as a sacrifice. But we knew it would be just a temporary lifestyle change while we worked on getting to where we really wanted to be.

Back in New York, I met a young investor at a bank foreclosure auction. He had bought several run-down properties and was fixing them up nicely. He had also arranged for some government rehabilitation loans, and it seemed as if he knew what he was doing. Since I was going to hold the mortgage on the properties in New York, this was an important consideration. We spent months negotiating, and at least ten times I thought we'd settled on a deal only to have him come back a day or two later with a totally different proposal. This bugged me, but I was motivated seller, and I was trying hard to stay on schedule with my goal of moving to Florida. Of course, today I know the difference between being goal-oriented and just plain stubborn, but back then I was determined not to let anything get in my way.

I sold a few of my properties to a couple of investors I had worked with before and finally agreed on the purchase terms for the rest with the young investor I had been negotiating with for so long. He was getting a great deal, and we set the closing for January 29. I planned to close on the deal in the morning and be in my car with my family—my wife, my toddler daughter, and my infant son—heading to Florida by lunchtime.

When I arrived at my attorney's office, thinking all I had to do was sign a few papers, I was slapped with the news that the buyer wasn't ready to close. In an obvious stall, he claimed his attorney still had to review some points in the contract. But he generously assured me it was a minor detail, and he would manage the properties until we closed.

I had a bad gut feeling about the deal, but everything was packed, we had the apartment building in Florida, and we were ready to go. So I arranged for my accountant and attorney to handle the money. The buyer was to collect the rents and turn them over to my accountant for deposit, and to submit any request for maintenance monies to my accountant.

Six months later, we still hadn't closed. Worse yet, the properties that had showed such a handsome profit when I managed them were now operating almost at breakeven. I flew back to New York to find that my so-called buyer was ripping me off royally. He had arranged for unnecessary maintenance at absurdly high prices. He wasn't responding to legitimate maintenance requests from tenants. He wasn't bothering to turn over utility bills to the accountant, so they were going unpaid. He was also reporting rented apartments as vacant and pocketing the money himself.

I have no idea how much money he made from my properties during that time with his unique brand of management, and even today I don't like to think about it. However, I did learn a valuable lesson about absentee management of low- and moderate-income properties. It's difficult to manage these properties from a distance. Over the years I've owned virtually all types of real estate in just about every income range, and I'm comfortable using management companies for commercial and upper-income residential properties, but low- and moderate-income units need an owner or a managing partner nearby.

So I formally advised my "buyer" that I was backing out of our deal, and I went to work correcting the damage he'd done and looking for legitimate buyers. It took another six months—a year after we'd moved—before I sold all my New York properties and was able to realize the cash flow from holding the mortgages that I had originally anticipated. This was a serious setback, but I don't consider it a failure. It was a learning experience for me—and I hope for you, too.

While all of this was going on in New York, I was figuring out how to survive and prosper in sunny Florida. My money was tied up in New York, and I didn't have a lot of cash. The market was different from what I was used to. Even more critical is that Florida, because of the transient nature of its population, is a difficult place to establish banking relationships. Let me tell you, going in a matter of weeks from comfortable financial independence to worrying about how I was going to support my family was emotionally devastating. I felt as if I didn't have a choice, so I started looking for a job.

The job I found was selling vending equipment on commission. I had to travel around the state, and I spent about three months getting nowhere fast. I quit that job and got a real estate license. My logic was that I would have an "in" in the local market and I could present my own offers. I would also have the opportunity to try to sell some properties for the commission.

My low and no-money-down offers were being rejected as fast as I could make them. The properties I was trying to represent as a real estate agent were vacant lots—not an area in which I had much expertise. I wasn't very successful there, either. I was discouraged and frustrated. I had been so successful in New York; why couldn't I repeat that performance in Florida?

LEARNING FROM GETTING OFF TRACK

I finally got fed up enough to figure out what my problem was. I had been flailing away at things I didn't know much about and that hadn't made me much money. My success in New York had been built on income properties; it was a comfortable and natural environment for me. So why was I messing around with all this other stuff?

The answer was that I had allowed myself to get off track. I knew where I wanted to be and I knew what I had to do to get there, but I wasn't heading in the right direction. And I wasn't really sure how I'd gotten turned around.

When people get off track, they rarely do it a mile at a time. If they did, their mistakes would be noticeable and easy to correct.

People get off track an inch at a time. Then, inch by inch, they get farther away from the track until they're off a mile, but because they did it so gradually they don't realize what's happened. All they know is that they're lost.

I had gotten off track because I'd refused to recognize the differences in the market and in the bankers in Florida. It would have been the same if I'd gone to any other part of the country; every area has its own business personality, and you have to learn that personality before you can successfully do business there. I had gotten farther off track by focusing too much time and energy on areas I didn't know enough about. Once I realized this, I was able to get myself back on track in a hurry. I decided to get back to the basics of what I knew would work, and that was dealing in various aspects of income properties.

IF IT WORKED THE FIRST TIME, IT CAN WORK EVEN BETTER THE SECOND TIME

I sat down and reviewed the things I had done in New York that had worked and mapped out a plan to make the most money in the least amount of time. I set long-term goals, then broke them down into monthly increments. I made detailed to-do lists outlining the daily and weekly tasks that were necessary to reach those goals. I developed a plan that would turn $1,000 into $4.7 million in just eighteen months. As I go along, you'll see how you can follow the same plan, regardless of where you are, and start building your own personal fortune immediately.

START BUILDING YOUR LINE OF CREDIT RIGHT NOW

We'll discuss credit in detail later, but I want to make this point now: you need to build your credit rating and establish relationships with lenders, and you need to start today.

Whether you have good credit, bad credit, or no credit, follow the advice in chapter 17 to establish and strengthen your credit rating and expand your personal line of credit—that is, the amount of money you can borrow (either secured or unsecured) to use to build wealth.

Once I had established my creditworthiness, plenty of institutions were happy to lend me money. And I was happy to take it, then use their funds as my springboard to financial independence and wealth both in New York and again in Florida. You can do the same thing.

GETTING ON TRACK CAN MAKE YOU $3,000 IN LESS THAN TWO MONTHS

While I was building my banking relationships, I was also busy looking for property. I found a run-down four-unit apartment building with an asking price of $75,000. Other similar properties nearby were appraised much higher, so this was clearly a good investment.

I bought the building with a 10 percent down payment. I was able to make the purchase with this relatively small down payment because the seller was willing to hold the mortgage, and sellers don't typically require as high a down payment as a conventional lender does. Then I immediately had the property cleaned up and painted and some minor repairs done. A little bit of new landscaping provided a finishing touch. I paid for this work using the line of unsecured credit I had established.

A month later, I had the property appraised at $130,000. I applied for a new mortgage based on the improved value. At the time, banks were willing to lend only 75 to 80 percent of a property's appraised value, so I was able to get a loan for $106,000 (81 percent of the appraised value). I used that money to pay off the original mortgage of $68,000 (which was the asking price of $75,000 less my down payment and the credits I received at closing) plus the $5,000 in signature loans that paid for the fix-up.

My new monthly mortgage payment was $815.04; my rental income was $2,000 a month. Even after paying the additional expenses of taxes, insurance, water and sewer, trash collection, and so forth, the building produced a positive cash flow. The bottom line was that I now had some independent income—money that would come in month after month without me having to go to an office every day—and I had more than $33,000 in nontaxable cash to use as I pleased. I used that run-down property that plenty of other people had overlooked to achieve a financial goal and provide the capital to do more, and it was easy.

I was definitely back on track.

HOW TO GET A BANKER TO GIVE YOU
A HOUSE PLUS $3,000 IN CASH

You've probably heard over and over that the best form of advertising is word of mouth. That's true in every business, especially real estate. When you provide a service that people need and you do a good job, deals will come to you. That's what was now happening to me, I've seen it happen to my students, and it will happen to you if you follow my plan.

A fellow I met through the real estate office I worked in approached me one day with a deal he thought I might be interested in. He told me about a lady who owned a home in Cape Coral that was being foreclosed. She had lived in the house with her husband, who had abandoned her and disappeared without a trace a year or so earlier. The memories she associated with the house were pretty horrible, so she moved out. Her son moved in with several other guys and a pack of dogs and cats. They made payments for a while, but eventually stopped and then moved out.

I went to look at the property immediately. It had three bedrooms, two baths, a Florida room, and a den that would also work as a home office. But its condition was a classic example of cosmetic distress. Animal excrement was on every bit of carpeting, garbage was strewn everywhere, the rooms were still full of discarded junk and clutter, and the lawn was overgrown and out of control. It was perfect!

The next step was to meet the owner. She was very open with me. She had bought the house new nine years before. Her parents had loaned her $14,000 for the down payment, and she currently owed $22,000 on the mortgage, which was held by a local savings and loan. They were about six months into foreclosing, so it wouldn't be long before she lost her entire interest in the property. There were some other legal complications because her former husband's name was on the deed, and she had put the house in the hands of the court, which had appointed a court master to act in good faith for her.

Her primary concern was recouping the $14,000 her parents had loaned her, and she didn't care how it was paid. So I made an offer to take care of the $22,000 existing mortgage either by assuming the old one or getting new financing, which would stop the foreclosure. I would also pay her $14,000 in the form of a second mortgage over twenty years at 11 percent. On the second mortgage, there would be no payments for two years, and no interest would accrue during that time. I explained that I needed those two years of freedom from payments to be able to take care of the repairs and improvements the house obviously needed to make it livable.

The owner accepted the offer, so I submitted it to the court master and the judge, who also approved the deal. While I was waiting for their decision, I went to the savings and loan that held the mortgage to see what it could do. Several things were working in my favor. It would save the bank money if the house was sold before foreclosure. Also, the house was in such disgusting condition that the bank would have to sink about $10,000 into it before it could reasonably expect to put it on the market. The market was slow at that time, so the bank would probably have to hold it for quite a while before it sold.

Here is something important you need to know about banks and other lending institutions: they are not in business to foreclose on property. They don't want to foreclose, and they will usually work with just about anyone in a good-faith effort to avoid a foreclosure. They know, and you need to realize, that their business is lending money, not managing or marketing property. So when you offer a banker who is facing a foreclosure an opportunity to avoid it, you'll get his attention and probably his cooperation. And that's what happened to me in this situation.

After several meetings, the bank's branch manager and I made a deal. He would give me a new $30,000 mortgage. With the proceeds, I would satisfy the old $22,000 mortgage and pay $5,000 toward the legal fees and costs the bank had incurred. The branch manager and I had agreed I would need some money to get the house into shape, so at the closing I received $3,000 from the loan proceeds. I used that money to clean, paint, and put in new carpet. When I was finished, the house was appraised for $63,000—a ready-made equity of $19,000. It was so nice that Ingrid and I moved into the house ourselves and put tenants in our apartment.

It may seem odd to you that a bank would agree to this kind of financing deal, where the buyer walks away with cash from the loan. This is actually common. The key was that I figured out the numbers ahead of time. I knew what the house was worth in its present state, what it would be worth after I fixed it up, how much those repairs would cost, and how the monthly mortgage payments would fit with my debt-to-income ratio. When I went in to talk to the banker, I was able to give him all this information before he asked and show him why this was a good deal for everyone.

I now had two bank mortgages in Florida, which helped establish my credibility with other lending institutions and gave me some borrowing power. I also positioned myself as an outlet for that bank with other foreclosed properties. The loan officers recognized the favor I was doing them by taking these run-down properties off their hands, and that motivated them to be a little more lenient with me in terms of financing.

I was geared up for a new surge of success. While I continued looking for more income properties, I went to work putting the other elements of my moneymaking plan into action.

HOW TO CASH IN TWICE ON ONE SMART BUY

I've already mentioned that the first building I bought in Cape Coral was a six-unit apartment building we purchased by assuming the existing mortgages and asking the owner to hold a mortgage. The purchase price was $198,000; I put up approximately $4,000 in cash and got credited for $12,000 down (an easy technique I'll show you later); assumed a first mortgage of $42,000, a second mortgage of $67,000, and a third mortgage of $45,000; the seller held a fourth mortgage of $32,000. It was a good deal, but I wasn't altogether happy with the terms of that fourth mortgage, which required semiannual payments of $5,000 each. As the due date of the first payment on that mortgage approached, I was strapped for cash because of the problems I was having with my New York properties. I put the building on the market, but there were no takers.

I approached the bank that held the first mortgage about refinancing the entire $186,000 I owed, but it was willing to lend me only $145,000. The second mortgage holder was a fellow in his sixties, and twenty-two years were left on his note. I offered him $45,000 in cash to settle the $67,000 debt. While he was considering the deal, I offered the third mortgage holder $30,000 to cancel the $45,000 debt, and the fourth mortgage holder $18,000 cash for his $32,000 mortgage. I didn't really think they would all agree to my proposals, but if one or two of them did, I could take the new first mortgage, use the borrowed $145,000 to get rid of that fourth mortgage with its large payments, and comfortably keep the building—and the cash flow it produced.

To my surprise, they all agreed to discount their mortgages for cash rather than taking the payments over the next twenty to thirty years. I took the new mortgage, paid off the three junior mortgages, and immediately made $41,000 profit in equity just by asking for discounts. I also appreciated the bonus of improving my cash flow by $620 a month, since my payments on the four loans totaled $2,200, and after the refinancing, the payment on the new loan was only $1,600. When I later sold the property for $209,000, my profit was $64,000 instead of $11,000, thanks to those discounts.

This technique is called discounting mortgages, which simply means the mortgage holder is willing to accept a cash payment of less than the total mortgage to settle the debt in full. Many sellers—especially those middle-aged and older—do not really want to be long-term mortgage holders. It might have sounded good when they agreed to hold the note, or that might have been the only way they could get the property sold. In many cases, after a year or so of receiving payments, they're happy to "take the money and run." You get the cash to pay them off by refinancing the property with conventional mortgage money, which you'll obtain either after improving the property if it was distressed or after other loan money becomes available.

I use seller financing and discount mortgages as a strategy when I buy, especially during down market cycles. When the market is slow, sellers are motivated to hold mortgages to sell their property. When the market loosens up, they would often rather have a lump sum of cash than payments over the years. Whenever I purchase a property with seller financing, I make a note in my calendar to follow up in a year or so and offer a discount.

You'll generally have more success with discounting mortgages when dealing with a private or individual lender, but don't automatically assume this technique won't work with a commercial lending institution. Though most do not routinely discount mortgages, many will consider it, especially if the loan is shaky and the property is at risk of being foreclosed. This technique is known as a short sale—essentially, the property is being sold for an amount that is "short" of what's owed on it, usually because the outstanding obligations (loans) on the property are greater than what it can be sold for. You'll never know if the lender will agree unless you ask, and the worst that can happen is you'll be turned down. The best, of course, is that you'll make a handsome contribution to your personal fortune.

CHAPTER 5

TURN AN IDEA INTO A $1 MILLION BUSINESS

Success is simply a matter of luck. Ask any failure.
—EARL WILSON

As I was laying out my personal wealth-building strategy, I was guided by a philosophy I hope you'll take to heart, too. It's this: you make a living with your hands, but you become wealthy with your mind.

As I mentioned in the last chapter, I have made a lot of money buying run-down properties and fixing them up. Today, my investment strategies focus more on land development and commercial projects, but you can still benefit from knowing what I learned the hard way. In the beginning, I did a lot of the labor myself, but eventually I realized that my time was better spent on negotiating deals, planning future investments, and managing the various stages of my projects. Plenty of people are looking for part-time work, either students or other people who want to supplement their regular jobs, and will do painting and other fix-up work on the weekends at affordable rates. You don't have to pay a professional painter $30 or $40 or more an hour when you can get a teenager to do the same work for $10 or $12 an hour—provided, of course, that the painting or other work being done is not regulated by any laws that require special permitting or licensing.

When I or any of the trainers who work for my company ask students at our introductory sessions how many people in the crowd would be willing to spend a Saturday painting a house for $150, more than half the hands in the room go up. That distresses me. Earning $150 a day may be a reasonable living, but it's not, and will never be, wealth.

I'm not saying you should never do any of the work yourself on your properties. What I'm saying is that you need to think about whether slinging a paintbrush or hauling trash is the best use of your time if you want to become wealthy.

A SMALL BUSINESS THAT CAN REALLY MAKE YOU MONEY

When I began accumulating properties in Florida, I formed a separate corporation to operate as the management company. The properties paid the management company for its services, which included maintenance, repairs, and rent collection. I hired two people to handle the routine maintenance—changing locks on doors, cutting the grass, painting, or whatever needed to be done—but they weren't always busy. Rather than shortening their hours, laying them off, or paying them to do nothing, I approached other owners of moderate-income properties and negotiated contracts to provide management services for them.

To understand the tremendous opportunity here, you should know that most management companies don't do a particularly good job, especially if property management is just a sideline business for them. Most real estate companies have a property management department, but it doesn't mean they know what they're doing; often, it's just a service they offer to help them get listings. It probably works fairly well, too, because if the property is poorly managed, it may not be profitable, and eventually the owner may be glad to give the real estate office the listing to get rid of what has become a headache.

An independent property management company just doesn't have the interest an owner does. Also, many management companies, especially those associated with real estate offices, are geared more to middle- and upper-income properties. If you can offer quality management, particularly on low- and moderate-income properties, you'll find it fairly easy to get contracts from other owners.

For their services, management companies generally receive a percentage of the collected rents, but they may also work on a fee-per-unit or flat-rate basis, or a combination of a percentage and a flat fee. The range is typically 10 to 15 percent, with harder-to-manage properties commanding a higher fee. This fee covers keeping tenants in the units, accounting for rents, and arranging for necessary maintenance. Actual maintenance and repair expenses are billed back to the owner and have the potential to be even more profitable than your basic management fee.

One of my first management contracts was for a thirty-four-unit building. The rent averaged $400 per apartment (remember, this was back in the early 1980s), which meant the building generated $13,600 in gross revenue each month. The property was not in the best shape when I got the contract, so I negotiated a 15 percent management fee. That meant I had the potential to earn more than $24,000 a year on this building alone. It only took a few more properties to build a $100,000-a-year business.

I used the maintenance workers I already had on my payroll to handle the work needed on my contract properties. The first few times I sent them out to do maintenance, I simply billed the owner my actual cost. But then I found out how many other management companies and even the owners themselves handled problems: they looked in the telephone directory for companies that provided whatever type of repair they needed—and they paid top retail dollar for the service. To replace the washer in a leaky faucet, for example, they called a plumbing company that sent out a licensed plumber and charged $35 for the service call and another $35 an hour for labor, plus retail price on parts. I was charging $7 for my hourly worker, plus my actual cost for parts, which I bought with my contractor's discount.

I decided to start billing maintenance and repairs as though I had to hire out the work instead of using my own employees. I still gave my clients a better deal than they would get going through the telephone book, so it was a win-win situation for both of us. For example, my trip charge was only $15 to $20 and my hourly rate was less than half of what they might otherwise have to pay, but my markup was at least double my cost. I also started charging the owners retail for parts, even though I had gotten a discount; if they had bought the parts themselves, they would have paid the full price, so they were still saving some money, and I had the cost of making the purchase and billing it back covered by keeping the discount. This is the capitalist system at work, it's what makes the United States such a great country, and it's why anyone who is willing to do what it takes can become a millionaire.

The bottom line was that my clients were getting a better deal with me than they'd ever gotten before, and I was making more on maintenance than I made on management. And in a matter of months, I had created a management and maintenance company that was showing profits of hundreds of thousands of dollars a year.

When I started my property management company, I owned ten rental units in Florida—a fourplex and a sixplex—plus the house I lived in. Managing them was easy and didn't take much time. But they, and the knowledge I had gained over the years, gave me the credibility I needed to contact other property owners about managing their buildings. To find prospective clients, all I did was look around. When I saw buildings in less-than-top condition, I made a note of the address. Once or twice a month I went to the courthouse and looked up the owners in the public records. (Today, you can do that online in the comfort of your home.) I wrote the owners a letter offering my services, then followed up with a telephone call. Some weren't interested, but enough were that I was able to quickly build a business generating more than enough cash flow to support my family and finance other investments.

Another advantage of being a property manager is that I was almost always first in line as a prospective buyer if the owner decided to sell. Since I had already proved how well I could manage their properties, negotiating seller financing was easier. Starting a property management business is not only great for immediate cash flow, it also provides you with tremendous long-term investment potential.

This is just one reason I strongly recommend that any real estate investor, especially in the early stages, should manage his or her own properties. The experience will give you the knowledge you need either to start your own property management firm or to protect yourself if you should decide to hire such a firm later on. This theory should apply to any business; after all, you wouldn't buy a restaurant franchise unless you knew how to run the place.

A technical note: some states require property management companies to have specific licenses if they are going to be managing property for other people. Usually you don't need a management license for your own properties. Other states don't have any licensing requirements at all. Check with your state's department of commerce or department of business and professional regulations to determine what sort of licensing, if any, you will need. And don't worry about not being "handy." You don't have to be able to perform any of the maintenance chores yourself, you just have to be able to make sure they get done and take the checks to the bank.

INCREASE YOUR PROFITS BY ACTING AS YOUR OWN CONTRACTOR—EVEN IF YOU DON'T KNOW ANYTHING ABOUT CONSTRUCTION

You probably know that most general contractors are essentially project coordinators. When a general contractor is hired to build a house or add a room or do a major repair, he or she doesn't actually do any of the physical work. Contractors simply hire subcontractors (electricians, plumbers, roofers, painters, drywall installers, and so on) who come in and do all of the work for them. The general contractor determines the specifications (what needs to be done and who needs to do it) for the job and makes sure the work is progressing satisfactorily and on schedule. And he or she makes a healthy profit for doing so.

Within certain limits, you can act as your own contractor without a license as long as you own the property. If you own your home right now and something goes wrong with the plumbing, you can call a plumber to come and fix the problem. You don't have to go through a general contractor; essentially, *you* are the general contractor who is contracting with the subcontractor to get the needed work done. The plumber has to have a license, but you don't. The same thing is true with any rental property you may own. You can call a roofer, a plumber, a painter, an electrician—any subcontractor you need to get the work done. And you can contract with them directly without being a licensed general contractor as long as you are the owner of the property involved. (You can also do this if you are a co-owner in partnership with other investors.) You pay the subcontractor directly, just as any general contractor would, but you don't have to pay the general contractor's markup, which can be anywhere from 25 to 400 percent. Use that savings to increase the equity in your property.

For example, let's say you have a property that needs work. Right now, the property is worth $150,000. When you finish the work, it will appraise at $200,000. You call a general contractor and get an estimate of $22,000. But then you figure out that if you act as the contractor and arrange for all the workers, you can get the same work done for $12,000—which means you'll have increased your equity position in the property by $10,000 when the work is complete.

Instead of having a general contractor handle everything, do as much as you can yourself and hire the subcontractors who gave you the lowest estimates. Purchase your own materials and negotiate discounts if you can. Use a handyman for jobs that don't require a license. Look for experienced workers (such as carpet installers, painters, drywall installers, etc.) who are willing to moonlight and work for you on the side for a fraction of what you'd have to pay the company they work for during the day.

Hire students to do nonskilled labor such as cleaning, landscaping, painting, and minor repairs.

The rules about acting as your own contractor vary by state and generally apply when you are doing work that requires obtaining a permit with your local building department. There may be limits to the amount you can borrow when acting as your own contractor, and you may not be able to do this with investment property if it is currently rented or you are planning to sell it in the near future. Check with your state's department of business and professional regulations or professional licensing division to find out exactly how much you can do without a general contractor's license.

Whether you act as your own contractor or hire a general contractor, be sure to take several good-quality photographs of the property both before and after the work is completed. Include these pictures in your portfolio to show future lenders what you do with your investment properties.

EVERYONE INVOLVED CAN MAKE A PROFIT

Especially in recessionary times, it's much easier to get home equity and home improvement loans on property you already own than to get mortgages to buy new properties. In the early 1990s and well into the 2000s, we saw an abundance of funds available for existing property repair and renovation. Actually, these days, plenty of lenders are offering home equity loans that can be used for anything. When you borrow against your real estate—whether it's your own home or investment property you own—only use that money to make more money. Use the money to improve the property you're borrowing against or to invest in or improve additional real estate. Do not use those funds on depreciating assets that will be worthless long before they're paid for.

A bonus that comes with creating your own property management company is that you may become eligible for commercial discounts at building supply stores, both independently owned stores and large chains. As you accumulate properties, your commercial discounts can become sizable, so call the stores you'll be buying from and find out how their discount program works before you start your first improvement project. What's more, you can use your discount for anything you purchase, even items for your own home. Do you see how even this small, informal business can both save you money and make you money on many fronts? It's not any one big deal that will make you rich; it's a series of deals and the small things that both save and make you money that will eventually add up to wealth.

Always be sure the property you are borrowing against will generate enough cash flow so that you cover your debt service and ideally have money left over. For example, let's say you have a four-unit building generating $3,000 a month in revenue. Your mortgage payment is $1,500, your monthly expenses (taxes, insurance, utilities, etc.) are $600. You have a $900-per-month positive cash flow, so you can afford to take out a home improvement loan as long as your monthly payments are less than $900. And it's possible your improvements may allow you to raise the rents and even increase your cash flow, in addition to increasing the value of—and therefore your equity in—the property.

On the other hand, if for the same apartment building your mortgage payment is $2,400, with monthly expenses of $600, you're breaking even, and you can't afford to increase your monthly expenses on the property. In this case, consider a home improvement loan only if you are convinced you will be able to raise your rents enough to cover the debt.

If for some reason you're having difficulty qualifying for a loan, find a partner who can. Show him or her how he or she will make a profit when the property is improved, and how the property will take care of repaying the loan. You'll both be winners.

HOW TO MAKE $200 TO $5,000 AN HOUR

Once you get started on a wealth-building program, you'll find that more opportunities than you can handle will drop in your lap. Success truly does breed success, so take advantage of it. When I got back on track and started prospecting properties, I was running into more good deals than I could buy. Once you train your eye and mind to see what the 95 Percenters overlook, you'll realize many great deals are out there.

As you begin buying properties, you'll be excited and you'll talk about it to people you know. As they see you accumulating real estate—and wealth—they'll want to know more about what you're doing and how you're doing it. And that can make you even more money.

My first experience with making money from my market knowledge was in New York when an insurance agent I'd known for a while came to talk to me about buying a policy from him. He asked me what I did and how I did it. I told him I invested in real estate and earned anywhere from a 30 to 100 percent return on my money. I explained the process to him the same way I'll show it to you in chapter 7. He got excited and wanted to know how he could do it, too.

At the time, I had several property deals I was working on, but I knew I didn't have the cash to buy them all. So I offered to pass one or two of the deals along to him—for a small fee, of course. There are two ways to do this. If you have a real estate license and the properties are listed, you can simply sell them as an agent and make a commission that way. If you don't have a real estate license and/or the properties aren't listed, but you have negotiated a good deal someone else would like to get in on, offer to turn it over to him or her for a fee. You can either mark the property up or change an hourly rate or a flat fee for your consulting time.

If you go the hourly route, charge at least $150 per hour; even $250 is not unreasonable for the service you're providing. I found it more profitable and easier just to add a premium of $3,000 to $5,000 to the price of the property; today, I'd probably add a premium in the range of $4,000 to $7,500. Even with that, everyone can win.

One of my first clients as an investment advisor was a church pastor I knew who told me he was interested in doing some investing to supplement his income. I had several deals in various stages of negotiation, but I knew I wasn't going to be able to complete them all. (It's always a good idea to have more deals in the works than you think you can do; you never know if one of them might not go through, and you always want other deals to fall back on.) One particular deal I had in the works fit the pastor's parameters exactly, so I showed it to him. He bought it and paid me a $5,000 consulting fee. Five years later, he still owned the property, had more than doubled his investment in equity alone, got a good tax write-off every year, and enjoyed a few thousand dollars a month in positive cash flow.

The method for doing this is to get the deal under contract and assign the contract to another buyer; it's commonly known as wholesaling, and we teach an entire advanced course on it because it's so profitable. You simply nail down all the details, write the contract in your name and/or assigns (or your company name and/or assigns), then assign the contract to another investor for a fee. This is done by creating a simple one-page agreement that stipulates you are assigning all of your rights under the contract to the other person for the compensation described.

You can handle the compensation any way you want. You can insist on full payment when you assign the contract, you can split it part on assignment and part on closing, or whatever works for you and the buyer. And believe me, there are plenty of potential buyers out there who are happy to pay you a fee for finding and negotiating their investments for them.

What's especially great about this type of investment advising is that it is truly a part-time activity that requires absolutely no cash to do. It's a great way to build up your bank account so you have the cash to do the deals that require it. Just a few hours of your time can be worth several thousand dollars. Or you can approach other investors and offer your advice and management skill for a part ownership. In my early days of investing, I had many profitable deals where someone else put up the money, I did the work, and we split the profits. Today, I'm more likely to be the funding source in a deal like that.

PARTNERS CAN BE WORTH
THEIR WEIGHT IN GOLD

In one case, a fellow I had bought a property from had another run-down building he wanted to sell. He saw how well I'd taken care of the first property, so I had his confidence. The only problem was that I couldn't get a loan because all the bankers in town thought I'd been borrowing too much. We decided that I would take half ownership in the property for overseeing the rehab. He qualified for a home improvement loan, and I used the money to get the building in great shape. It wasn't long before it was generating positive cash flow, and thanks to my half ownership, I made a nice profit when we sold the property a short time later.

A couple of my students in Lancaster, Pennsylvania, used this approach with their first investment. They found a house that had been condemned by the city and was in terrible shape. Their investor partner put up the cash to buy the house and get it fixed up, my students did the work, and they split the profits. They were able to purchase the house for $5,000 and the repairs cost $50,000. Once the repairs were complete, the house appraised at $74,900, which means that my students and their partner will share the $20,000 profit. Even more important, my students say they've gained the trust of the city's redevelopment agency and expect to work with that agency on future projects (see chapter 16 for more on how the government can help you become wealthy). In addition, they've proved to their families that my techniques work, and now their family members are out scouting deals for them. With just a few deals, these students expect to make enough money so they won't need funding partners in the future.

So don't stop prospecting when your personal investment plate is temporarily full or when you don't have cash of your own. Instead, let these skills continue working for you by expanding your prospecting to other investors and helping them build wealth, too.

SIMULTANEOUS CLOSINGS
WILL NET YOU THOUSANDS

As an alternative to just turning a deal over to another investor, you can buy property yourself and immediately sell it at a higher price. It's called a simultaneous or double closing, and here's how I do it.

I make an offer to purchase a good piece of property but make it contingent on financing and closing in ninety days. This contingency, which is included in the contract to purchase, means that I don't have to buy if I can't get financing, and I've given myself three months to find the money. Sometimes the seller doesn't want to give me ninety days; that's fine—depending on the deal, we can negotiate for a shorter time period. Then I talk the property up to the people I know and sometimes even advertise it. If I can find a buyer, I arrange for the two closings to be held simultaneously. The property is transferred briefly to me, then to the new owner. I don't have to come up with any cash, and I walk away with a nice profit for my efforts.

This is a technique I used often in my early days of real estate investing. Back then, most title companies would handle a simultaneous closing. Today, many will not, and you have to shop around to find one that will. But those title companies are out there and worth looking for.

BEYOND BUYING AND SELLING PROPERTY

When I first started investing in real estate, I had no idea that I would eventually be an owner or a part owner of dozens of companies, including the CEO of a public company with annual revenues of approximately $179 million and growing, or that I would have been involved in such a variety of businesses along the way. I was just looking for a way to build a financial future for myself and my family.

It didn't take me long to realize that while I could build substantial wealth with real estate investing alone, creating some ancillary businesses and even diversifying beyond real estate would provide greater opportunity and security. I began with the contracting and management companies I just told you about. Even though these were sole proprietorships that I owned and operated, setting up my business this way, rather than just doing everything as an individual investor, provided a variety of benefits. The separate entities made it easier to track my costs and profits, as well as identify various business patterns. As an individual, I had to pay full retail for rehab materials; my contracting company qualified for professional discounts, credit lines, and additional special services from paint stores, home improvement stores, and other suppliers. Having these companies also made it easier to borrow money for my investments. At the time, lenders were far more reluctant to approve loans for self-employed individuals than they are today. As an employee of a company—even one that I owned—I was viewed as a better risk than as a self-employed independent investor. It was absurd, but I knew that if I wanted to borrow money, I had to play by the rules of the lenders.

While my initial purpose in creating these companies was for the benefit of my own investments, I quickly realized that I could provide services to other investors and create additional income for myself.

After a few years of real estate investing and related business activites, I had the opportunity to get involved in a buyers' cooperative. Unfortunately, that company failed, but it provided me with a valuable education about running a business—knowledge that I'm still using today.

DIVERSIFICATION CAN TRANSLATE TO DOLLARS—LOTS OF THEM

Even after I was back on track and successful in Florida, I was still reading and studying how-to books and realized I had infor-

mation to share that wasn't in any of the books on the market at
the time. So I decided to write my first book, *Overcoming the
Hurdles & Pitfalls of Real Estate Investing*. The manuscript was
rejected by several major publishing houses before I struck a deal
with a company to publish the book if I would go on the lecture
circuit to promote it.

This led to my first venture into the publishing and public
speaking industries, and I loved it. I was working hard, traveling
around the country giving talks on real estate, and making a lot
of money—but more important, I was helping people change
their lives for the better. I wanted to be able to give people more
in-depth information, so I created my own training company. I
also created my own publishing operation to produce my books
and tapes. These operations gave me the opportunity for some
terrific on-the-job training in two new businesses, and I was excited.

I decided that if I could do this for myself, I could do it for
others. So I found other bright people with good information to
share and helped them set up training programs and put together
support materials in the form of educational books, tapes,
videos, and live instruction. As the seminar and publishing businesses grew, it made sense to set up a mail order operation and
expand our sales that way.

As those companies thrived, I continued looking for additional opportunities. Intuitively, I understood the value in diversification. I had achieved my goal of becoming a millionaire at the
age of twenty-seven, but I had no intention of stopping with that.
And it wasn't just for the money—all of my businesses were making a difference in the lives of my customers. My tenants had safe,
secure, sanitary housing. My students were learning how to invest in real estate and build their own financial futures. The trainers I worked with were helping people and making money for
themselves. And my companies were providing good jobs for
people. So it just made sense to me to keep building my business
empire—even though I didn't think of it in those terms at the
time.

I made a trip to Canada to study the real estate industry there and was introduced to the concept of biweekly mortgage payments. In 1985, I created Equity Corp. to offer a system to help people pay off their mortgages sooner, which also reduced the amount of interest they paid. We developed software called the Mortgage Reduction System and recruited consultants to sell the service. Today, the program is known as the Mortgage Payoff Acceleration Program (MPAP), and it's saving consumers literally billions of dollars in home mortgage interest.

In developing Equity Corp., I saw an opportunity to get into the computer business. In the mid-1980s, few people owned personal computers. People who wanted to become consultants for Equity Corp. could either buy just the software package, or, if they didn't have a computer, we would sell them a system bundled with all the software and peripherals they needed. Because we didn't want to restrict our computer sales to Equity Corp. consultants, we created a separate company that was on the leading edge of the personal-computer revolution.

TAKING THE LEAD IN EDUCATION

When I first got into the real estate education business, the training was delivered primarily through books and tapes and some weekend seminars. I developed a number of those products, and even though they sold well, I began to realize through customer feedback that people needed more. So I put together an intense weeklong training program called Millionaire U that I only offered four or five times a year. It started on Monday and ended on Friday, and the students spent eleven or twelve hours a day in the classroom and then had homework every night. We took them into the field to look at property and put together offers. Many of them actually bought properties during their training. We also taught them business, finance, marketing, and salesmanship. My goal was to teach them everything they needed to know to successfully invest in real estate in that one week. The students loved the program—it was exhausting but exhilarating. Most of them did well, but they didn't have the success ratio I wanted them to have.

In the mid-1990s, I decided to step back from the real estate seminar business. I was involved in some other businesses, I still had my own real estate investments to manage, and I was tired of spending so much time on the road.

Sometimes, a little distance is all it takes to see things clearly. I realized that I needed to restructure my seminar business into more of an education company and model the training after conventional education programs.

If you're familiar with the biblical story of Noah and the ark, you have probably thought about what Noah felt like when he was following God's instructions to build a boat in an area where people didn't even know what rain was. I had moments of feeling a little that way as people tried to tell me that what I wanted to do wouldn't work.

Of course, it wasn't the first time in my life I'd had to deal with naysayers. And this wasn't some idea that I came up with on the spur of the moment and decided to implement on a whim. I did a lot of research and study and invested a significant amount of time, resources, and money in converting the company to the new training format.

We launched the new program in 1996, and the wisdom of the decision was immediately apparent. Our students experienced a higher degree of satisfaction with their training, along with quicker and greater success in their real estate investments. In 1997, our training revenue under the new format was $5.56 million. Two years later, revenue topped $26 million. By 2002, it had jumped to $62 million; it more than doubled two years later with approximately $135 million in revenue in 2004; 2005 closed at approximately $179 million. We fully expect revenues to continue to increase at a similar rate for the forseeable future. We are doing something no one had done before, and it is obvious we are doing it right.

In 1998, Whitney Information Network Inc., the parent company of Whitney Education Group, went public. Over the next several years, we made a number of strategic acquisitions that helped drive our amazing growth. And as the public company was growing, I was still making personal real estate investments, some of which turned out to be the best deals of my entire career.

Shortly after I began buying raw land, I realized there was an opportunity in subdividing the land and building houses. I started by contracting with a builder, and it wasn't long before I was selling so many houses that the builder couldn't keep up. He was a great builder, but he needed help with the other aspects of his business. Instead of just bringing in another builder and splitting my business between the two, I suggested that the builder and I create a construction company. We brought in two more partners and made sure we had all our bases covered: operations, management, marketing, and sales. The four of us each have a percentage of ownership in the company. Currently, we're building more than 350 houses a year—and growing. This construction company is making millions of dollars a year and was profitable from the start.

It's important to note that the builder went from being a 100 percent owner of his company to being a part owner of the construction company we put together. But when he was running his own show, the best he could do was to build about forty houses a year, and he was running himself ragged. With our partnership, he's not working as hard, he's much less stressed, and he's getting a handsome share of the profits of a company that's building more than 350 houses a year. Our company is operating more efficiently, and that has a direct result on the bottom line. By being in partnership with me, this builder is making ten times more than he made in business by himself, and he's enjoying life more than ever.

It's also worth noting that I, personally, don't know how to build a house. I understand the general process, but I don't know how to mix and pour the foundation, how to put up the walls and install the roof trusses, or how to install electrical wiring or plumbing. But not knowing how to build a house has not stopped me from owning a highly profitable construction company, because I do understand the concept of how to start with a piece of vacant land and end up with a house a few months later.

In addition to the construction company, I also have a real estate development company; a mortgage company; a syndication company that puts together deals for investors to purchase acreage and other types of real estate; an interest in a title company; several small corporations that buy, sell, and develop real estate both domestically and internationally; and a number of other businesses.

CHOOSE THE BUSINESS THAT IS RIGHT FOR YOU

Most of the businesses I am involved with as an owner or an investor are related to education, training, real estate, and development. That makes sense for me, because those are the industries where I have expertise and experience. But it doesn't mean that I wouldn't consider an opportunity in another industry.

My general rule is this: if an opportunity comes along in an industry I don't know much about, I look at the numbers. Financial statements are financial statements, regardless of the business—and I know how to read financial statements. If you don't, you need to learn.

When I review a financial statement and the numbers look good, and I decide it's something I want to do, I look for an operating partner. I find someone with experience in the business and I give him an equity stake in the company. He also gets a salary and expenses, but because he is an owner, he has a strong motivation to make it succeed. And in doing this, I'll learn what I need to know about the business.

Regardless of the industry, I have certain guidelines that a deal must meet before I'll consider it. The primary one is that the deal has to generate a profit (or annual positive cash flow) of at least $1 million. If it won't, it's generally not worth my time.

Certainly this is a different position from what I took when I first started investing at the age of twenty. At that point, I would do pretty much any deal that was profitable. I did low-income re-habs, single-family properties, small apartment buildings, room-ing houses, small lease-option deals—all of the things that I have taught students how to do over the years. I didn't buy my first piece of investment property and then decide that I wouldn't do another deal unless I could net $1 million from it. If I had, I'd still be sitting where I started in New York with just one piece of property.

But as I continued investing and as I gained business experi-ence, I demanded more from my ventures. Remember, your in-vestments—whether property, stocks, or businesses—should work for you, not the other way around.

I have partners in many of the businesses I own because it makes sense. I'd rather own a piece of many bigger pies than all of just one or only a few small pies. And we all benefit. All in-volved make more money as part of a team than if they tried to go it alone. The various companies can grow faster, be more prof-itable, create more jobs, and contribute more to the community because they are well funded and well managed.

I hope you are starting to see the multitude of ways you can begin creating your personal fortune, regardless of where in life you are right now or where you've been.

CHAPTER 6

THE QUICKEST WAY TO BUILD A MONEY MACHINE

Opportunity is missed by many because it is dressed in overalls and looks like work.
—THOMAS EDISON

I've made fortunes in a number of businesses, but I know from personal experience that real estate is the simplest, fastest, and most productive way to generate significant sums of immediate cash, and it can help you lay the groundwork for even greater profits in the future. This is especially true for beginning investors.

Take a look around the area where you live right now. Is real estate more expensive than it was fifteen years ago? The answer is yes. Is real estate more expensive than it was twenty-five years ago? Yes, again. And is real estate more expensive than it was two hundred years ago? Definitely yes. In fact, America's Founding Fathers valued real estate ownership so highly that in the country's early days, the legal right to vote was limited, with few exceptions, to landowners.

The story is the same virtually all over the world. Real estate has steadily and consistently increased in value. If you want to build wealth, you simply cannot ignore an investment with this kind of track record. Of course, there have been cycles when the value of real estate has leveled out or even dipped slightly. But it always comes back, and comes back stronger than before.

One more question: If you had some money to bet right now, would you wager that in ten years real estate where you live will be more valuable than it is today? I'm not a gambler, but this is a bet I'd be willing to make.

A home is the largest single investment most people ever make in their entire lifetime, but I have found through talking with thousands of people that most homeowners don't have any idea why or how they bought their house. Maybe somebody told them owning is better than renting, or they just decided they should do what other people do and buy a house. So they go out, maybe with a real estate agent, shop around, find a house or a condominium they like, figure out how to get a loan and handle the closing, and suddenly they own a home.

The same process can apply to your second property, your third property, or even a business you might want to buy. You shop, you do research, you make commonsense decisions, you figure it out and get it done. It's that simple.

Think about this: If your home is the largest single investment you're likely to make in your life, doesn't it make sense that buying two or three other houses could, over time, have a significant and positive impact on your financial security? And if you could buy one house, don't you think buying a second one would be easier than the first? By the time you get to the third or fourth, you'll have plenty of confidence and expertise. Even if you don't net any positive cash flow and just let tenants' rent pay the mortgages off, in twenty or thirty years you'll have a substantial net worth and assets you can sell if you want to.

I became a millionaire in my twenties in New York. I did it all over again when I moved to Florida. And if I had to do it again, I would do it the same way. I have studied the techniques used by some of the world's wealthiest people, especially things they did to become wealthy, and I am convinced that my program is a "best of the best" combination of methods to build financial security.

Rich people who are also famous are the exception, not the rule. There are millionaires all over the world you've never heard of, and when you meet them, you wouldn't think they are wealthy. Most of them made their money with a combination of their own businesses and real estate. Here's what you need to know to make real estate your initial wealth-building vehicle.

HOW ECONOMIC CYCLES CAN MAKE YOU WEALTHY

Our economy moves in fairly predictable cycles, which include a period of high prosperity and growth, a slowdown, a recession, a gradual increase in activity, and then high prosperity again. We run through this cycle every seven to ten years. Learning to recognize these cycles and adjusting my strategies accordingly provided a major boost to my wealth-building plan. If you're going to become wealthy, you need to learn this, too.

You've probably heard that, especially during a recession, rich people get richer—and it's true. When the economy hits a downswing, most people tighten their belts and prepare to ride out the tough times by not doing anything. But wealthy people have the cash to take advantage of the bargains a recession offers. They buy up real estate and other assets at rock-bottom prices. And because they have money to start with, they can afford to hang on to those assets until the market comes around. And the market *will* come around—it always does.

Another point about economic cycles is that when times are good, banks are willing to lend more. It's easier to borrow 80 to 95 percent of the value of a property. When times get tough, you'll have to search for even an 80 percent mortgage. On the surface, that looks as if you need tremendous amounts of cash to take advantage of a recession, but that's not necessarily true. During lean times, more sellers are willing to hold mortgages (that is, let you make the payments to them rather than to a conventional lender) because it's the only way they can get rid of the properties—especially ones that are run-down. And seller financing can be much more flexible than most conventional loans will ever be. With seller financing, you don't pay points or other loan-origination fees, there is rarely a credit check, and the closing can usually occur much faster than with a bank or a mortgage company. There's also the opportunity to profit by discounting the mortgage later on.

By understanding economic cycles and using creative techniques, you can consistently build wealth in good and bad times. The object is to not fear economic cycles and to recognize that each stage of a cycle has its special benefits. The wealth-building techniques I'm sharing with you are timeless. They can be adapted to work in good times and bad.

THE BUY-LOW, SELL-HIGH MYTH

Most people think the best real estate strategy is to buy in a down cycle and sell in an up cycle. Though that is a good strategy, it's limited, because those cycles come around only every seven to ten years. If your plan is to buy low and sell high, it can take you a long time to make any money.

When I began investing in real estate back in the early 1980s, I wasn't buying because we were in a recession and it was a good time to buy—though certainly that was true. I understand that now, but at the time I was buying because I'd learned a technique to buy run-down properties, fix them up, and rent them out to build a positive cash flow that would cover my debt. The theory was that as my equity increased, so would the value of the properties, and maybe in twenty years I'd be wealthy.

I have since learned how to make money *right now* on real estate, regardless of the cycle. I've personally made plenty of money in the up cycles—and plenty in the down cycles. I used techniques like seller financing, discount mortgages, assigning contracts, and several others that I'll explain as we go along.

People tell me I was lucky, and to a degree I was. I had accumulated quite a few properties, and when the economy picked up, I was able to quadruple my money on many of them. But let me make two important points: First, I was "lucky" only because I took action. If I hadn't bought that first investment property, I would probably still be working at some menial job for slightly more than minimum wage. Second, I would have made money doing what I did at any point in the economic cycle because I bought run-down properties and fixed them up to create value. I also chose properties that could support themselves while they made money for me.

Once you understand economic cycles and have either lived through one or two of them or studied their patterns, you'll see that they don't present obstacles to wealth building. Instead, economic cycles are tremendous opportunities. All you have to do is take advantage of them.

I'm not advocating that you run out and buy every piece of real estate you can find as soon as the economy shows signs of slowing down. In fact, I don't recommend buying a property that must be sold immediately to produce profits. If we are in a down or flat cycle, and you buy and must sell right away to make a profit, you could lose your shirt. But if you buy properties that have enough cash flow to pay the expenses and have a little left over, you can afford to wait until the cycle comes around. So look for properties that can support themselves (and you) with positive cash flow, and ones that will make money for you whether you keep them or sell them. We'll talk about how to choose the right properties a little later on in this chapter.

What's important now is that you understand that every recession has been followed by a period of prosperity, every period of prosperity has been followed by a recession, and there's no reason to expect that pattern will change. It's one of the natural laws of our economic system, so don't sweat the tough times. Recognize and take advantage of the fact that tough times create great opportunities. In fact, it's during the tough times that wealthy people set themselves up to hit major financial home runs when things turn around.

THE THREE TYPES OF PROPERTIES

There are only three types of investment properties you can buy. The first is low-income property. The second is middle-income property. The third is upper-income property. I figured this out early in my investing career. It doesn't matter if you're buying a single-family home, a duplex, a multi-unit apartment building, or even commercial real estate—the property will fall into one of those three categories.

When you go into the low- or even moderate-income areas, you'll find the price of real estate is lower than in other areas. And if the property is cosmetically run-down, it will be even cheaper to buy. But what's interesting (and profitable) is that the rents in low-income areas are not much different from those in middle-income areas, where the price of real estate is higher.

Think about this and tell me if it makes sense to you. If you can charge pretty much the same amount of rent but pay significantly less for the building, will you have a greater positive cash flow? Of course you will. When you pay less for property, your mortgage payment will be lower and you'll have a better chance for a positive cash flow.

On the other hand, you're probably thinking that you don't want to have to collect your rents with a gun. But *low-income* doesn't necessarily mean "crime-ridden." As long as the human race has existed, in every economic system there have been low-income people, and there always will be. Someone has to provide housing for them—and that housing ought to be safe, sanitary, and decent.

Over the years I have owned plenty of lower-income properties, and I have no horror stories to tell. Low-income people may not have a lot of money, but they do have an immense amount of pride. If they are treated with respect and given a decent place to live, I have found they will care for their apartments as well as any middle- or upper-income person—sometimes even better. The landlords of low-income housing who have horror stories to tell are the ones who don't paint, fix the leaky faucets, or keep the lawns trimmed. You can't expect someone to take better care of your property than you do yourself. But if you take pride in your property, your tenants will, too.

Several years ago, a woman came to work at our company as a receptionist. She needed extra cash, so she volunteered to work overtime on the weekends as part of the support staff in our training programs. Her bonus was learning what we teach—and she took it to heart. She quickly accumulated more than fifty low-income units (all purchased with no money down) and began teaching at our Millionaire U. course. Those units generated more cash flow than she had ever dreamed she could make when she was looking for a job as an office worker. But the real point I want to make is that while they were low-income properties, she kept them maintained, and she wasn't afraid to go into the neighborhoods to collect rents and deal with other management and maintenance issues. Her tenants respected her and they appreciated that she was a high-quality landlord. Consequently, they took care of the apartments and referred good prospective tenants when they knew one of her units was vacant. While she owned those units, the cash flow supported her in a comfortable lifestyle, helped put her daughters through college, and allowed her to build her cash reserves. After several years, she sold most of her rental property and used the proceeds to invest in a business she had dreamed about for years.

In short, low-income properties can be serious cash-flow generators. They will appreciate over the years along with the rest of the market, and you can force their value up somewhat with improvements, but their primary advantage for the real estate investor is cash flow.

Middle-income properties have a higher unit price than low-income ones. Because you have to pay more for the property, your mortgage payments are more, but rents are not dramatically higher. The result is less positive cash flow, but the appreciation aspect will likely be better than with low-income properties. As the market goes up, middle-income properties will appreciate faster than low-income ones. Use middle-income properties to balance your portfolio *after* you've accumulated plenty of cash and a positive cash flow.

The final type of property, upper-income or prime, does not present any special opportunity for beginning investors, as a rule. Though the rents are higher, the per-unit cost is usually proportionately higher, too. The result with most upper-income properties is a break-even or negative cash flow—and that's not something I would advise as part of your wealth-building strategy. Upper-income properties are usually purchased by investors who are looking for shelters for their money but don't want to do any of the hands-on work. These are usually doctors, lawyers, and other highly paid professionals who often don't even know what's going on with their real estate. I have students who have been the exception to this, and they have made substantial profits buying and selling upper-income property. If you find a deal on upper-income property, definitely check it out—but be sure it will be profitable before you get involved.

Never buy a property solely as a tax shelter. You never have to lose money on real estate just to get a tax break, because with the right property you can have a positive cash flow and tax benefits at the same time.

INGREDIENTS FOR A SUPER PURCHASE

Though real estate is in general a great investment, you must be selective about what you buy. Any one or a combination of the following ingredients could mean you've found a moneymaking property or business.

Distressed Seller. A distressed seller is probably one of the most lucrative circumstances an investor will have the good fortune to come across. For our purposes, distress doesn't necessarily mean tragedy, but distressed sellers are under a tremendous amount of pressure to sell—much like I was when I put my New York properties on the market. This gives you as the buyer a great deal of leverage, and the ingredients are the same whether you are looking at a property or a business. Examples of distressed property sellers include someone who is facing foreclosure; a couple going through a divorce when neither partner can afford alone what they had together, or when they just want to get rid of a place that represents unhappy memories; an owner who is experiencing some sort of personal crisis, such as an illness, that has created a need for immediate cash; a property owner who has died, so that the heirs must sell and divide the proceeds; an owner who may be elderly and no longer able to handle the property or the business.

Let me make it clear that I'm not recommending that you take advantage of or try to cheat anyone. But if someone is facing foreclosure, and your below-market offer is the only one they've gotten and it will prevent the total loss of their investment and a bad credit rating, then you've both made a good deal. Remember, they may be distressed, but they are not obligated to accept your offer; they have the option to hold out for something better.

It always pays to find out why the owner is selling. You may have to dig a bit for this information, since some sellers may feel that admitting to distress lessens their bargaining power. Pay attention to subtle clues and innocent comments that may tell you more than they mean to say.

Distressed Property or Business. In most cases, a distressed property or business doesn't take a lot of probing to discover. It's usually blatantly obvious: the grass is overgrown and the landscaping is shabby; windows are broken; the building needs paint; if it's a business, inventory is low and the shelves are bare. When owners of a distressed property or business are willing to sell, they are usually realistic enough to know they can't expect to get full market value. You can buy at a good price, make improvements, and create a positive cash flow for yourself for a good investment to sell at a profit to someone else.

Distressed properties and businesses are often owned by distressed sellers, and that's a good combination for you. If the seller wants out bad enough, he'll help you structure a good deal and may even be willing to hold a major portion of the financing.

Lack of Management. Falling somewhere in between a distressed seller and a distressed property, lack of management has effects that are not always readily visible, but they can be capitalized on. The building may or may not be in good shape, and the seller may or may not be motivated. But when good management is lacking, there is an opportunity for the buyer.

In one case, I came across an owner of a four-unit building who had become friendly with two tenants who had lived there for a number of years. At the time, the neighborhood commanded about $550 in rent for comparable apartments, but these tenants were paying only $310 because the owner felt uncomfortable about raising the rents. When I negotiated the purchase, I did so with the current numbers and justified a lower purchase price based on the existing cash flow. Once I'd bought the building, I raised those rents to fair market value (legally, according to the leases, and with reasonable notice to the tenants) and created an additional $5,760 in annual cash flow. That was like finding an extra $500 a month, just because I knew the market would support the higher rents.

I have also found properties suffering from mismanagement because the owners either didn't know what they were doing or didn't want to take the time to manage efficiently and profitably. They may have failed to make simple repairs that would have reduced other operating costs, such as leaky faucets that drive up water bills, or air-conditioning and heating units that use excessive energy because they need to be cleaned and serviced. They may have spent top dollar on the services they did provide, instead of finding a way to accomplish the same thing for less money. And their inattentiveness may have resulted in a higher-than-necessary vacancy rate. You'll see similar situations with businesses that are for sale, where owners want to retire, move, or for any reason just don't want to run a business. All of this gives you leverage as a buyer and the opportunity to increase your cash flow as an owner.

Lack of Owner Interest. Lack of owner interest can be due to a variety of reasons on the part of the seller. He may have bought the building and then realized he doesn't like managing rental property, but rather than sell, he just let it go. He may have a full-time job or another business and is just not willing or able to take the time and energy to do a good job. He may live in another city; distance is one of the biggest problems property owners face. Or he may have bought the building as a tax shelter without realizing that rental properties don't run themselves. Owners lacking interest are not usually looking for a big windfall profit; they just want to sell and get out.

A classic example of this was a property I purchased with one of my students back in the early 1990s. It was a twenty-unit apartment building in Marietta, Georgia (a suburb of Atlanta). I only had to put $9,000 down, and the property generated $4,100 a month in positive cash flow. The seller was the chief executive officer of a bank, and he lived more than an hour away from the property. He just didn't want to bother managing it anymore and wanted out. He was willing to hold the financing, so I didn't have to shop or qualify for a loan. My student/partner in the deal was twenty-two and had a job making about $22,000 a year; on this property alone, he would net more than $24,000 a year and have plenty of time to work on other ways to get wealthy. In other words, this property meant financial independence for my student, and he found it just by looking. And this sort of deal is not unique; it happens all the time. You just have to be on the lookout for these opportunities.

These are the circumstances that will make a super purchase for you. But take a moment to think about how these circumstances could be turned around. In other words, take care not to let yourself become a distressed seller or the owner of distressed property. If you do, you'll only be helping someone else become wealthy—at your expense.

HOW TO KNOW YOUR MARKET

When you see one or more of the ingredients for a super purchase—a distressed seller, a distressed property, lack of management, or lack of owner interest—you've got the potential for a real estate or small business bargain. But to know for sure, you must *know your market*.

There are no shortcuts and no exceptions to this rule. You've got to get out in the field and look at all types of properties. Read the real estate section of your local newspaper. Get comfortable with the language of real estate and the jargon most investors use. Know what the current market values are in various parts of your community for both property and rents. Go online and learn how to access the public records quickly and efficiently.

Establish relationships with several real estate agents. You'll find they have different areas of expertise and differing opinions of the market. Learn from all of them. Let them know what you're looking for—ideally you should be starting with distressed low- and moderate-income properties—and that you're willing to look at any property, regardless of its condition. Remember, looking doesn't commit you to buying, and each time you look at a piece of real estate, you'll learn a little more.

Once you know your market, you'll be able to recognize and take advantage of bargains when they come your way. Remember, all of this can be done part-time. You don't need to quit your job; just make your off hours more productive by accumulating information and knowledge to get comfortable with real estate investing. And, who knows, you might just find a great deal in the process—because deals are out there in abundance, being snapped up every day by people who are smart enough to look for them.

THE GOLD MINE AD

Shopping for real estate investments can be time-consuming, but it doesn't have to be. As your experience and confidence increase, you'll find ways to streamline your efforts. In the meantime, I'll share with you some of the shortcuts I've learned to find great deals fast.

One of the most effective methods I've found is what I call my Gold Mine Ad. It is a small classified ad I placed in either the "Income Property for Sale" or "Real Estate Wanted" sections of the Sunday newspaper. It reads like this:

```
Private investor wants to buy income property.
Will look at all, any condition. 333-555-1234
```

If you try this ad, be prepared for calls from plenty of interested people. I've had many students tell me that when they ran this ad, the response was so overwhelming that they didn't have time to follow up on all the leads they got.

Be prepared, too, to discuss prospective properties as a knowledgeable investor. You have the psychological advantage, because people are calling you rather than the other way around. But if you don't sound as if you know what you're doing, you could scare off a good prospect and a potential steal on a bargain deal.

You'll get calls from people with single-family homes, duplexes, triplexes, multi-unit apartment buildings, businesses, commercial buildings—just about every form of real estate there is. Your conversations with these people will give you tremendous insight into the seller mind-set and its many variations, so pay attention. Take notes; in fact, I suggest completing an APOD (Annual Property Operating Data) sheet for each call. A sample is on page 91.

Here are the basic questions you need to ask:

Is the property listed with a Realtor? Find this out immediately. The best deals are usually the ones not listed, but don't automatically rule out a property that is. Just keep in mind that the seller will have the added expense of paying a commission (if he has not reserved the right to sell the property himself), and that may have an impact on the offer he will accept.

Where is the property located? Get the full street address, and if you don't recognize it, ask what part of town it's in.

What is the asking price?

What is the appraised value and the market value? You can ask the seller for this information, but it's also a good idea to confirm it by calling a real estate agent or checking the property records, which can usually be done online.

How many units?

Are they currently rented?

What are the gross rents?

Who pays the utilities?

What are the expenses? Specifically, you want to know the costs of taxes, insurance, water and sewer, licenses or permits, heating and/or air-conditioning, garbage collection, other utilities, and any other expenses of managing the property.

What are the present mortgages on the property? You need to know the balance of any mortgages on the property, the interest rates, the payments, the years left to pay on the loans, and if they are assumable—that is, if you can take over the payments. Though it's rare, in some cases people may be hesitant to provide you with this information; if you encounter resistance, just be firm and let them know you can't make an intelligent evaluation of the investment without having all of the applicable data. Usually this bit of firmness will get you the answer to the question and the needed respect for future negotiations on the property. If it doesn't, you're going to have plenty of other callers, so just move on.

Is the seller willing to hold some of the mortgage? You'll get a variety of answers to this one, and you may have to explain that your policy is to look for the seller to hold at least some of the mortgage.

Why are you selling? Listen carefully to this answer to be sure you get the real reason. If necessary, probe further to find out how motivated (and possibly distressed) the seller really is.

How can I reach you? Get telephone numbers (home, work, cell) and determine what are the best hours to call. If the seller works during the day, you don't want to waste your time calling his home while he's away.

Wrap up the call by telling the seller you want to have your appraiser take a look at the property, and if you're interested, you'll call him back. Having an appraiser sounds professional and organized; the seller doesn't need to know you do your own initial appraising. Then analyze the numbers (calculating return on investment and cash flow are explained later in this chapter) and decide if the property has good investment potential. If it does, go take a look. If not, move on to the next call.

OTHER WAYS TO LOCATE BARGAINS

The Gold Mine Ad brings the opportunities to you, but you'll also find some great deals by looking for them yourself. Here's how:

Keep Your Eyes Open. You can find distressed properties just by keeping your eyes open. Carry a pad and pen or a small tape recorder wherever you go. When you see a distressed property, jot down the address. When you're back at your computer, look up the owners' names in the public records. Then write the owners a letter asking if they are interested in selling and follow up with a phone call. You'll find the response will vary. If they're not interested right now, ask them to keep your name and contact information, then put the details on the property in a file and check back with them in six months or a year. If they are interested, find out how much they want for the property and try to negotiate a mutually profitable deal.

Get to Know Your Building Code Officials. Another way to uncover distressed properties is to visit your city or county building code enforcement agency. Let the people there know you are in the business of rehabilitating older, distressed properties and ask them about their files on buildings that are condemned or have multiple violations. You'll be amazed at how helpful they can be. With this information, you can contact owners to discuss potential deals.

Pass Out Business Cards and Flyers. If you're going to be a serious investor, print up business cards and flyers. The printing itself is a nominal expense; it's an affordable way to enhance your image and get your message out. One of my first cards read, "I buy houses, duplexes, multi-unit apartments, and commercial. I will look at all in any condition," and then it listed my name and phone number. Another early card listed a business name, R & I Enterprises, along with my name and phone number. "We buy" was printed in the upper-left corner, and directly under that was "Houses, apartments, commercial, terms, any condition." I handed out these business cards to anyone who would take them, because I never knew where a good deal was going to come from.

I also had flyers printed up with similar information, and every so often I'd pay one of the neighborhood kids a few bucks to pass them out. You never know when someone will stick that flyer in a drawer or their car's glove compartment, then pull it out six months or a year later and call you with a property. I also put a flyer into every piece of mail I sent out, including my mortgage payments, utility bills, credit card bills, and so on. You never know who is opening that mail and what their circumstances are. And I have gotten calls and ultimately purchased property from people who received my flyers that way.

Read the Newspaper. Your newspaper is, of course, a great source of bargains and an excellent way to keep in touch with the market. You'll find some great leads in the "For Sale by Owner" and "Investment [or Commercial] Property for Sale" sections, but don't overlook the foreclosure ads and bulletins in the legal section. Keep in mind that when a property is in the newspaper, other investors see it, too, so the competition for these deals is greater.

Ask for Referrals. Finally, never underestimate the value of referrals. In any business, referrals are the easiest and most productive way to grow. The only way I know of to build a strong referral base in real estate investing is to spend time in the business and do some serious networking. Let people know what you are doing and offer to pay $100 for any lead they bring you that you buy.

DO YOU NEED A LICENSE?

Something I learned very early is that there is a major difference between real estate brokers and real estate investors. Real estate brokers and sales agents earn a living (sometimes a good living, sometimes a poor one) by representing sellers and buyers in real estate transactions. Real estate investors become wealthy using real estate as their profit-making vehicle. I'm not recommending that you pursue a career in real estate sales, but you might consider getting a real estate license for a few reasons.

First, the knowledge you'll have to acquire—usually through any of a number of real estate schools—to get your license will help you with the nuts and bolts of buying and selling.

Second, when you find a property that is listed with an agent, you will be entitled to share the commission if you, too, are a licensed agent—even though you are also the buyer. This bonus money can make a big difference in the amount of money you'll have to pay out of pocket to purchase the property.

Third, some states require property managers to have real estate licenses. If you are considering a management and maintenance business, a license may be helpful.

A real estate license is easy to get; most state require the equivalent of a weeklong course that focuses primarily on real estate law, followed by a licensing exam. If you can read at the eighth- or ninth-grade level, this is not difficult.

If you have an active real estate license, you must divulge that fact on your purchase offers and sales contracts. It's usually a nonissue, and most people don't care one way or the other, but you do have to tell them. The primary drawback to having a license is that you may find it difficult to get other real estate agents to look for deals for you since they might view you as a competitor rather than a client. With your own license, you could make more money on each transaction; but by using other agents, you could do more transactions and make more money overall.

My advice is to get your license and try it both ways. You can always place your license on inactive status if that works better for you.

THE BUSINESS OF BEING A REAL ESTATE INVESTOR

Successful real estate investing is more than just buying and selling. While you own the properties, you must manage them effectively if they are to continue to generate positive cash flow for you.

You could hire a property management company to handle this aspect for you, but I don't recommend it in the beginning. No one manages property as well as the owner, because no one else has the vested interest in it that the owner has. When I left New York and moved to Florida, I sold all my properties because I didn't believe I could have maintained the quality my tenants had become accustomed to if I became an absentee owner. For the maximum return on your investment, manage your own real estate at least until you accumulate a number of prime properties and have a substantial cash flow.

There are a number of good books on the market that deal with residential property management, and I suggest adding two or three of them to your personal library. You could also take property management training through Wealth Intelligence Academy™ (see "Resources" for details). You should also join a property managers' association. It will give you an opportunity to network with and learn from others. Such associations have publications and programs that address common problems and serve as a resource for members' needs. You may also find this a good source for leads on properties you might be interested in purchasing.

The most important part of property management is to keep an eye on the property. I'm not talking about military-style inspections here, but you should visit every property you own regularly to make sure the tenants are keeping things up and no special maintenance is needed. Multi-unit buildings have to be seen more frequently than single-family homes because of the number of tenants. The idea is to catch small problems and correct them before they turn into major, costly repairs. This also helps you maintain a positive relationship with your tenants and keeps your units rented.

Keep your vacancy rate low by maintaining attractive exteriors on your buildings, adding improvements based on tenant input whenever feasible, and setting rents at fair market value. If you have a reputation as a conscientious owner and provide quality housing, you'll rarely have apartments vacant longer than it takes to clean them between tenants. Encourage your existing tenants to provide you with referrals when vacancies do occur; you may want to consider giving a small, onetime rent discount to existing tenants who bring you a qualified new tenant. Otherwise, when you have a vacancy, post a For Rent sign and consider placing an ad in the classified section of your local newspaper and in whatever online resources are available. Do this as soon as the departing tenant gives notice; don't wait for the unit to be vacated to begin screening prospective tenants.

In multi-unit buildings, you may consider arranging for a resident manager to collect rents, show vacancies, and handle janitorial and landscape maintenance. Unless you have a very large complex, this does not have to be a full-time job and can be compensated with a rent allowance. And you will continue to be primarily responsible for your property because you'll be handling any major issues that arise.

Every one of your tenants should have a lease or a rental agreement—no exceptions! If you buy a building that has units rented without leases, draw them up immediately. You can find standard lease forms in most office supply stores, as well as in the software program we provide to our real estate investment students. Also, remember that most tenants expect rent increases when a building is sold, so don't be reluctant to do this. The key is to do it right away, within the bounds of existing leases.

Always maintain a cordial but strictly business relationship with your clients. You have agreed to provide them with safe, sanitary, well-maintained housing. They, in turn, have agreed to pay rent on a specified date and to exercise reasonable care with your property. In other words, "no ticket, no laundry." If they don't pay their rent, or if they violate other terms of their lease, you must take appropriate action up to and including eviction. Treat your property business as if it were a Wal-Mart or a grocery store. It's okay to be friendly with your tenants, but never let "friendship" get in the way of your initial business agreement.

Real estate is a business much like any other business, but it's different because it has a significantly lower risk level. If you're thinking about going into business for yourself but you haven't quite made the decision, try a small rental property—either a single-family house or a duplex, for example. You'll have to do everything you would have to do in any kind of a business, from management to marketing to record keeping, but on a small scale. That will give you the chance to get a feel for how you'll do in business for yourself. If you like it, you can either buy more property or another business of your choice. If you don't like it, you can sell the property, and you will have learned your lesson probably without having lost any money—in fact, you'll likely show a profit on that educational experience. Is there any other arena that will pay you to get an education without any future obligation? And, who knows, you might just create a small personal fortune along the way.

TAKING THE NEXT STEP UP

Once you have established yourself as a real estate investor and refined your skills, move up to the next level. I built my early wealth on low- and moderate-income residential real estate, but those types of properties are no longer in my portfolio. I now focus my energies and resources on land development and larger commercial projects.

Low- and moderate-income residential real estate is a great way to get started, but it's also management-intensive and you can get burned out. You'll find that some of your best deals on income property come from owners who are just tired of the management routine. Don't let this scare you away from investing—it's the natural process. It's happened to me, and I've watched it happen to my students: Start with low- and moderate-income properties because they can be purchased if you have little or no capital. Learn the business as you build your portfolio and net worth. Then gradually move up to higher-income residential properties, commercial real estate, and land development deals—and sell your low- and moderate-income properties to a new investor who needs to learn how to do it.

ANNUAL PROPERTY OPERATING DATA

❖ ❖ ❖

Property Name _____

Property Address _____

Type of Real Estate _____

Number of Units _____

Appraised Value   Land $_____   _____%

                         Improvements $_____   _____%

                         Personal Property $_____   _____%

                         TOTAL: $_____   100%

Source of appraised value (attach verification): _____

Financing

Type	Balance	Payment	Pmts./Yr.	Int. Rate	Term	Annual Payment

Total _____

Income	Yr. 1	Yr. 2	Yr. 3	Yr. 4
Gross Rents				
Other Income				
Total Income				

Note: If any category does not apply to your subject property, place "N/A" in the spaces.

continued

Operating Expenses	Yr. 1	Yr. 2	Yr. 3	Yr. 4

Accounting & Legal _____

Advertising & Promotional _____

Office Supplies _____

Phone Expenses _____

Property Insurance _____

Employee Insurance _____

Property Management @ ____% _____

Payroll—Resident Manager _____

Payroll Taxes _____

Maintenance Supplies _____

Pest Control _____

Cleaning Supplies _____

Swimming Pool Expenses _____

Painting Expenses _____

Trash Removal _____

Services (lawn, snow) _____

  Other _____

Utilities

  Gas & Oil _____

  Water & Sewer _____

  Electric _____

  Vacancy Allowance _____

Miscellaneous _____

Total Operating Expenses _____

CHAPTER 7

ANALYZING YOUR DEALS

*To be what we are, and to become what we are
capable of becoming, is the only end of life.*
—ROBERT LOUIS STEVENSON

When I'm teaching people how to make money with real estate, the questions I hear the most often have to do with problems. What do you do if a tenant moves out, what do you do if the furnace breaks down, what do you do if something else happens? My best answer is to remind you that every business has its problems.

If you own a store, you'll probably lose some merchandise to shoplifting. Wal-Mart tops the Fortune 500 list of publicly traded companies with sales of $288 billion and growing. Right now, as you're reading this, somewhere in the country, someone is shoplifting something at a Wal-Mart. And there may even be a cashier stealing a few dollars from a cash register or running a bogus credit card charge through. But when Sam Walton started his company, he didn't say, "Gee, I think I'll give up this $288 billion in sales and close down all my stores because I might have a problem now and then." Instead, he set money aside in a reserve account to cover losses from theft; it's called the cost of doing business—and whatever your opinion of the way Wal-Mart operates, the company is a classic American success story and the late Sam Walton's achievements should inspire you.

When it comes to real estate, remember that people have been renting property for hundreds of years. Owners have been making profits from renting property for hundreds of years. Just because you buy a rental property doesn't mean all the tenants are going to move out or the building will fall down.

Will you have an occasional problem? Sure. Everybody has problems. They're not special gifts reserved for an unfortunate few. But think about this for a moment. What are problems? Is it a problem when we can't buy a new car or pay our bills? Is it a problem that we can barely afford to take one vacation a year, not the four or five trips we'd really like to go on?

Those are problems. Also a problem is facing retirement with an income at or below the poverty level. A problem is not being able to give your kids the opportunities you'd like. A problem is driving an old car that breaks down once a week because you can't afford a new one. A problem is a boss nagging at you and having to punch a time clock. A problem is when lack of money causes so much stress in your marriage that you end up getting a divorce.

A tenant calling because of a drippy faucet is not a problem, it's progress. Having to put an ad in the paper to fill a vacant unit is not a problem, it's an opportunity. These are simply circumstances that go with the territory of being in business and building wealth.

The bottom line is that it doesn't matter what business you're in, you'll have problems occasionally. Set aside a little money so you can handle them, collect your profits, and live a happy, abundant life.

EVALUATING THE PROPERTY

Something that often scares newcomers to real estate investing is how to tell when a property needs too much fixing up to make it a good investment. I have bought and sold hundreds of properties, and I rarely come across any in such bad shape that they are beyond repair. The reason is simple: if the property is in really bad shape, the owner may be motivated to sell way below the market value of a similar property that is in good condition. If you are dealing with an extremely low sale price because the property needs repairs, you have more borrowing power for your repair or rehab loan.

However, you have to train your eye to know the difference between cosmetic distress and serious problems. A building might look so neglected that you're afraid it's going to fall down around you, but in reality a few trips to the dump, a fresh coat of paint, and some cleanser and disinfectant may revive the property to fair market value. Here are a few things to watch out for:

Structural Damage. Outside, look for a dramatic lean in any direction. Inside, look for floors slanted toward a corner of the house. These are indications of a possible foundation problem. Before you reject the project, call in several contractors and get free estimates on repairs, then use that information to negotiate a better price.

Termite Damage. Termite damage usually scares off investors, but termites can take up to ten or fifteen years before they do irreparable damage. I once bought a house that had severe termite damage in the supporting beams in the basement. The property had been on the market a long time and was bargain priced. Obviously the termite damage had scared off many other potential buyers. After I bought the property, I had a contractor replace the beams using mobile jacks as support; it was not particularly complicated or expensive. I pulled money out of the property up front with the rehab, then made $15,000 a few years later when I sold it. You can make good deals on termite-infested properties. Just figure the cost of replacing the bad wood and exterminating the termites. If you can do that and still make money, buy it.

Roof Damage. Always examine the roof. You might also ask several roofers to do it for you. Pick their brains until you become proficient enough to do your own evaluations. Roofers make money by selling you a roof, so keep that in mind as you consider their recommendations. If it looks as if the roof will need replacing in the near future, calculate that into your offer—but wait until the roof starts leaking to replace it.

Major Plumbing. When you are evaluating a property, turn on all the faucets, flush all the toilets, and make sure all the drains run freely. The most common way plumbing can become a problem is in older buildings with galvanized and/or cast-iron plumbing. After years of use, this type of pipe collects sediment, which builds up and causes a loss of water pressure and stopped-up drains. I have found a product called Drain Snake, available in professional plumbing supply stores, which seems to remedy the problem. (When using this or any other chemical product, always use caution and follow the directions on the label to avoid personal injury or property damage.)

Furnaces. In larger multi-unit buildings, you may have one furnace that heats the entire building. Be sure it operates efficiently or that the cash flow will support the heating bill. Get a heating and air-conditioning contractor you trust to do the evaluation for you.

These are the areas in which you could have a major expense if there is a problem. In most cases, roofs and plumbing and heating units need major repairs or replacement only every twenty to twenty-five years, so problems with them are the exception, not the rule, but it's always good to check. When you do see a major problem, don't automatically rule out the property. If you can cover the repairs and still make money, the property is a good investment. If you can't, it isn't. The whole process is just that simple.

You might want to hire a professional inspector in the beginning to confirm your opinion, but eventually you'll get to the point where you can accurately evaluate a property on your own.

CALCULATING RETURN FOR A SUPER BARGAIN AND GREAT PROFITS

There is only one hard, fast rule about when to buy and when not to buy: if you will lose money, don't buy. And you can figure out just how profitable a property might be with basic, elementary school arithmetic.

To evaluate a property's profitability, you need to look at four areas:

Net Profit. The easiest to see and most simple to calculate, net profit is the amount of money you have left over after all your expenses are paid.

Appreciation. This is the amount your property increases in value. There are two types of appreciation: natural, which is the amount the market goes up; and forced, which is adding value with improvements or a higher and better use. During periods of moderate growth, natural appreciation usually ranges between 5 and 10 percent annually; in high-growth cycles, it could be well over 10 percent, and sometimes as much as 20 percent or even higher; in low- or no-growth cycles, the value may remain the same or increase only by 1 or 2 percent. To find out the current rate of natural market appreciation, call a couple of real estate agents. It's their job to know these things, but it's also always wise to check with more than one to be sure you're getting an accurate picture. Forced appreciation is the area through which the bigger and more short-term profits are usually made. Most real estate will appreciate naturally to a small degree if you do absolutely nothing; if you put a little money and effort into the right property, you can make significant gains.

Equity Buildup. A portion of each mortgage payment you make (which the tenants actually pay with their rent) is applied to reducing the principal balance of the mortgage. When rents are paying the mortgage, you can consider the equity buildup as part of your overall profit.

Tax Shelter. Real estate investing is a business, and you are therefore entitled to take a variety of business-related deductions on your income tax. Often these deductions will offset income earned from another source and reduce your overall tax liability. The deductions you can take by owning investment property include depreciation, interest (the interest portion of your mortgage payments), maintenance, and any other expenses related to

managing your property, such as gas or car expenses for driving
to and from the property, cleaning supplies, bookkeeping supplies, forms, and other administrative materials. Though we
know that real estate typically goes up in value, the IRS will allow
you to take a tax deduction for the depreciation based on wear
and tear on the building (not the land). The formula for calculating investment-property depreciation can change with revisions
in the tax laws, so check with your accountant.

Now, let's look at how you use these areas of profitability to
determine the return on your investment (ROI). Calculate your
ROI by dividing your profit by the amount of cash it took you to
achieve that profit. To illustrate ROI, I'll use the four-unit building I told you about in chapter 4. I bought the building for
$75,000 (this was a long time ago—the numbers would be higher
today, but the math is the same, and that's what you need to
learn). The owner was willing to hold the mortgage and take a 10
percent down payment, or $7,500. By arranging to close on the
third day of the month (after collection of that month's rents, of
which I would get a prorated share), I was able to purchase the
building for $3,700 cash out of pocket. The building was fully
occupied, and each unit rented for $500 a month. This is how the
numbers worked:

Net Profit—Add up the gross rents. Add up all the expenses
(taxes, insurance, maintenance, utilities, vacancy allowance,
and so on) and debt service (mortgage). In our example, we're
using 5 percent for the vacancy allowance, which is the amount
of time each year we can expect the units not to have tenants. To
determine the vacancy rate for your area, contact a Realtor or a
property management company. You can ask the seller for documentation on the other expenses. Then subtract the expenses
from the rents. That will be the net profit (or loss) for the first
year.

CALCULATING NET PROFIT

Monthly gross rents (4 units at $500 each)	$2,000
Annual gross rents (12 × $2,000)	$24,000
Monthly expenses	$800
Annual expenses (12 × $800)	$9,600
Gross annual operating profit	$14,400
Debt service (12 × $596.75, the monthly mortgage payment)	$7,161
Net overall operating profit	$7,239

Your first-year ROI is the net profit divided by the cash out of pocket it took for you to buy the property, which is $7,239 divided by $3,700, or 196 percent return on investment.

Appreciation—If you know your market, you will be able to estimate how much specific improvements will increase the value of your property. Appreciation turns into a cash profit when you sell or refinance.

Original purchase price of property	$75,000
Cost of improvements	$1,300
Revised appraised value of property	$130,000
Forced appreciation	$55,000

Appreciation ROI on this property was 1,486 percent (the amount of appreciation divided by the investment, or $55,000 divided by $3,700). In this example, I used forced appreciation only—that is, I forced the value of the property up by improving it. When adding in natural market appreciation, contact a real estate agent for the figure that applies in your area.

. . .

Equity Buildup—As rents pay down the mortgage balance, the equity increase is considered profit. It is a paper profit until you sell or refinance, but it is there for you to use when you need it.

Initial loan amount	$68,000
Amount applied to principal	$500
New principal balance	$67,500
Equity buildup	$500

Equity buildup ROI is 14 percent (the amount of equity divided by the investment, or $500 divided by $3,700).

Tax Shelter—With investment real estate, most of the time your expenses will offset most, if not all, of your income for tax purposes. You will make additional income gains by deducting depreciation and letting that offset the taxes on income from other sources. How much of a tax shelter you will receive depends on your tax bracket and sources of income. Generally, you can count on a 5 to 15 percent ROI from the tax shelter area.

Now let's go back and total up the first-year ROI from the $3,700 I used to buy this building:

Return on cash invested	196%
Appreciation	1,486%
Equity buildup	14%
Tax shelter	10%*
Total ROI	1,706%

* average estimate

And this doesn't even consider the money I made later by refinancing the building on the increased appraised value. Is it any wonder so many great fortunes have been built through real estate?

On any investment, I look at the first-year anticipated net profit, and if that doesn't give me at least a 20 to 30 percent return on my investment, I don't usually go any further. The exception would be if there is a tremendous upside to the building—something I know will give me a greater return in the future. It might be that the building has a lot of vacancies I know I can fill, or that nearby property-use trends are changing and I can benefit from that. In chapter 12, I'll explain how to find out about future land-use plans in a given area that could have an impact on your investments. Don't put anything in concrete, but always have a sound basis for your decisions; be flexible and use logic and reason to make a good deal.

INCREASING YOUR CASH FLOW

It's critical that you look at all the expenses of a property. The owner should be able to provide you with documentation for taxes, utilities, water, sewer, trash collection, licensing, and any other permits you may be required to have. You may also require the seller to give you records detailing maintenance costs and actual vacancy rates.

After you purchase an investment property, you must always be on the lookout for ways to increase your cash flow. Here are some techniques I recommend:

Contract with individuals rather than businesses for any work you don't do yourself. In other words, don't call a painting contractor to paint your building; find two or three people who can handle a paintbrush and put them to work. If you use a painting contractor, you will also be paying his overhead and profit, and that will eat into yours. Find a good handyman to do the bulk of your maintenance. It's a lot less expensive to have a $12- or $14-an-hour handyman replace washers in faucets than to call in a licensed plumber to do it. Once you own enough properties to keep a handyman busy full-time, consider putting him on your payroll.

Look for hidden costs. Worn-out washers can cause drippy faucets that run up your water bill. Windows that don't close tightly can increase your heating and cooling costs. (Check with your city or utility company on the availability of grants to pay for energy-conservation improvements; see chapter 16 for more details on how various government agencies can help make real estate investing more profitable for you.) If you use a Dumpster for trash collection, be sure it is just large enough to accommodate your tenants' needs; don't pay for more service than you require. This is just plain good management, and it puts money in your pocket.

Buy used appliances. When it's time to replace items such as stoves and refrigerators, shop for and buy used appliances. Your best deals will come from individuals, but shopping for and negotiating those deals is more time-consuming than working with used-appliance dealers. If you're purchasing from a dealer, let him know that you're a property owner and that he can expect repeat business from you; that will give you some leverage for a better price and/or a better warranty.

Analyze all expenses. Never accept an expense at face value without researching the amount to be sure you're getting the best price possible. Shop around and negotiate for good deals.

Raise the rents. Keep your rents in line with the market; don't charge lower rents just because a tenant has been with you a long time. When your leases come up for renewal and you are aware from your knowledge of the market that rental rates are increasing, adjust your rents accordingly. Be sure to give your tenants adequate and legal notice of the increase.

Verify the accuracy of your tax bills. Take the time every year to check your tax bill on every property you own—including your home. Get copies of the tax bills for comparable properties in the area (this is public information and you should be able to find it online, usually at the tax assessor's Web site). If your taxes are higher, file a protest with your tax collector; this is every taxpayer's right, and it can result in a lower tax bill. You can get instructions for the specific procedure for doing this by checking the local tax collector's Web site or calling its office.

CHOOSING THE RIGHT WEALTH VEHICLE

A question I'm frequently asked is what's the best type of real estate to start with. Should you invest in single-family homes or multi-unit buildings? Both can be profitable, and I would recommend a balance of different types of properties. Remember, when you have a vacancy in a single-family home, that property is 100 percent vacant. When you have a vacancy in a four-unit building, that property is only 25 percent vacant and is still producing cash flow. The trade-off is that single-family homes generally require less management attention and often appreciate faster, so put both types of properties in your portfolio.

My advice is to start with small multi-unit buildings, build a healthy cash flow, then diversify and add single-family homes to your holdings.

AVOID THESE MISTAKES BEGINNERS OFTEN MAKE

That you're reading this book says that you're willing to learn from others. That's great. But experience has taught me that beginners tend to make the same mistakes. Here are some things to do—and not do—that reflect common mistakes beginners make.

Don't fall in love with your investment property. This isn't your home, you're not going to live in it, and it doesn't need to reflect your personality. Don't go overboard with your fix-up. Walls and carpets should be in neutral colors—and don't go to the added expense of wallpaper when paint will do. Fixtures should be serviceable and of reliable quality but also neutral. Do what's necessary to create a safe, sanitary, attractive home for your tenants, but don't lose money with unnecessary enhancements.

Know your market. Take the time to learn your market before you buy your first property. Failing to know the market and understand what's driving it can cost you dearly.

Do your due diligence. Nothing can take the place of thoroughly researching a property before you buy. Do your inspection, study the history, know the costs, and, as I just said, know the market. Skipping over some details can be an expensive shortcut.

Don't pay too much. Don't be shy about making below-market offers on property. This is your business, it's how you make money, and if you can't buy at the right price, don't buy—move on to the next deal.

Do a thorough screening on all of your tenants. Most landlord complaints revolve around bad tenants. You can keep your percentage of bad tenants to a minimum if you screen them before you let them sign a lease and move in. Set standards and stick to them.

Don't break your own rules. You should have a good reason for setting your rules and policies—and that means you should also have a good reason for consistently enforcing those rules and policies. If your rental agreement calls for a late fee, collect it—no matter what the tenant's problems that have contributed to the late payment are. If your rules say no pets or no cars parked on the grass or no whatever, be sure every tenant follows the rules or faces the consequences.

INDEPENDENT THINKING

Once you begin accumulating real estate investments, you'll have to consider the question of how long to own each property. There are two traditional schools of thought on this: the "keeper" theory and the "nonkeeper" theory.

The author of one of the first real estate books I read subscribed to the keeper theory. Essentially, his theory was buy, buy, buy, and never sell. His strategy was never to sell anything, but instead to wait until you have enough equity in the properties to either refinance them completely or take another mortgage out and let the rents cover the mortgage payments. The money you get from a loan is not taxable because it's not income. The income you get from rents is taxable, but if you follow this strategy, it will be offset by the deductible interest you're paying on your mortgage. In other words, you keep pulling your money out of the property in the form of mortgages.

That is a good strategy, but not for your entire portfolio. You need income, and you need capital to go into bigger deals that require more money.

When I first began investing, I didn't realize there were many investment theories and that different circumstances required different approaches. Because I was successful from the start, I was loyal to most of the literature that gave me the specialized knowledge to do what I had done. I treated the advice in some of those books as gospel and followed it to the letter—especially the keeper theory.

In retrospect, if I had sold a few properties and cashed in on the equity, I could have grown twice as fast because I would have had more working capital. And though money from loan proceeds is not taxable because it's not income, which is great from a tax-strategy angle, there's a negative aspect to making all your money this way. When you approach lenders, you'll find that they frown on making loans to people who show no income on their tax returns, and that makes getting financing difficult. Don't choke your growth by following the keeper theory exclusively.

Following the nonkeeper theory exclusively has some drawbacks, too. When you turn over properties quickly, you don't derive all the benefits of ownership, such as positive cash flow and tax deductions for depreciation. Also, the profit, or capital gains, you make when you sell is taxable as ordinary income.

Most important is the reality that the nonkeeper theory is based on buying low and selling a little higher. It sounds great, but I don't believe that anyone could consistently find enough properties at low enough prices to buy and then sell and turn a profit to have this approach be their only source of revenue. And if you're depending on the sale to make your money, what happens if you can't find a buyer?

At times, turning a property quickly will be very profitable. I've done it many times and made as much as $5,000 on a property by owning it for just an hour or so. But also at times your wisest move is to hang on to a property for years. So don't subscribe exclusively to either the keeper on nonkeeper theory. Instead, do what I learned the hard way: be an independent thinker.

Set up your investment goals to include a diversified game plan. Start with one or two of the techniques you've learned, master them, and move on to another one. Shelter as much of your income from taxes as possible, but show enough income to be considered a good credit risk. Hire competent attorneys and accountants and listen to their advice, but make your own decisions. Consider partnerships and joint ventures as sources for seed capital. Remember, too, that it's easy to get emotionally attached to the first few deals you make. Don't do this! Be willing to sell properties when the time is right to increase your wealth.

Everyone will have an opinion about how you should run your investment business. That's fine. They're entitled to their opinions, and they might even have some positive input you'll benefit from. But the final decisions are yours. You decide when to buy, when to keep, when to sell—and ultimately, when to become wealthy.

CHAPTER 8

HIGHER AND BETTER USE

Do not follow where the path may lead. Go instead
where there is no path and leave a trail.
—UNKNOWN

In chapter 3, I told you how I turned a single-family house into a rooming house, which created what I call a higher and better use of the property. This concept can be applied to a variety of situations, and it's an excellent way to increase value and cash flow.

You could change an old warehouse into an office building, a house into apartments, or an abandoned factory into retail shops. You see this over and over in cities all across America. Older buildings frequently have a special charm and character, and people are often delighted to have the opportunity to move themselves or their businesses into these facilities.

Here are a few specific suggestions for higher and better use: always look for ways to turn unused space into a revenue source and to maximize the revenue you do get. If you find a duplex with a large attic, create new value by turning that space into an income-producing unit. One of my students bought a triplex and turned it into a remarkable rooming house. He converted each apartment into three individual rooms, creating a nine-unit rooming house with a common kitchen and bath for each three units. It was positively luxurious for a rooming house and exceptionally easy to rent and maintain.

Another of my students lived in an area where two-bedroom, two-bath homes averaged $60,000 and three-bedroom, two-bath homes averaged $75,000 to $80,000. He looked for two-bedroom homes with large, enclosed porches on the back. With an inexpensive partition and a little cosmetic work, he would add a third bedroom and create an additional $15,000 to $20,000 worth of value. Other students have profited by converting small multi-unit buildings (both residential and commercial) from rentals to condominiums. That's what you can get by thinking in terms of higher and better use.

Pay attention to neighborhood trends and use your imagination. Learn to look at buildings from a different perspective. With a little foresight and determination, you can use the higher and better use concept to rake in the money.

HOW TO CREATE A ROOMING HOUSE

One of the easiest ways to apply the higher and better use concept is by converting a single-family home into a rooming house. This is most commonly done with older homes located in neighborhoods that are in what is called a transitional stage. Such neighborhoods usually have a mix of single-family, multifamily, and commercial properties. Often these neighborhoods are close to downtown or industrial areas; sometimes they are near colleges and universities.

If the neighborhood has a mix of single-family and multifamily homes, it's a fairly safe bet that zoning won't be a problem. If the property is not already zoned for multi-unit, call your local zoning board to find out how to make the change. You can also make your offer to purchase contingent on getting the necessary zoning to accomplish your higher and better use goal.

In many cities, officials welcome the addition of rooming houses, which are often referred to as SROs (single room occupancy). People with limited incomes (the elderly, students, young people in the early stages of their careers, etc.) have trouble finding a place to live because they can't afford to rent an apartment or buy a house. But they *can* afford to pay $75 to $100 a week for a nice, clean room in a decent building. By creating a rooming house, you can provide a tremendous community service while you make money for yourself.

How do you do it? It's not complicated. In most older homes, the bedrooms are all upstairs, which means you'll have little, if any, remodeling to do there. What you do with the downstairs will depend on the floor plan you're working with, but you want to convert as much as possible to revenue-producing space. Leave the kitchen as is, because tenants appreciate kitchen privileges, and it will give your facility more value. Also, create a small common room as a sitting area or a gathering space for tenants. They'll appreciate a comfortable, safe place they can use outside their own rooms. For the remainder of the downstairs, erect partitions and hang doors to turn the rooms into bedrooms. Be sure to plan your partitions so every room has a window, if possible. (Some areas require a bedroom to have at least one window; check your local building codes to be sure. Remember, too, that windows are easy to install—just cut a hole in the wall.) Your tenant/bathroom ratio will depend on how many baths the house has. Rooming house tenants expect to share bathrooms.

Once your partitioning is completed, you'll want to clean, paint, make any necessary repairs, and install new door locks. I recommend using locks from Weiser Lock and having a master key made. Each tenant gets a key to his or her room and the front door, but your key opens any door in the house. If anyone moves without turning in their key, just switch the locks with another unit—something that's easily done by a handyman and doesn't require a locksmith but still provides security for your tenants. You'll also want good locks on the bathrooms to protect tenants' privacy. You may also need to install an extracapacity water heater and add some cosmetic touches to the exterior.

Your last major expense involves furnishings. When you're buying eight or ten rooms of furniture, you can usually negotiate a good price. Shop at secondhand stores, check out the used-furniture sales departments of furniture-rental companies, and watch for hotels that have recently remodeled and are selling their old furnishings. (These are the same techniques hotelier

Conrad Hilton used when he was running rooming houses.) When choosing rooming house furniture, go for function and sturdiness over style. Each room should contain:

- ❖ A full-size bed (frame, box springs, and mattress). Single beds are not as well received, so unless the room is extremely small, go with the full-size.
- ❖ Curtains or blinds. Windows must be covered for privacy and insulation.
- ❖ Nightstand.
- ❖ Dresser with mirror. Or you may choose a chest of drawers and hang a mirror on the wall.
- ❖ Lamp. If there is no ceiling light fixture, you must provide a lamp.
- ❖ Sitting chair. If space allows, provide a comfortable chair.

Furnish your common room with some easy chairs, a few small tables, and maybe a used television (consider offering basic cable as well). You might also check into the feasibility of installing a public telephone here, although these days, it's likely that most of your tenants will have cell phones.

MANAGING YOUR ROOMING HOUSE

A rooming house is more management-intensive than an apartment building, but many of the same basic principles apply. Here are the essential details you'll need to know.

Advertising for Tenants. Once you're open for business, place an ad in your local paper (either the daily or a neighborhood weekly) under "Rooms for Rent." Note the key amenities, and include the general location, price, and contact information. If your newspaper organizes ads in alphabetical order, try to start your copy with an *A* word to get it at the top of the listings. These are two examples I have used:

```
AA—Downtown, private rooms, kitchen
privileges, cable TV, all included,
    $90 per week—222-555-1234


  A private room, central location,
all included, $80 per week—222-555-1234.
```

Screening Tenants. In rooming houses, you can't expect to screen for an upper-income clientele or you'll run a higher-than-necessary and quite unprofitable vacancy rate. My advice is to make sure that applicants are working and that their personal hygiene is decent. Other than that, the only qualification is cash. With experience, you'll develop a sense for the type of tenant who will meet his or her obligations. Many city and county governments are passing laws about where convicted sex offenders are allowed to live; it's a good idea to check to see if such a law is in place and, if so, find out if your property is located in an area that would require you to screen prospective tenants for sex offender status.

Rental Agreement. The rental agreement stipulates the amount of rent and the rules of the rooming house. You will find rental agreement forms in office supply stores, or you can create your own; as with any legal document, have it reviewed by an attorney to be sure it conforms with your state laws.

Deposit. A deposit will help you compensate for incorrect judgment decisions in screening. If you feel a prospective tenant might not be of the best quality but you want the rental, ask for a $200 deposit on top of the first week's rent. On the other hand, if your instinct tells you you've got a decent prospective tenant but he is short of cash, you might allow him to move in by posting just one week's rent as a deposit. In any case, never let someone move in without paying a deposit.

Rental Proration. It's more efficient to have all your rents due on the same day. Because Friday is payday for most people, I have found that's the best day to collect rents. When people move in during the middle of the week, prorate their rents by the day for the partial week. Remember that rents are always paid in advance, not in arrears.

Master Key. Master key all of your units, not just the rooms. It's much easier to carry one key that will get you into any of your units, rather than several jangling key rings.

Manager. Each rooming house should have a resident manager to enforce the rules and make sure the common areas are kept clean. It's best to train the manager to *manage*, not to be a maid for the other tenants. (Tenants are expected to clean up after themselves in the kitchen, bathrooms, and sitting room; this stipulation should be part of your rental agreement.) The manager should have a strong attitude and some leadership qualities. Offer this person a $30- to $45-a-week rent allowance for assuming these responsibilities.

Collecting Rents. Rents may be due on Friday, but that doesn't mean you'll collect them all on that day. Take steps to instill a pay-on-time attitude among your tenants. One way to accomplish this is with a $4- or $5-per-day late charge. Another way is to charge $110 rent for your $90 room, with a $20 discount if the rent is paid on time. I have found that rewarding tenants for paying on time rather than punishing them when they're late is more effective.

Despite the best screening and the most creative incentives to pay on time, you're going to have the occasional tenant who doesn't pay. This happens in every business, and it shouldn't deter you from using rental property to pursue your dreams. Just be prepared to handle it, and my advice is to not let a late payer slide. When the rent is due on Friday and not paid by Saturday, issue a written late-rent notice that day. This can be a simple form that reads:

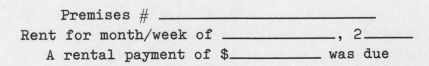

```
     Premises # _____
   Rent for month/week of _____, 2_____
       A rental payment of $_____ was due
```

on _____. According to our records,
a payment has not been received. Kindly
arrange to make payment at your earliest
convenience. If you have already mailed
your check, please disregard this notice.
The Management

The best time to go after late payers is early Saturday morning. Knock on their door at eight. because they would probably prefer to sleep until ten. They'll get tired of you waking them up and start to pay on time.

If you haven't received the rent by Monday, post a "24-Hour Notice to Vacate or Pay Rent" notice on the door and put one in the mail. Here's what that document should look like:

24-Hour Notice to Vacate or Pay Rent
This notice made this _____ day
of _____, 2_____.
To: _____ (name of tenant)
_____ (address of premises)
_____ (city and state)
You are hereby notified that you are indebted
to the Landlord of the premises above
mentioned in the amount of _____ dollars
($_____) for unpaid rent of said premises
from the _____ day of _____,
2_____, to the _____ day of
_____, 2_____, which you are required
to pay within 24 hours of receiving this
notice or vacate said premises. If payment is
not made or premises are not vacated, the
Landlord will take appropriate legal action
to recover possession of the premises.

_____ (signature)

If by Tuesday you haven't received payment or a suitable explanation from the tenant, open the unit to see if he has vacated. If he has, you know where you stand. By leaving without notice, he has forfeited his deposit (this should be stated clearly in your rental agreement), so you are covered for the week's rent. Clean the room and find another tenant.

Sometimes a tenant may give you a sob story that may be true, false, or partially true but exaggerated. You may be sympatheic, but remember that you're in business. Stand your ground, be firm, and remember that to run a profitable business of any kind, you have to get paid. If the tenant still doesn't pay, refer to and enforce the terms of your rental agreement.

Remember, rent collection problems are the exception, not the norm. Rooming houses can be a very profitable real estate investment; just one or two of them can give you the financial independence you need to quit your job and start building your wealth. So don't let the fear that you might have to deal with an occasional late payer stop you from becoming wealthy.

NET $3,000 A MONTH WITHOUT MANAGING ANYTHING AFTER WORKING FOR 60 DAYS

Creating and operating a rooming house can be a source of significant and profitable cash flow and a great way to apply the higher and better use strategy, but there are other ways to benefit financially from this investment. Once you've got the rooming house up and running, you can earn a large cash profit and establish long-term income by selling it to another investor.

Let's say you bought a property for $150,000 and turned it into a rooming house generating $1,500 a month in positive cash flow—that is, $1,500 a month more coming in than you have to pay out. You could realistically put the rooming house on the market for $225,000. The monthly payment on a loan of $75,000 at 8 percent for twenty years is $627. (Use the mortgage loan calculator under student tools at www.russwhitney.com to figure out the payments for a different principal amount, interest rate, or term.) That means the person who buys the property will have to pay $627 a month more than you're paying now, but he'll still be netting more than $850 a month from the income the rooming house generates, and he's stepped into a literal turnkey operation.

You can sell the property for a minimal down payment, as low as $5,000, on a wraparound mortgage. That means you hold the financing and are still responsible for paying off the original mortgage. But the buyer will be making his mortgage payments to you and you'll have more than $600 a month left over after you make the payments on the original mortgage. That money will come in every month for the next twenty years, and all you have to do is a few minutes of bookkeeping.

The buyer will net more than $10,000 the first year, which is better than a 200 percent return on investment for him. When you show a buyer that kind of profit, it's hard for him to justify trying to drive you down on either your price or your down payment because his return is so great to start with.

Of course, if the buyer has the means to pay cash or get new financing, that means you can pay off the original loan and walk away with $75,000 in cash that you can use for other investments.

A word of caution about wraparound mortgages: many conventional lenders insert clauses into their mortgage contracts prohibiting this technique, so if you have a conventional mortgage on your rooming house, you'll need to check this out. When you buy with seller financing, however, you won't have this obstacle. Also, remember that the primary concern of all lenders is getting their payments on time every month, and even conventional lenders may be willing to negotiate with you if you want to sell the property with a wraparound mortgage.

The only thing that can possibly go wrong is if the buyer defaults on his payments and you have to take the property back and foreclose. In a good, well-written wraparound contract, you don't have to go through a formal foreclosure; the process is more like an eviction, and it can happen quickly if it's done right. Get a good real estate attorney to help you with the paperwork. If the buyer defaults several years into the deal, you're taking back property that has gone up in value and is probably producing higher rents and more cash flow than it did when you sold it. And you can either go back to managing it yourself or resell it for a higher price.

This technique is great for any property you buy with the higher and better use concept, and it's something that doesn't take any special skill or a lot of capital to do. You just have to focus on the project and get it done. If you did just one of these deals a year for the next five years, you could set yourself up to get $3,000 a month for the next twenty or thirty years without having to manage anything. Do more than one a year, and you'll quickly build a mind-boggling amount of passive income.

MAKE MILLIONS ON
APARTMENT-TO-CONDO CONVERSIONS

One of the more popular trends in real estate investing these days is apartment-to-condo conversions—a classic example of higher and better use. Let's say you find a sixty-unit apartment complex for $3.5 million. If you convert those apartments to condominiums and sell them for $100,000 each (a total of $6 million), your gross profit will be $2.5 million. You could even do this on a much smaller scale, say with a four- or eight-unit building.

I don't recommend this technique for a beginning investor, but it's well worth considering once you have some experience. Though apartment-to-condo or co-op conversions have tremendous profit potential, you must do your homework before you buy. You need to have the proper zoning, and you'll need permits if you're going to do any major repairs or remodeling. You should put together a complete business plan for the project, including a comprehensive market analysis and your plans for marketing the property after the conversion.

GROW BIG DOLLARS ON RAW LAND

I used to advise my students to avoid raw land and stick to investing in existing buildings. I did that because that's what I was taught and I've made millions buying existing buildings. But then I began to realize that there is plenty of opportunity for investing in raw land if you know how to do it—I've figured it out and made more millions in this arena. As with conversions, this isn't for beginners. It takes experience, knowledge, and cash, but I recommend that it be a part of your long-term strategy.

We'll talk more about this in chapter 12, but my point for mentioning it now is this: always keep the higher and better use concept in mind when looking at property. Make asking yourself "Is this the highest and best use for this building or parcel of land? Is there something I can do to increase its value and profit potential?" a standard part of your investment decision-making process.

CHAPTER 9

How to Borrow Money and Build Your Own Personal Fortune with It

It is one of the most beautiful compensations of life that no person can sincerly try to help another without helping themselves.
—Ralph Waldo Emerson

You've learned how to borrow varying amounts of money, but before you run out and begin applying for loans and credit lines, know the amount you're going to need and how much that money will earn for you.

Let me illustrate. Suppose I offered to give you a temporary job to help you acquire seed capital for your business, whether it's real estate or something else. We agree on your duties and that you will work for me for thirty-five days. But then I offer you your choice of compensation plans: I will pay you either a straight $1,000 a day or a penny a day, compounded daily at 100 percent. That means your pay rate will double every day.

Which would you choose?

The arithmetic on the first plan is simple: thirty-five days times $1,000 a day equals $35,000. Not a bad sum for five weeks' work, and it could well be just what you need to get you on your way to financial independence.

The arithmetic on the second plan is a little more complicated

and is based on the principle of compounding. That means the
money you earn immediately starts to earn more money for you.
Let's see how the numbers work out:

DAY	DAILY AMOUNT
1	$ .01
2	.02
3	.04
4	.08
5	.16
6	.32
7	.64
8	1.28
9	2.56
10	5.12
11	10.24
12	20.48
13	40.96
14	81.92
15	163.84
16	327.68
17	655.36
18	1,310.72
19	2,621.44
20	5,242.88
21	10,485.76
22	20,971.52
23	41,943.04
24	83,886.08
25	167,772.16
26	335,544.32
27	671,088.64
28	1,342,177.28

continued

DAY	DAILY AMOUNT
29	2,684,354.56
30	5,368,709.12
31	10,737,418.24
32	21,474,836.48
33	42,949,672.96
34	85,899,345.92
35	171,798,691.84
Total earned:	$343,597,383.68
	(over $300 million!)

When I present this proposition to students, most people choose the penny-a-day option, but only because they suspect a trick. When I ask them to tell me how much money the penny will turn into in thirty-five days, they never even get close. They guess $100,000, or even $1 million, or occasionally as high as $10 million, but no one has ever guessed $343 million.

My point is this: if you don't have money, or even if you do, you may want to borrow the funds to get your business started. But first take the time to understand the principles of compounding, and make sure you apply them to your investment. Look for ways to double that borrowed money quickly, then double it again, and again. That's a great way to build your own wealth with someone else's money.

You may be thinking that investing your money so it will double—and double quickly!—sounds good, but that it's not really possible. On the contrary, it happens every day. In chapter 7, I used a real property I purchased to show you how to calculate return on investment—and my ROI on that property was 1,706 percent! That was a good deal, but it wasn't an unusual deal. Those kinds of properties are out there all over the place, in every city and town in the country, just waiting for you to pick them up and make money.

As a simple example, let's say you put a $5,000 down payment on a $100,000 piece of property. A year later, it appreciates 5 percent (which is realistic in most markets), and you sell it for $105,000. Your initial $5,000 investment has earned you a profit of $5,000, which is a 100 percent return on your money in just one year.

Most people think that getting a 100 percent return on investment in real estate means you buy a property for $100,000 and sell it for $200,000, but you don't have to see the property double in value to double your money. Real estate is bought using mortgages, so you measure your return on investment based on the amount of cash you have invested, not the total amount of the purchase.

Real estate brokers generally won't tell you this because in many cases even they don't understand it. I even tried to explain it to a member of Mensa (the high-IQ society), and she didn't get it at first. The problem is not that it's complicated but that it's so simple it tends to escape most people.

This works in plenty of businesses other than real estate. For example, retail markups are tremendous. Most consumer goods—clothing, jewelry, furniture, electronics, etc.—are marked up anywhere from 100 to 300 percent. The process generally works like this: Items are manufactured and then sold in truckload or train-car-load quantities to a broker, who adds 10 to 15 percent to the manufacturer's price. The broker sells to a wholesaler, who tacks on a 30 to 50 percent markup before selling to the retailer. The retailer adds another 100 to 150 percent, so by the time the item gets to the consumer, it has been marked up 200 to 300 percent. When a retailer buys a pair of shoes for $20 and sells them for $40, he's making a 100 percent gross profit.

DOUBLING YOUR MONEY

When I make an investment, whether it's in a business or a property or anything else, all I want to know is how much I have to put up and how much I'm going to get back, period. Everything else is incidental.

Do you see now that it is possible to double your money in a short time? Getting a good return on an investment is compounding in action, and compounding is one of the main keys to wealth. But remember, if you take the money out of the process too soon, you'll kill the compounding formula and put yourself back at square one. That's what happens to most people when they start building wealth. They make a little money and are so pleased that they "reward" themselves with jewelry, clothes, cars, and trips—and destroy the compounding formula. It's the same principle as when someone who is dieting loses five pounds and eats a hot fudge sundae as a reward. Don't reward your success by undoing what you've accomplished; reward your success by staying on track and achieving even more.

During my first year in real estate, I made $117,000, but I kept my job at the slaughterhouse for another full year. With that kind of money, why was I willing to spend eight hours a day doing hard physical labor in a disgusting environment? For two reasons.

First, I hadn't yet shaken off my middle-income, blue-collar mentality that required a job for security. Second, and most important, I was determined to reinvest that $117,000 in appreciating assets that would compound at 100 percent annually. Ingrid and I lived on the money I earned at the slaughterhouse, and I put every nickel of that $117,000 back into real estate. By the end of the second year, I had made $234,000, and a year later I had turned that into $500,000. My penny-pinching days were over. At that point, I could easily have pulled out $100,000 for a new Rolls-Royce and still continued to increase my net worth. If you, too, exercise the discipline to keep your money working for you until you have amassed your first significant amount of wealth, you will be able to afford all the toys and luxuries you want while your bank account continues to grow.

Take another look at the penny-a-day compounding example. If you spend $100 on day 15, you've spent a major portion of your income. But by day 30, you can spend thousands of dollars and not be seriously affected by it. So make your seed money work for you until it grows into a money tree.

Remember, financial independence is within your grasp—today. You just have to borrow smart, invest in appreciating assets, compound your money at a rate as close to 100 percent as possible, and don't touch your seed capital until you've turned it into a money tree that will be your own personal fortune.

OPM IN ACTION

Shortly after my wife and I were married, we found an old house that was in such terrible shape that it was unlivable. There was no back door, the bathroom was on the back porch, and the only useful item in the kitchen was an old tub sink. We bought this palace in 1977 for $18,000. We used our hard-earned savings to make a $4,000 down payment, and the owner agreed to hold a $14,000 fifteen-year mortgage at 8.5 percent.

I knew absolutely nothing about home repairs and remodeling, but I learned as I went along. With my brother-in-law's help and a lot of sweat, we made the house livable. The initial purchase price was well under market value because of the poor condition of the house, but we quickly built up "sweat equity" with the repairs we made. Then I went to a bank and asked for a loan to install aluminum siding at an estimated cost of $4,000. With the improvements I had already made, I felt certain the house was now worth $25,000 to $30,000, and I owed only $14,000.

The bank appraised the house and offered to lend me $18,000—which was 72 percent of its assessed value—as a first mortgage. That meant I would have to pay off the existing $14,000 mortgage the seller was holding. Now, this was not an especially good loan for me; it was great for the bank, because it was well secured. You can easily borrow 75 to 80 percent on investment property these days, and 90 to 95 and even 100 percent on your own home. But at that time, I only knew to ask for the actual cost of the aluminum siding I planned to install. That was one mistake I'll show you how to avoid.

When I decided to accept the loan, I was operating under the strong influence of two important factors: first, I wanted more cash out of the deal, and second, I had been doing my homework. So I called the man I'd bought the house from, told him that I'd done a great job making improvements on it and that I was planning to add aluminum siding. Then I asked him to come out and take a look at the house.

Keep in mind that as the mortgage holder, he had a vested interest in the condition of the property. When he came out, I showed him what I had done. I explained that I had to borrow the money for further improvements, but the bank wanted a first mortgage position. I offered to give him $7,000 in cash if he would hold the other $7,000 I owed him in a second mortgage for twenty years at 8.5 percent. I'd already been paying him on time and the house was in better shape than it had been in years, so the offer was clearly a good, safe deal for him.

At the closing, the banker showed up with two checks: one payable to me for $4,000, and one payable to the seller for $14,000. We closed, the banker left, and the seller and I completed the deal. He gave me back $7,000, and I signed a second mortgage over to him. All of the paperwork was prepared by attorneys, so it was safe and legal for both of us. I walked away from the closings with $11,000 in tax-free cash. The whole deal took about three weeks.

Think about that. In less than a month, I had as much cash as it normally took me a year to earn. Of course, out of that cash, I paid for the aluminum siding to be installed, but that increased the value of my house, and I still had $7,000 to use for other investments.

The name of this technique is "seller subordination," which means that if you have a property on which the seller is holding the first mortgage, you ask him to subordinate his mortgage position to second place so you can obtain other financing on the property.

At the same time I did this, I decided to try buying a distressed income property to fix up and rent out. I used part of the $7,000 I had left after paying for the siding as a down payment on a shabby duplex that was structurally sound but looked awful. Ingrid and I painted the outside, paneled the hallways, did some landscaping, and were able to raise the rents high enough to cover not only the mortgage payment on the duplex but the one on our home as well. Essentially, we were living free thanks to the money that we had borrowed from the bank and that our tenants were repaying.

This is just one small example of how to build wealth using other people's money—a phrase popularly abbreviated to OPM. And the more money you make, the easier making money will become.

Though I first used this technique (buying run-down property, fixing it up, and then letting the rents pay the mortgage) on an inexpensive house in a low-income neighborhood, it works just as well on higher-priced property. Plenty of upper-income neighborhoods have one or two run-down houses. Even in my current neighborhood, where the houses go for $1 million and up, there's a shabby, neglected house that's a real eyesore. I've tried to buy it, but the owner doesn't want to sell. But you'll find enough owners who *will* sell in all types of neighborhoods to use this technique successfully over and over, as I have.

LET YOUR IMPROVEMENTS
PAY FOR THEMSELVES

When you're buying distressed property, it's not difficult to close the deal with little or no money down. But then you need money to pay to get the property fixed up so you can either rent it or sell it. If you put together a solid loan application package (which I'll explain in more detail in chapter 13), you shouldn't have any trouble getting a home improvement loan.

If the property you're fixing up has a mortgage on it, you may need to get that mortgage holder to subordinate his or her mortgage to a second position to allow the new lender the first mortgage position. You'll rarely find a conventional lender willing to lend with anything other than a first mortgage position on a rehab/construction loan. But plenty of other lenders, such as sellers who hold their own financing and second mortgage companies, will assume a second or even third mortgage position. Shop for them online or in your telephone directory; look under "Mortgage Companies," "Mortgage Brokers," and "Finance Companies." You should also check the "Money to Lend" section of the classified ads in your local newspaper.

The key is to be sure your property will pay for the improvements. Get your estimates, figure out how much total money you need and how long it will take to do the work, then what the property will be worth and how much cash flow it will generate when the rehab is done. Your cash flow should easily cover your anticipated debt service; if it won't, don't do the project.

ONE PROPERTY CAN IMPROVE ANOTHER

Once you own real estate, you can use the equity in one property as collateral for a loan to improve other properties. You just have to be able to demonstrate that the income from the encumbered property can support the debt. For example, let's say you have a duplex that's generating $300 a month in positive cash flow, is appraised at $175,000, and you owe $145,000 on it. You've just bought another duplex that needs $15,000 in rehab. You can borrow that $15,000 against the first duplex—a fifteen-year loan at 7 percent will mean monthly payments of $135, which the first property can easily support. When the rehab on the second property is finished, refinance it and use the proceeds to pay off the loan on the first property.

CONSIDER A DIFFERENT TYPE OF LOAN

My experience in applying for rehab/constructions loans taught me an important lesson. When you approach people at a bank and ask for a specific type of loan and are told they aren't making that loan right now, but they have other types of loans, listen carefully to the terms of the loan and think about how you can apply it to what you're doing.

Years ago, I was trying to get a relatively small new first mortgage on a property I was going to rehab. The deal was good and my track record was established, so the loan should have been easy. I was stunned when it wasn't. The first five lenders I approached turned me down. At the sixth bank, a small community bank, the senior vice president of commercial loans took the time to enlighten me about what was going on in the banking industry at the time. He explained that the banks were basing their lending decisions on economic cycles and that it would be easier to borrow commercial mortgage money if I were seeking an amount nearly three times what I needed; commercial lenders weren't going to get excited about the amount of the loan I was looking for.

I thought I was going to lose the deal, then this banker said he would make the loan. But instead of a traditional thirty-year mortgage, he said he would amortize my payments over twenty-five years but the loan would be callable in one year. What that meant was I would make monthly payments as though I had a twenty-five-year mortgage but at the end of one year I had to pay the loan in full.

This was a so-called balloon loan, and the terms made it extremely risky for me. But the potential reward was sufficient for me to take the chance. My plan was to do the rehab work and then look for permanent financing. As it happened, I wasn't able to secure the necessary financing when the loan came due at the end of one year.

This is an aspect of balloon loans that scares many people,

and it used to scare me. However, after I had a few balloon loans that I couldn't pay—such as this one—I realized there's nothing to fear. All you have to do is remember this: the banks don't want the property, they want their money. And if you've been making the payments on time, they're usually happy to renegotiate your loan. They may try to bluff you at first and insist that the loan is due. Just be firm, businesslike, and honest. Offer them their choices: they can extend the loan, or they can have the property back. You'll find that you usually won't have a problem getting the loan extended. On this particular property, I was able to extend the loan on the same terms, which I maintained until I found a buyer and sold the property at a handsome profit.

The real point of this is to stress that just because you can't get the specific type of loan you want doesn't mean you can't get the money to do the deal.

TAKE ADVANTAGE OF SELLER FINANCING

Often, sellers of distressed property are forced to hold the mortgage because traditional lenders will not lend money on real estate in such poor condition. (The same can apply to a distressed business; many businesses are sold with seller financing.) Sellers are also motivated to do their own financing when conventional mortgage money is tight; it's often the only way they can sell their property. No matter what its condition, whenever you buy a piece of real estate, always ask about seller financing. And always try to get the seller to hold as much of the mortgage as possible before you look for other money.

Once you have seller financing, you can pull money out of the property a number of ways. One is seller subordination, which is what I did with my first house. As I described at the beginning of this chapter, we bought the property, improved it, and refinanced it. Part of the refinancing included asking the seller to subordinate his mortgage position and take back a *second* mortgage. If you've been making your payments on time and you combine this proposal with some cash, most reasonable sellers will go along with you. Other ways to pull money out of property are to completely refinance the property or to borrow against the equity as you build it up.

Perhaps the most exciting part of making money with other people's money is that you help them make money, too. Building wealth with the right kind of debt is a win-win situation.

CHAPTER 10

A MILLION IN DEBT IS A MILLION IN NET

The first person gets the oyster, the second gets the shell.
—ANDREW CARNEGIE

There are only two times a banker will call you sir or ma'am, and that's when you have $1 million on deposit, or when *you* *owe* the bank $1 million.

As long as you make the payments, banks are happy to have you indebted to them. And you must understand that the only way to get wealthy is with debt—but it has to be *good* debt. If you owe $1 million or more on appreciating income-producing assets, your wealth will increase in direct proportion to your debt. Ideally the income should cover the debt service, and the assets will gain in value as the amount you owe decreases. When the loan is paid off, you will have an asset that has paid for itself; it can continue to generate revenue for you, or you can sell it.

This principle works on any scale, from a small house to a multimillion-dollar development. If you buy a house for $100,000 and rent it for enough money to cover the mortgage and other expenses, when your mortgage is paid off, you'll have an asset worth $100,000 plus whatever appreciation in value it's gained over the life of the loan. If the house's value rose by only 2.5 percent a year over the period of a twenty-year loan (which is a conservative figure), you'd have an asset worth $150,000 and your tenants would have paid it off for you.

The same thing applies to larger, multi-unit properties. It also works on businesses other than real estate. When you buy an appreciating asset, you start out with a big debt, but you use the income from the asset to pay the debt and ultimately turn it into a sizable net worth. If you purchase an income-producing, appreciating asset for $100,000 and it increases in value just 10 percent, you've made $10,000 over and above whatever profits the asset produces. If you purchase an appreciating asset for $1 million and it appreciates at that same 10 percent, you've made $100,000.

When you start or purchase a business, always try to buy the real estate as well, instead of just leasing. A woman I know bought a commercial building for her own business. She got a good deal on the building, and her business did well. When she decided to retire, she made more selling the building (she netted $1 million) than she did selling her business. I've seen this happen over and over: the business generates the cash flow, but real estate creates the true wealth.

Have you ever thought about how nice it would be if you could charge something and have someone else make the payments? That's how buying income-producing assets work, because the cash they generate makes the payments. And when those assets go up in value, your net worth has increased that much more.

Just remember that debt for appreciating and income-producing assets is a great way to build your personal fortune. By contrast, consumer debt *never* turns into net worth. It always turns into net loss—always!

I've had students proudly tell me that their only debt is their mortgage and they pay cash for everything else. While it's good that they have no consumer or credit card liabilities, these people are not going to get wealthy until they change their attitude about debt. Used properly, debt can be one of your greatest wealth-building tactics.

HOW WEALTHY PEOPLE GET WEALTHIER

Wealthy people consistently use other people's money to make more for themselves. More fortunes have been built on borrowed money than in any other way. After more than three decades as a real estate investor and business owner with a net worth in the millions, I still never use any more of my own money than I absolutely have to when I'm executing business deals. And neither should you.

In fact, I see using other people's money to make money as a game. It's fun, it's challenging, and it's a profitable way to play. And the wealthiest people do it all the time. The big players who have the biggest money all use borrowed funds. They take on huge debt, because the larger the debt, the bigger the asset—and the more awesome their net worth becomes. Of course, the asset must be an income-producing, appreciating asset to accomplish this.

The other aspect of this policy is that I rarely, if ever, use anything but totally disposable income to purchase *depreciating* assets. I don't buy clothes or household furnishings with borrowed money. I don't finance my vacations. If I can't pay cash, then I do without the consumer item and focus on making enough money so I *can* pay cash. I owe money only on assets that will make me more money than I borrowed to buy them in the first place. And so should you, especially in your beginning stages of wealth building. Once you begin to accumulate money, you can blow some of it on frivolous things, but don't do that until you have it.

Let me clarify that when I use the term *paying cash*, I don't necessarily mean actual currency. It's perfectly fine to use credit cards to complete the transaction when you are buying depreciating assets as long as you pay the bill in full when it comes in.

A technique that has worked well for me over the years is to designate the positive cash flow from a particular asset for a specific purpose. I would, for example, look at the cash flow from a

given rental property as money for solving a financial problem—
such as paying for a vacation, buying a new car, or providing luxuries for my family.

HOW TO GET YOUR NEXT AUTOMOBILE FREE

After I'd bought my first few properties, I realized I needed a new
vehicle. The car I had wasn't in the greatest shape, and a pickup
truck would have been more convenient, anyway. I had just purchased a building with a positive cash flow, and I found a great
deal on a new Toyota pickup truck. I used a $5,000 line of credit
a bank had sent me (totally unsolicited) to buy the truck and used
the cash flow from the property to pay it off. To me, that was like
getting the truck for free, because the apartment building made
the payments on it.

Even when you get to the point that you can afford a luxury
vehicle, I recommend that you not use it when conducting your
real estate business. Don't drive around low-income neighborhoods in a $100,000 car or arrive at a property in that same car
ready to make a below-market offer. It's human nature for someone to look at things like an expensive car or flashy jewelry and
think that if you can afford that, you can afford to pay more for
the property or take less in rent or whatever. Drive a serviceable,
midrange vehicle and leave the ostentatious jewelry at home
when you're dealing with buyers, sellers, and tenants.

WHEN TO TURN THE BANK DOWN

The advent of credit cards and the lack of education about how
to use them has increased consumer debt to record levels. The result is that many of us have a negative perception of credit and
debt, even as we run up the balances on our accounts. Many will
never get out from under their credit card debt, but *you* can.

You just have to understand that credit is both good and important, that debt can be positive, and that even credit card debt is okay if it's used for appreciating assets instead of consumer goods.

Here's the rule about borrowing money: *borrow money only when you can use those funds to make more money*. Use borrowed money to invest in appreciating assets, that is, only assets that will increase in value. Use borrowed money to invest in income-producing assets—preferably ones that show a positive cash flow, meaning that you have money left over after meeting your loan payments and expenses each month. For example, if you borrow money to purchase a rental property, your rents must be higher than the total of your mortgage payment and expenses. You learned how to analyze a property's profitability in chapter 7; what's important now is that you understand and accept the policy of borrowing money *only* to purchase appreciating and income-producing assets.

Never use borrowed money to purchase consumer goods. Never buy clothing, jewelry, or new cars with borrowed money. And if banks or other credit companies try to lend you money and you don't need it, don't take it. Ask them if they will establish a line of credit so you will have quick access to the funds when necessary, but never borrow money you're not going to immediately use to make more money with.

Big merchandisers such as Sears, Kmart, and Wal-Mart, along with the credit card companies, continue to spend millions of dollars on advertising campaigns to entice you to charge up your cards with consumer items. They want you to take vacations, go out to eat, and buy frivolous items with money you borrow from them at exorbitant interest rates. And they know you'll never pay the money back. You'll pay the interest, month after month, and you'll never be able to reduce the balance, so you'll be paying them forever. Who's getting wealthy with that deal?

Consumers are getting an incredibly mixed and confusing message. On the one hand, merchants and credit card companies are saying, "Buy, buy, buy." On the other hand, economists are saying how bad things are because we owe so much money. But nobody is pointing out that owing money on the right kinds of things is positive and productive.

Have you ever seen any of the major credit card companies air a commercial that suggests you use your credit card to invest in a good piece of real estate? No, and you probably never will. The reason is simple: if you make a few good investments and start building your personal wealth, you'll have enough money to pay cash for the things you want and you won't need to use their credit cards—or if you do, you'll pay the balance in full every month. It's much more profitable for them to encourage you to charge consumer goods, so you'll stay in debt and they'll keep on raking in the bucks.

You're being bombarded with the "buy now, pay later" message hundreds of times every day, but it's for consumer items. If you listen to it, it will keep you broke. I'm going to bombard you with the "buy now, pay later" message, too, but I'll teach you to focus on items that will generate positive cash flow now and will go up in value while you own them and on terms that are set up so someone else pays the debt for you. If you listen to me instead, I'll help you build your personal fortune.

Which would you prefer?

INTEREST RATES DON'T REALLY MATTER

Credit card companies justify their high interest rates because they are essentially offering unsecured loans at a higher level of risk than other types of loans. That in itself is understandable, and my problem with credit cards is not the interest rate but the type of purchases that are generally made with plastic.

I'd like to tell you a story that clearly expresses my feelings and policy about interest rates. Not too long after I'd reached financial independence and quit my job, I applied for a loan at the bank I'd been doing business with since I first got started at the age of twenty. I was surprised when the people there turned me

down and totally shocked at their reason. They said I was growing too fast, and they thought I should slow down.

I argued with them. I pointed out that my property business
was in beautiful condition, every unit was rented, every building
was profitable, and I was making all my payments on schedule. If
anything, I thought I should speed up so I could make more
money, both for me and for the bank. I was so insistent that they
finally agreed to make the loan I wanted but at a higher interest
rate because they claimed I was risky. Interest rates at the time
were fluctuating between 7 and 8 percent; they charged me 16
percent. I was too naive to know I could negotiate this; I needed
the loan for a good property, so I analyzed the deal and took the
money on the terms they offered.

But here's the point about interest: if you have money left
over after you pay your mortgage and expenses, don't worry
about the interest rate. When that banker offered me the money I
needed at 16 percent, I calculated my rents and expenses, fac-
tored in my down payment, and figured out that I would still
have a 100 percent return on my investment in the first year—
even paying twice the going interest rate!

This was another advantage being a high school dropout
gave me. If I had been too educated, I might have realized the
bank was taking advantage of me, and I probably wouldn't have
accepted the loan on those terms—and I would have missed out
on a profitable investment. What's more, the entire situation
taught me a valuable lesson about conventional thinking. Insist-
ing on the lowest interest rate can stop you from making money.
Though I do try to get the lowest rate I can, I'm willing to pay
more if I'm going to get a good return on my money. It's just
something that wealthy people do.

This is the principle that made many people wealthy with investment bonds in the 1980s. Basically, bonds are loans. The people issuing the bonds want to borrow *your* money, and they'll
usually pay a higher rate of return than a conventional savings institution because you're taking a risk with their idea, project, or
business. The reason they're able to pay higher interest is that if

whatever deal they're attempting to finance works out, they'll make even more than the 12 or 15 or 18 percent they're paying on the bonds.

I was young and naive, and it hadn't been long since I had been dirt-poor, but I had the common sense to realize it was worth paying a higher interest rate on that loan because I would still get a good return on my investment. Wealthy people know this. It's the people stuck in the middle who either don't understand or aren't willing to take advantage of this exciting money-making concept.

CHAPTER 11

WALK AWAY FROM THE SETTLEMENT TABLE WITH CASH EVERY TIME YOU BUY

Every problem has within it the seeds of its own solution. If you don't have any problems, you don't get any seeds.
—NORMAN VINCENT PEALE

For many people, one of the most memorable and gut-wrenching parts of a real estate or business purchase is the four- or five-digit cashier's check they are required to bring to the closing. But these purchases don't always mean you have to shell out big bucks. You can buy a property at a fair price, make a reasonable or low down payment, and still *make money* when you close.

I had to try this technique of financing several times over a span of years before it began working for me. No one ever showed me how to do it; I had to figure it out myself. But I'm going to show you. It may seem a little complicated, so study it carefully before you use it. It needs the right combination of circumstances to work, but you can create those circumstances with many income-producing assets. Your goal with this strategy is to get the seller to sell you his property, take his down payment out of the mortgage money, and allow *you to make money* at the closing. You'll get your best results with a highly motivated seller, a cosmetically distressed property, and any other circumstances that will encourage the owner to participate in creative financing. Show the seller the improvements you plan to make and convince him to allow you to finance those improvements out of the closing proceeds.

The mechanics of this technique usually involve the use of a promissory note from the buyer to the seller that represents your down payment. A promissory note is a negotiable instrument that can be bought and sold like cash. It is the instrument you sign along with a mortgage that is essentially an IOU. The note is your promise to pay; the mortgage is evidence of the collateral.

Begin by locating the property and deciding how much you want to offer and the amount of the down payment. The terms of your offer are that the seller will hold a second mortgage on the property contingent upon your obtaining a suitable first mortgage. On the offer the lender receives as part of the mortgage application, you show your down payment. But rather than cash, the seller has your promissory note for the agreed-upon down payment.

At the closing the bank will give the seller the first mortgage check. The two of you (seller and buyer) go to your title company's office, where the seller writes you a check for whatever the agreed cash-back balance to you is. Then you give the seller a second mortgage totaling the down payment amount plus any cash you received. Once this is completed, the seller returns your promissory note because you have now satisfied it with the second mortgage and a new note for same. Essentially what happens is that instead of giving the seller a cash down payment, you've agreed that the down payment can be made over time instead of at the sale, and you've secured that agreement with a second mortgage.

This type of financing, which years ago was commonly called overfinancing, is usually used with large, multimillion-dollar deals, although it can work effectively on smaller properties and even businesses under the right circumstances. The reason you don't see it more often on smaller deals is that people either don't

SAMPLE PROMISSORY NOTE
GENERAL FORM

❖ ❖ ❖

$ _____   _____

(city, state)

_____

date

FOR VALUE RECEIVED, I [or we, jointly, jointly and severally] promise to pay to the order of _____ the principal sum of _____ dollars ($_____) in lawful money of the United States, with interest thereon from _____ at the rate of _____% annum until paid, payable on _____ and _____ thereafter, and if not paid as it becomes due, to be added to the principal and become a part thereof and to bear interest at the same rate.

_____

(signature)

_____

(signature)

_____

(witness)

_____

(witness)

know about it or don't think they can do it. But it's a practical and useful technique that can be used to complete a deal that might not otherwise happen.

It's true that overfinancing was part of the problem with the bad real estate loans many S&Ls made that led to the S&L crisis of the 1980s. But it wasn't the technique that was bad; it was a lack of ethics that caused the problem. People got their money up front, then hung the banks for the loans. If you decide to overfinance, be prepared to meet your obligation and make the commitment to yourself to follow through.

Before you try this technique, be aware that some banks insert clauses into their mortgages that restrict you from obtaining secondary financing on the property without their approval. I don't understand the reason or need for this clause, because any junior mortgages you might add to the property will not affect their position as a first mortgage holder or the security of their loan. But since some banks do this anyway, you can make it a point of negotiation. If you see the clause, tell the banker that you may eventually want to seek secondary financing and ask that it be removed. At the very least, demand additional language to the effect that permission to obtain secondary financing will not be unreasonably withheld by the bank.

HOW CREATIVE FINANCING WORKS IN REAL LIFE

The first time I successfully used this technique was to purchase a wood-frame, two-story, single-family house. The property had minimal cosmetic distress and was ideal for an inexpensive conversion to a rooming house. The seller wanted to leave the state and be near her family, so she was motivated.

She was asking only $32,000 for the property and was willing to hold a second mortgage. I needed $5,000 to pay for the improvements. I agreed to pay her full asking price and give her a $15,000 down payment, which would come out of the $20,000 first mortgage money that I would seek and secure. She would hold a second mortgage for $17,000. At the closing the banker gave her a check for $20,000; she gave me $5,000 of that money, and we drew up the note for the second mortgage. Here are the terms of the offer:

Purchase price	$32,000
Down payment (promissory note until closing)	15,000
First mortgage	20,000

Here's the end result:

Purchase price	$32,000
Down payment	15,000
First mortgage	20,000
Cash to buyer (me) at closing	5,000
Second mortgage at closing held by seller	17,000

The property was now financed for $37,000. Though that was $5,000 over the selling price, I walked away from the deal with $5,000 in cash, and the improvements I made with that money quickly forced the value up to exceed the loan amount. It was a great deal for everyone: the woman was able to sell the house; the bank made a good loan that was eventually paid off; and I was able to finance the property with enough money to make the necessary improvements to generate a substantial cash flow as a rooming house. Note that because this was a deal I did many years ago, the numbers are smaller than they would be for the same property today, but the process is the same.

This financing method works best with a motivated seller and a property that can be improved to enhance its value. This example is for a modestly priced property, but the creative financing formula can work equally as well with million-dollar properties. Just use caution and common sense; be sure your cash flow will cover all of the debt that's created with this technique; and consider having your documents reviewed by an attorney to verify that the deal conforms to your state laws.

This technique is also more likely to work when you are dealing with a repeat seller. This is when you have bought a property and the seller is impressed enough with the transaction to contact you when he or she has something else to sell. Not only do you go into the deal with confidence and respect already established, but you are operating from a position of strength because the seller has come to you.

CASH BACK TO YOU

Another way to get money at a closing is with a repair and redecorating allowance. This is the money the seller gives you out of the sale price to cover the cost of repairing or redecorating the property. To actually take cash away at the closing, you need a seller who is willing to accept a purchase price that is less than the appraised value and who will work with you to put together the deal. You can also use a repair and redecorating allowance to reduce your down payment.

Once you've agreed on the amount the seller wants, the repair and redecorating allowance is added to the price and presented to the lender for financing. At closing, the seller turns the amount of the allowance over to you from the loan proceeds.

Let's say you find a house appraised at $200,000, but the market is slow and the seller is motivated, so he or she agrees to accept $177,000. You write the offer to show a sale price of $198,000 with a $21,000 repair and redecorating allowance. Then you apply for a mortgage based on 90 percent of the sale price, or $178,200, which just about any bank will be happy to provide on a property appraised at $200,000 if it's going to be owner-occupied.

At the closing, the bank gives the seller $178,200 and you give the seller $19,800 as your down payment for a total sale of $198,000. Then the seller gives you $21,000 back for the repair and redecorating allowance. You don't have to physically exchange thousands of dollars, you can just have the seller bring

$1,200, which is the difference between the amount of the mortgage and the sale price, and you walk away with that cash. Had this been a purchase of investment property with financing of only 80 percent available, you could have used the repair and redecorating allowance to significantly reduce the amount of cash you need to make the down payment. If the seller is worried about paying taxes on the repair and redecorating allowance, you can ease his or her mind by explaining that it may be written off as an expense related to the sale.

This is often done with both residential single-family and multi-unit buildings, as well as commercial properties. A friend of mine who is a real estate agent has used this technique to make some great deals for himself and his clients. No one dictates just how much work really needs to be done on the property, or how much it will actually cost, as long as the numbers work for everyone involved. It's a simple and easy way to reduce the down payment, and it sometimes even allows you to get cash at closing, especially when you are buying the property with the intention of living there.

When you come to the negotiating table with a sound knowledge of techniques like these, you have a distinct advantage over most buyers and sellers. With the clout and power this knowledge gives you, you can make great deals happen.

LET THE SELLER MAKE YOUR DOWN PAYMENT

When you are buying occupied rental property, always arrange to close (take ownership) on the third or fourth day of the month. The logic is simple: Most rents are due on the first, which means that whoever owns the building on the first is obligated to collect them. But rents are paid in advance, so if ownership transfers a few days after those monies are collected, the new owner is entitled to receive a prorated share of them.

Two longtime friends of mine, construction workers who became millionaires by investing in real estate, purchased their first multi-unit building using this technique and walked out of the closing with a check for $6,000 and a building that generated $800 a month in positive cash flow.

Here's an example of how this worked for me. Earlier I told you about a run-down four-unit building I bought for $75,000 with a 10 percent down payment. But I didn't have $7,500 in cash. I did, however, have a $5,000 signature line of credit available. Obviously that wasn't enough, and I also needed additional cash to handle the needed repairs. So in my offer I stipulated that the closing take place on the third of the month.

The building was fully occupied, and the rents totaled $2,000 per month. To determine the daily rents, I divided the monthly total by the number of days in that particular month. In a thirty-day month, that meant daily income of $66.67. By closing on the third, that meant the seller would owe me twenty-seven days of rental income, or $1,800.

Here's another consideration when purchasing occupied rental property: the owner collects and holds security deposits on each unit. The amount of the deposit will vary depending on the location and the lease, but it's usually one month's rent.

Let me be very clear here: That money belongs to the tenants. But it is held by the owner, and when you become the owner, the funds are transferred to you. That meant another $2,000 the seller had to give me at closing. Check with your state laws to see if there are any special requirements about the handling of security deposits. You may need to maintain the deposit money in a separate escrow account, or you may be allowed to use the deposit money until you sell the building or a tenant moves out and you refund his or her deposit. But remember, even if a tenant moves out, you'll soon have another moving in with a new deposit.

I was able to make a $7,500 down payment with only $3,700 cash out of pocket after deducting the monies the seller had to transfer to me at closing. I still had enough money to pay for the improvements necessary to increase the value of the property and qualify it for new financing, so I could pull $33,000 out of the deal just one month later. At that point, I could have sold the property for no money down, held the mortgage, and walked away with all the cash and no debt.

Even today, I make a practice of closing on the third, fourth, or fifth day of the month when I purchase multi-unit buildings, because it's always worthwhile to get the benefit of the prorated rents. One thing you need to check on is that the rents are due on the first, and not a different day. It's rare, but sometimes rents are due on the fifteenth, or sometimes the owners use an odd lease by which the rents are staggered throughout the month. Rents due on any day other than the first will affect the amount of prorated dollars you can take off your down payment, so check it out.

Also, if you're buying a business of any sort, do some research on the payables and receivables to see if you can take advantage of prorations.

Most sellers will never question the closing date. If they do and want to close on the first of the month, or at the very end of the month when there would be little benefit from prorations, just tell them you won't be available. You don't need to give a reason; just say that because of your commitments, the closing must take place on the third, fourth, or fifth. Remember, your choice of dates will rarely be challenged, but if it is, all you have to do is be firm. There's no reason to be afraid of losing the deal over this issue. When you're confident of your own knowledge and ability, you can accomplish just about anything at the negotiation table.

CHAPTER 12

COOKING UP PROFITS IN RAW LAND

I'm very determined and stubborn. There's a desire in me that makes me want to do more and more, and to do it right. Each one of us has a fire in our heart for something. It's our goal in life to find it and to keep it lit.

—MARY LOU RETTON

When I first started investing in real estate, all of the so-called experts at the time advised against buying raw land. Their logic made sense, because they pointed out that vacant land couldn't be rented out; hence, it wouldn't generate income, and you'd have to pay the mortgage and the taxes while you were waiting and hoping for the value to increase to the point that you could sell it and take your profit. I figured that because I had followed their other advice and had made money, I should follow their advice in this arena, too.

When I make a mistake, I'm the first person to admit it. And to totally ignore land as an investment was a mistake.

I have made more money investing in raw land in the past few years than I did in the total of the first fifteen or twenty years I was investing. I don't want you to wait as long as I did to take advantage of this lucrative opportunity.

There are a number of ways to profit from raw land. One is to buy and hold the land while the growth in the area drives up the value, then sell it. This is not an investment strategy, it's luck—and wealthy people don't depend on luck. You have absolutely no control over what will happen with this approach. While it's possible to make money accidentally by investing in raw land, you'll make more—lots more—if you use my proven strategies.

When I started investing in raw land, nobody was teaching people how to do this. I looked for books on the subject, and all I could find were thick technical volumes that focused on the processes of development, not on moneymaking strategies. As an investor, I don't need to understand how to install roads or utilities; I need to know how to profitably buy and sell the property. Once I figured that out, I took what I learned and wrote *The Millionaire Real Estate Mindset,* which was the first mass market book that showed how even new investors could profit with raw land. Then I created a course that we added to the curriculum offered by Wealth Intelligence Academy™. In that course, we teach seven strategies for investing in land, and I'm going to give you an overview of each of those strategies in this chapter.

You don't have to be a big development company to profitably invest in land. Small investors are making millions every day because they've taken the time to learn how to do it, and you can, too. Let's take a look at the basics.

UNDERSTANDING HOW LAND IS PRICED

Single-family and smaller multi-unit residential properties are priced based on the total land and building. Commercial properties are often priced by the square foot, and raw land is generally priced either by the square foot or by the acre. This type of pricing makes it a little easier for you to compare costs.

If you found a three-bedroom, two-bath single-family house in a neighborhood and the seller was asking $150,000, it would be a fairly simple matter to check the property records and see what other three-bedroom, two-bath single-family houses in that neighborhood had sold for within the previous six months. With that information, you can evaluate the asking price in terms of the market value of the property. It's not as easy when it comes to commercial property and raw land.

Let's say you found a five-acre tract of land on a corner for sale with an asking price of $100,000. Two of the other corners are already built out; on the fourth corner is a thirteen-acre tract that sold six months ago for $300,000. There are no other vacant five-acre tracts in the area for you to use as a price comparison, so instead you calculate the per-acre price for the thirteen-acre tract to get a sense of the market values. When you do the math, you'll see that the thirteen-acre tract sold for $23,076 an acre. The seller of the five-acre tract is asking $20,000 an acre. If your other research into what you expect the market to do confirms potential growth, the five-acre tract is probably priced below market. Note that I said *probably*—there might be reasons for the lower price, such as zoning limitations, no water or sewer, or an endangered species of animal or plant on the property that will restrict what you can do with it. Find out before you make the purchase.

For smaller parcels, do the math the same way by calculating the price per square foot. There are 43,560 square feet in an acre. Let's say you're looking at a half-acre lot that's on the market for $75,000. That's 21,780 square feet, and the seller is asking $3.44 per square foot. There are no other half-acre lots in the area, but a one-acre lot sold for $130,000 four months ago (about $3 per square foot) and a three-quarter acre lot sold for $125,000 last month ($3.83 per square foot), so the half-acre lot is competitively priced. See how it works? It's not difficult.

HOW TO BUY AHEAD OF GROWTH

It's easy to say "buy ahead of growth," but how do you know where the growth is going to be? Simple. One way is to take a look at aerial photos of the county. Most local governments take aerial photos of the entire county each year and keep them on file in the county clerk's office or the property appraiser's office. These photos are public record, and anyone can ask to see them or get copies of them. Ask for photos going back five or ten years, spread them out, and look to see what's changed. You should be able to see clear patterns, and that will help you identify which areas are in the path of growth. You'll also be able to see where the vacant land is.

Or you can figure out where the potential for growth is by reading your town, city, or county's comprehensive plan.

THE COMPREHENSIVE PLAN CAN BE A CRYSTAL BALL

Every city or county is covered by a comprehensive plan that provides policy and planning guidance on the physical development and redevelopment of a community. The plan usually looks at current land use in relation to population and economic data and describes future land-use plans based on the anticipated growth of the community. This is one way you find the information you need to buy ahead of growth.

Comprehensive plans are public information, and many are available online. To get a copy of the comprehensive plan for the area in which you want to invest, contact the community development or economic development agency's planning department. Comprehensive plans typically consist of these elements:

- ❖ Foreword or vision statement—an introduction to the plan that may also summarize the goals and policies of the local government unit.
- ❖ Capital improvements—outlines the major capital expenditures planned that are needed to purchase, construct, replace, and maintain public facilities and services.
- ❖ Community services—deals with plans for utilities and community facilities such as sanitary sewer services, storm water management, water supply, solid waste disposal, on-site wastewater treatment technologies, recycling facilities, parks, telecommunication facilities, power plants and transmission lines, cemeteries, health and child care facilities, and other public facilities such as police, fire and rescue, libraries, and schools.

❖ Economic data—this is usually made up of a compilation of objectives, policies, goals, maps, and programs designed to promote the stabilization, retention, or expansion of the economic base; it will typically include an analysis of the labor force, describe desirable new businesses and industries, identify economic development programs that apply to the local government, and more.

❖ Future land use—this section will include the objectives, policies, goals, maps, and programs that will guide the future development and redevelopment of public and private property.

❖ Historic preservation—will identify areas designated for historic preservation and discuss how those areas are incorporated into the overall plan.

❖ Housing—the plan will identify and prioritize the community's housing issues and trends and outline short- and long-term solutions.

❖ Parks and recreation—identifies plans for public parks and recreational facilities, including the need to expand or rehabilitate existing facilities or to create new ones.

❖ Transportation—addresses issues related to the future development of various modes of transportation, including highways, mass transit, transportation systems for people with disabilities, bicycle paths, pedestrian walkways, railroads, air transportation, trucking, and water transportation.

Most counties and cities have determined the ideal and best use of each property as part of their master plan. The master plan is integrated into the comprehensive plan and serves as a guide for investors and developers.

Another component of the master plan that you'll use is the future land-use map, which is a geographical representation of future growth plans. Regardless of a particular property's current zoning, never make a purchase until you've reviewed the comprehensive plan and future land-use map so you know if any zoning changes are planned.

Let's say you find a parcel of land that's zoned for commercial, but it's on a two-lane road and does not have city water or sewer services. You check the comprehensive plan and see that the road is scheduled for widening in one year and the property is scheduled to get water and sewer services in two years. These will generally force up the value of the land. You could buy that property, hold it for two years, and make a substantial profit when you sell.

I did this with twenty acres I purchased for $1.46 a square foot. The property did not have water and sewer, but I knew from the comprehensive plan that these services would be coming in about eighteen months. I don't know if the seller knew about the comprehensive plan, but he made it clear that he just wanted to get rid of the property. So I paid $1.5 million, held the acreage for two and a half years, then sold it for $8.8 million. I did absolutely no improvement to the property—the city did all the work necessary to drive up the value.

Another way to use the comprehensive plan and future land-use map is to improve the zoning on property to bring it up to its highest and best use. You might, for example, find land currently zoned for agricultural and bring it up to residential, multi-unit residential, office, or retail. Or you might find something zoned for a residential duplex or fourplex that you can bring up to retail or office.

Keep in mind that most counties and cities have already determined what their planners believe to be the highest and best use of each parcel as part of their master plan. The actual rezoning may not yet have occurred, but you can see from the future land-use plan what it will likely be. If you want zoning different from what the future land-use plan indicates, you are going to have to go through the rezoning process.

IT TAKES WORK, BUT IT CAN BE DONE

Any zoning change that deviates from the future land-use plan will probably have an impact on the city's master plan, which has likely already planned for schools, parks, fire and police stations, retail shopping, light industrial, and so on. That doesn't mean it's impossible to get zoning changed—in fact, it's done all the time. But to do it, you need to go before the local zoning board, and in some cases it will have to be reviewed at the state level. Have all your proverbial ducks in a row and be ready to show why the zoning change you want is good for the community.

When I say that you go before the zoning board, the reality is that you don't actually do that yourself. You hire an engineering firm that specializes in land development and rezoning issues. You want a firm that does this for a lot of clients, that's established in your area, and has a relationship with the government leaders and knows what information they want and how to present it.

How to apply for a zoning change could be a book by itself, but you don't have to know the minute details of how to get it done—you just have to hire someone to do it for you. What's important for you to understand at this point is that if you can demonstrate a true higher and better use of the property with a positive impact on the community, in most cases you'll get the zoning change you want. You need to do your research and put together a comprehensive application. Be prepared for a process that could take several months or longer.

ENTITLEMENTS AND PERMITTING

An entitlement is a right generally to some sort of benefit granted by law or contract. In real estate, properties can be entitled with rights related to zoning, roadway access, property tax matters, economic incentives, permitting, density, and other restrictions and designations. Securing entitlements for a property can increase its value and your profits.

I have done a number of deals where I purchased a tract of land, obtained entitlements such as rezoning, new roadway access, and building permits, then sold the land to a builder for millions of dollars in profits. Could the builder do what I'm doing? Sure. But most would rather not. They're happy to let me—and investors like me—make plenty of money doing the preliminary work so that they can just step in and start building. One reason is that builders don't want to get their money tied up in land banking—they want to be able to immediately begin building and selling, which is what they do best. Most builders don't care how much money you're making as long as you're bringing them a deal that they can profit on, too.

PROFIT FROM DUE DILIGENCE

With any real estate purchase, you can write a due diligence (or inspection) period into your contract. The phrase *due diligence* essentially means doing your homework and conducting the research necessary to make sure you have all the facts you need to confirm your analysis of the deal and decide if you want to go through with the contract. If you own a home, you probably did that when you made your purchase offer if your contract stated that the offer was contingent on the house passing inspection and that you would arrange to have the inspection done within a specified period. I teach my students to put similar contingencies in all their contracts so that you can walk away from the deal if you realize it isn't going to work out the way you thought.

There's another advantage of the due diligence period, especially when it comes to vacant land. With land purchases, it's customary to have anywhere from 90 to 180 days from the time you sign the contract until the time you close to conduct your due diligence. That gives you time to consult with zoning authorities, engineers, architects, and other experts to determine if your plan for the land is workable. If it's not, you walk away from the deal and at most you've lost some money in consulting fees. If it is, you close on the deal and make money.

Here's how that worked for me: I put forty acres (half that was a lake, half that had been a dirt mine) under contract for $4 million. It was zoned for public works, and I wasn't sure if I could get it changed. During the due diligence period, my team went to work on both the zoning and on finding a buyer. Our plan was to get the zoning changed, but before we completed the rezoning and actually closed on the purchase, we found a buyer willing to pay $6 million with the current zoning—a gross profit of $2 million. Had we not found that buyer or not been able to get the zoning changed, we could have walked away from the deal under the due diligence clause in our contract.

DEVELOPING BIG MONEY

Take the concept of entitlements and permitting a step further by actually developing tracts of raw land. Buy the land; divide it into lots; improve the sites so they are ready for building; build roads, sidewalks, and curbs; install water, electric, and cable lines; install a sewage or septic system; and build the required public facilities. Each lot will usually sell for many times what it cost you to buy and develop the land.

Being a developer takes more resources and work than simply buying and selling property, but it's well worth the effort. If you don't have the experience and confidence, I recommend partnering on your first few deals with someone who does.

A key to successful development is to know your market, both as it is right now and as you expect it to be in the future. Leading economic indicators that can predict the rise or fall of a local market are readily available. You need to know if the local economy is on the upswing, which increases the demand to buy and creates appreciation; on the downswing, which increases the demand to rent and creates cash flow; or flat.

You can obtain studies and forecasts that will guide your development decisions at little or no cost; you just need to know where to find the information. Your local chamber of commerce can give you statistics on population growth and per capita income. The economic development agency can tell you about new business coming into the area as well as trends in specific business sectors. The building department has information on building permits and what the trends are showing. Apartment occupancy information can be obtained from the local apartment owners association or from the housing agency; the building owners and managers association can tell you about office occupancy. You can also get all this information from an urban planner (and I'll explain more about what urban planners do and how you should use them shortly); you'll have to pay his fee, but it will be worth it in time savings for you.

Recently I bought 11.6 acres of vacant land that was an infill parcel at a shopping center that was anchored by a major grocery store. My staff had been watching this parcel for some time because we were aware of some major office developments going in behind the grocery store. We bought the land for $4.5 million with a plan to sell it to a department store. We couldn't come to terms with the store, but that turned out to be a blessing in disguise, because we found another buyer who was willing to pay more than we were originally asking. We ended up owning this land for about a month, sold it for $6.3 million—a gross profit of more than $1.8 million. We were able to do this because we pay attention to the market, we study the economic indicators, and we always buy with a clear strategy in mind. This isn't difficult; it's something anyone can learn to do. With a little experience and education, you can be using these techniques to do the same kinds of deals where you live.

OFFSET YOUR HOLDING COSTS

As I mentioned earlier, the primary reason so many real estate "experts" advised against buying raw land is because it doesn't generate revenue for cash flow and yet you're still paying the mortgage and taxes. While it's true that a tract of vacant land doesn't have houses, apartments, or offices to rent, there are things you can do with land to offset your holding costs. This makes it a little easier to buy property that you know is in the path of development.

Some of the uses you may consider include mining any valuable minerals (it's a good idea to hire an engineering firm to assess the potential ancillary value of geological resources); selling lumber if the land has trees; selling fill dirt and boulders; or creating a short-term sod farm. Even though you don't have buildings, you might be able to rent the land for others to use for storage or parking. For a nominal investment, you could set up a driving range for golfers or a target range for shooters. Stock any water areas for fishing and charge for their use. Or lease the land for grazing or farming.

Of course, before you buy property with the idea of doing something like this to offset your holding costs, check with the appropriate sources (the zoning board should be able to tell you) to make sure you can legally do whatever it is that you have in mind.

DON'T DO THIS ALONE

In my early days of investing, I bought most of my properties alone (or jointly with my wife). When you're investing in land, you need a team of knowledgeable people to help you make good decisions. I have learned that an urban planner is a valuable resource, because this person (or firm) has access to the information that can quickly help you determine what the best use for a particular tract of land is. Urban planners tap into all of the statistical data, analyze it, then tell you what the highest and best use of a particular property is and why.

Once the urban planner has done his job and you're ready to move forward, you'll need an architect, a civil engineer, an environmental engineer, a market research analyst, and possibly a few other types of experts to help you complete the project. Don't let this part of the process intimidate you. These are the people who will actually do the work while you make the money. Their businesses depend on people like you retaining them regularly, so they want to do a good job for you so you'll hire them again. Just remember that it's easy to buy a house or a small apartment building by yourself; don't try to do that with raw land.

SEVEN STRATEGIES FOR PROFITING FROM VACANT LAND

At the beginning of this chapter, I told you that I have developed seven proven strategies for profiting with vacant land. I stress that these are *proven* strategies—they are techniques I have done time and again, and they can work for you, too. In my book *The Millionaire Real Estate Mindset,* I detailed many of the specific deals that I completed with these strategies and the millions of dollars of profit those deals generated.

Here are the strategies that will allow you to create and control value, drive pricing, and make a market:

Strategy 1: Create value by platting acreage

Make the land ready for development by platting it. A plat is a map or a chart of a piece of land with present or proposed features, such as lots and streets. Don't worry if you look at a piece of land and can't see anything but the land—the urban planner and the rest of your team of professionals can help you develop a vision for the property. The ideas for what to do with vacant land don't have to be yours; plenty of people are happy to help you with this. An engineering firm can help you prepare a plat map of the lots and their exact dimensions; the building footprint of each lot (the space on the ground the building is allowed to cover); the locations and dimensions of streets, sidewalks, sewer access, retention areas, ingress to and egress from the development, easements, wet areas, and open space. Once you have come up with an idea and a design and platted the land, you can sell it to a builder/developer who will then do all the construction.

I did this with a five-acre parcel that I brought for $35,000. An urban planner came up with the idea of dividing this parcel into fourteen quarter-acre homesites surrounding a park the size of a football field. We platted the land and did some renderings to show what it would look like, then I took the idea to a builder. I told the builder that he wouldn't have to pay for the land until he had built and sold each house, but he would have to prep each of the homesites and build the park. I sold the land to the builder for $40,000 for each quarter-acre homesite—that's $160,000 an acre for land I paid $7,000 an acre for. I bought this five-acre parcel for $35,000, platted it, then sold the land and the idea to a builder for a total of $560,000, or a $525,000 profit.

Strategy 2: Create value by entitling/permitting

We've already discussed entitlements and permits. You can increase the value of land by securing entitlements and permits that will allow a builder or a developer to step in and immediately begin construction. They are happy to pay a premium for the work you'll do in advance.

Strategy 3: Use of the city's comprehensive plan to buy ahead of growth or infrastructure

As you've already learned, use tools such as aerial photos and the city's comprehensive plan to identify growth patterns, then look for land in areas where growth is likely to occur in the relatively near future.

Strategy 4: Create value by improving zoning

Bring the zoning up to its highest and best use. The value of the land will be greater after a zoning change and will create a substantial profit margin. For example, you can have the property rezoned from agricultural to a duplex, a fourplex, or even a planned urban development (PUD). You can rezone from hotel or apartment to condominium or from retail to office. An urban planner can help you review the future land-use plan to evaluate the impact of your proposed zoning change and put together a proposal to take to the appropriate governmental authority.

Strategy 5: Create value by developing

The goal of development is to improve a platted subdivision so the lots are ready for a builder to buy them and immediately start construction. This is more work—and more profitable—

than just platting the land. When you develop the land, you make improvements that could include site preparation; building roads, sidewalks, and curbs; installing signage and lighting; landscaping; installing water, electric, and cable lines; installing sewage or septic systems; and building any public facilities such as a gatehouse, clubhouse, parks, pools, or tennis courts.

Assemble a power team that includes a partner with development experience to handle the details of the project; a managing partner; a marketing partner; and a contractor or a builder. Put together a plan, establish a legal entity (such as an LLC) for the project, raise the capital, and you're ready to go. When you have completed the development, you can sell the individual lots, build and sell the finished homes (or apartments, condos, or commercial buildings), or sell the entire project.

Strategy 6: Create value by selling to a builder/developer

All builders need land. Get to know the builders and developers in your area and keep records on what type of property they need and what they're willing to pay. Builders tend to operate in terms of a per-unit cost; they pay so much per unit that they can build. So if you find a parcel that can be zoned for thirty condominium units and you find a builder willing to pay $20,000 per unit, you can sell the parcel for $600,000. Whether that's a good deal depends on what you paid for the land. The point you need to keep in mind is that when you talk to a builder, speak his language and ask what he'll pay per unit.

When you find something that meets the parameters of the builders and developers you've gotten to know, put it under contract and take the deal to them. You can either purchase and re-sell the property, or you can just assign your contract to the builder/developer. In the latter case, you sell your rights to the property under your purchase contract and the builder/developer pays you for that and closes on the property. I did this with a parcel near my office. I knew a condo builder who had told me he was always looking for land, and I knew what he was willing to pay per unit. The parcel had the right zoning, so I put it under contract for $227,960 and took the deal to the builder. He was willing to pay $378,000, so I assigned my contract to him and cleared $150,040. He was happy to have the land, and he built some beautiful condos that I'm sure he made plenty of money on.

Strategy 7: Create value by selling the vision

Selling the vision takes platting a step further. Get the property under contract, consult with an urban planner to determine the highest and best use, then hire an architect to create a rendering (what I call a pretty-picture architect) of what the finished project will look like. You need to create a complete project presentation so potential buyers can clearly see the vision. You can sell the vision to investors as a developer/builder raising capital or to an entity that will buy the entire project and take over the developing and building.

KNOW HOW YOU'RE GOING TO GET OUT BEFORE YOU GET IN

Buying raw land to hold for a year or two (or longer) can be a sound investment strategy if you have done your homework, are buying right, and know what the market is probably going to do. But don't just buy vacant land with the idea that you'll see what happens and may be able to sell it for a profit someday. Always have a clearly defined exit strategy before you buy—and it's a good idea to have a backup for that. Use the strategies you've just learned to decide what you're going to do with property before you buy it.

For example, your exit strategy might be to sell the land in a targeted time after certain other things (perhaps road construction or the installation of water and sewer) have happened. But think about what you'll do if you can't find a buyer—you might need to consider developing the property yourself.

Developing your exit strategy will force you to think the deal through and do enough research so your risk is minimal and your profits have the potential to be substantial.

CHAPTER 13

INSIDER BANKING SECRETS

Can't never could.
—JIM PAYNE'S MOM

Banks are money stores. Just as a restaurant is in business to sell food and department stores are in business to sell clothes and furniture and other merchandise, banks are in business to sell money. Banks are for-profit enterprises with stockholders who want to see a profit on their investment. They make money in two primary ways: first, through interest on loans, charging points and origination fees for the loans, closing costs, and other service fees; and second, by making loans that are sold to other lenders who are looking for investments.

So loans are very important to banks, and bankers are under a tremendous amount of pressure to make them. But here's the catch: they are under a tremendous amount of pressure to make *good* loans—that is, loans that will be paid back on schedule. When a loan goes into default, all eyes turn to the guy who made it. Bankers have been known to lose their jobs when big loans or too many loans go bad. In fact, the whole S&L crisis of the 1980s was primarily caused by banks making bad loans and becoming insolvent as a result.

What you always have to keep in mind is that banks are not benevolent entities that lend you money when you need it just because you need it. They are *businesses*—just like the business you either have or will have—and they are in business to make a profit.

WHY ARE WE SO INSECURE ABOUT BANKERS?

Even though you may intellectually understand that by borrowing money from a bank you are a customer and the bank is making money on your loan, you may still be intimidated by bankers. Let's take care of that right now, once and for all.

Bankers work hard at projecting a respectable, conservative image. They dress in respectable, conservative gray, brown, or blue suits. They drive respectable, conservative automobiles. They belong to respectable, conservative professional organizations. And they do this because they work in what is supposed to be a conservative, respectable industry.

What's important for you to remember is that just as there is good and bad in any industry, there are good and bad banks, and good and bad bankers. Most bankers fall under the 95 Percent Rule: they go to work every day and do their job as best they can, but they will never stand out or achieve anything remarkable.

I'm not trying to make fun or be nasty or critical of the profession, but you need to know how the system works. Even the most important banker in town doesn't necessarily earn a lot of money. Many bankers don't even have a lot of business experience; they come out of college and go into bank training programs, and their knowledge of business and investing is more from textbooks than from practical experience. If you follow my methods, you'll probably make more on your first real estate deal than a junior loan officer makes in six months.

So why are so many people intimidated by bankers? There are several reasons. First, we don't understand banking, and it's common to be intimidated by something you don't understand. But let's put that into perspective. If you put a basic algebra exam in front of me, something that most high school seniors would knock out easily, I would be lost—and probably intimidated by all the *x*'s and *y*'s and other unfamiliar symbols. That's because I don't understand algebra; I never learned it. But I can look at the most complicated closing statement and figure it out fairly quickly, because I've taken the time to learn and understand closing statements.

Learning banking is just like learning anything else. For the most part, bankers are ordinary people who have learned their profession through college and on-the-job training programs. If they can learn it and be trusted to make loans, why can't you learn whatever it is the banker knows?

Getting to know your bankers personally can also take a lot of the mystique out of what they do. You can meet bankers by asking friends and business associates for introductions and by getting involved in your community. Banks encourage their senior staff people to be involved in chambers of commerce and other civic organizations. Join those same groups and begin building your banking relationships. Introductions made now will pay off in the future; you might meet a junior loan officer today who will become president of the bank in ten years, so keep in touch with him or her.

Another reason we're intimidated by bankers is that age-old fear of rejection. I'd like to tell you that bankers don't reject people, that they only reject bad loans, but that's not true. Certainly they do reject bad loans, but sometimes they also reject people. What I *can* tell you is that rejection isn't fatal, and if you get rejected by one banker, move on to the next and try again.

Bankers are human and they will discriminate based on their personal experiences and biases. A male banker in his sixties may decide that a thirty-year-old single mother who is applying for a small-business loan is too risky. A thirty-two-year-old female banker who is divorced and has children may applaud that same applicant's ambition and approve the exact same loan package. In my early days of investing, I had bankers tell me I was growing too fast and should slow down—the very same bankers who were reaping the benefits of my on-time mortgage payments. It doesn't always make sense and it certainly isn't always fair. But life isn't fair. Business isn't fair. Banking isn't fair. Sometimes you get turned down for a loan for no good reason, and when that happens, you'll just have to deal with it and not take it personally.

The reality is that rejection is an unavoidable part of the process of becoming wealthy, and that's why it's important to develop banking relationships with several bankers. Find bankers who can relate to who you are and what you're trying to accomplish. Search out bankers who have the authority to lend money and want to work with you. This is an ongoing part of being in business.

A third reason many people are intimidated by bankers is related to privacy. We don't know much about them, but through our loan application and credit report, they learn a great deal about us—sometimes things that even our closest friends don't know. But don't worry if your credit report is flawed by past financial problems. We'll examine the subject of credit in depth in chapter 17; for now, let me reassure you that your credit report can be a small part of any commercial loan application. Most people have had credit problems at one point or another, and bankers know that. Your primary concern should be to focus on the deal and put together a loan application package they can't resist.

THE TYPE OF LOAN YOU WANT IS MORE IMPORTANT THAN YOUR CREDIT

Banks are heavily regulated, and part of that regulation says they must have balanced portfolios. That means they can lend only so much money on particular types of loans. If the bank has reached its limit on the specific kind of loan you want, you won't get yours approved no matter how good it looks.

For example, let's say a bank makes loans for automobiles, boats, home improvements, and vacant land. The marketing department creates an advertising program that pushes land loans, and people flock in and the bank makes plenty of loans. But then a government auditor comes in and says the bank's portfolio is lopsided. Too much money is lent on land. If there's a dip in real estate, the bank could be in trouble. The auditor can actually tell a bank not to lend any more money on land and to focus on other types of loans.

What's more, when auditors think a bank's portfolio is not balanced, they can force the bank to do what is called a downgrading of the loans in the areas where it was lending too much money. By downgrading, the auditors are saying that the loans are not as safe as they could be. So the bank has to take money out of profits and post it to reserves to cover any bad loans. When this happens, investors tend to get nervous, the bank's stock may drop, and stockholders get upset.

What does all this mean to you? It means that you can go into a bank, and even if you have great credit, a good loan proposal, and a track record with that institution, it still has to turn you down if it's not lending that kind of money right then. And usually the loan officers won't tell you the real reason; they'll make it look as if there's something wrong with you. But you could take that same application to the bank next door and it could likely make you the exact same loan without any problem at all.

It may give you some comfort to know that even with all of my excellent banking relationships, I can't always get the money I want the first time out. That's okay—I just keep trying until I find a banker who needs to make the kind of loan I want.

BANKING GAMES YOU CAN PLAY

For the first ten years I was investing, I was like 95 percent of Americans in that I didn't understand how this banking game was played. It wasn't until after I was well established financially and had reached an age where the bank presidents and other senior officials were my peers that I finally learned the inside story. Because now that these bankers are my friends and we socialize together, they'll tell me the truth. And because I know how the system operates, when I get turned down for a loan, I can find out the real reason—even when it's one the bank doesn't want the general public to know. I see no reason not to share my inside knowledge with you.

If you present a great loan package and get turned down, try giving the banker a knowing smile and saying, "Portfolio's a little heavy on investment loans, is it?" The answer you'll get will probably be the truth.

Share some of the stories I'm telling you and let the bankers you deal with know that you know how the game is played. If they realize you know what you're doing, they'll be more comfortable sharing the real story with you. And it's refreshing for them to be able to do that, because there are few of their customers they can totally relax with. Though they may try to convince you otherwise, bankers are human, and they like to talk and gossip just like anyone else.

THINK COMMERCIAL, NOT CONSUMER

Remember when I said there are only two times a banker will call you sir or ma'am, and that's when you have $1 million on deposit or when you owe the bank $1 million? Well, 95 percent of Americans will probably never get to that point because they think like consumers. They see banks as a place to borrow money for cars, boats, and vacations. These loans are relatively small (definitely small in the bank's view), fully amortized, and usually paid back over two to five years. Keep in mind that a $15,000 car loan may be a lot of money to you when you're making only $30,000 a year, but it's not much money even to a small bank with $50 or $100 million in assets. When banks lump all their consumer loans together, they're very profitable; but taken one at a time, they're no big deal.

So when you go into a bank thinking like a consumer and ask to borrow $5,000 at whatever the going interest rate is, assuring the banker that you'll pay it back in monthly installments of

$159 over the next three years, he's going to discreetly cover his yawn, guide you to a clerk, and focus his attention on people who are talking about *real* money.

Commercial thinking is different. When you think commercial loans, you think of much larger dollar amounts. You generally think short term, often just six months or a year. You negotiate the payment schedule, which may be monthly payments, but it may also be no payments or interest-only payments until the note is due. You approach the banker with confidence; he's a peer, not a superior. He's not doing you a favor by lending you the money; you're doing *him* a favor by borrowing from his bank.

UNDERSTANDING THE DIFFERENT KINDS OF FINANCIAL INSTITUTIONS

So far we've been using the term *bank* in a generic way, but there are several different types of financial institutions. I didn't really understand this in my early days of investing. I got around and got things accomplished, but I could have done much better if I had had a clearer picture of the differences among the various institutions. Understanding what they do and how they operate will make dealing with them easier and more efficient and give you a significant edge.

Commercial Banks. This type of institution generally handles checking accounts (they call them demand deposit accounts), savings accounts, and certificates of deposit, as well as consumer, automobile, home mortgage, and commercial loans. They are usually well capitalized and more diversified in their services than savings and loan associations. Some banks provide brokerage services, annuities, mutual funds, and other investment services. The Federal Deposit Insurance Corporation (FDIC) protects depositors at commercial banks to a maximum of $100,000 at any one bank. Federally chartered banks are required to be members of the FDIC; state-chartered banks need not belong, but most of them do.

Savings and Loan Associations. Often referred to as S&Ls or thrifts, these institutions were initially created to house savings and offer home mortgage loans. During the 1980s, S&Ls attempted to diversify, which ultimately led to the infamous S&L crisis, during which many of these institutions failed. Many surviving S&Ls have returned to the operating guidelines they followed prior to the 1980s. Deposits are insured by the FDIC.

Credit Unions. Credit unions are nonprofit financial cooperatives that offer members many of the services provided by banks. They vary in strength, size, and assets. Membership requirements vary according to the institution and may be based on occupation, geography, employer, or some other requirement. Credit unions generally have lower overhead expenses than commercial banks and can usually offer more attractive savings interest rates and loan rates than commercial banks do. Deposits are protected by the National Credit Union Share Insurance Fund (NCUSIF), a federal agency that insures federal and many state-chartered credit unions the same way the FDIC insures banks. Generally the level of financial expertise and credentials is lower at a credit union than at a commercial bank.

Mortgage Companies. These institutions are in the sole business of lending mortgage money. Many mortgage companies are satellites of savings institutions based in another part of the country; others are individually owned and operated, with their own funding sources.

Second Mortgage Companies/Consumer Finance Companies. These institutions offer personal loans, home equity loans, and second mortgages at consistently higher interest rates than those charged by banks and S&Ls. Some, but not all, of these institutions may be more lenient with their lending requirements than a conventional bank, and some financial experts believe that their providing riskier loans than banks is one reason for their higher interest rates. They also do not have access to low-cost depositors' funds and must obtain their monies from commercial sources at money market rates. Often this type of lender is more willing than others to participate in creative financing packages.

Mortgage Brokers. Though mortgage brokers are not lending institutions, this is the best place to explain their role in the banking industry. Mortgage brokers are essentially middlemen who represent many lenders. They know who is lending what kind of money, and they can help you prepare a good loan package. Mortgage brokers are especially helpful to the beginning investor who may be insecure about dealing with bankers. I found them especially valuable when I was just getting started, since the broker dealt with the banker on my behalf, and the banker never had the chance to make a potentially negative judgment based on my age. Also, since mortgage brokers put together your documentation, if you're unsure of anything (though if you follow my advice, you shouldn't be), they'll be able to help you.

Mortgage brokers are paid a commission out of the closing proceeds of the loan; never use a mortgage broker who asks for an up-front fee. I learned this the hard way when I paid a broker a large fee (which the small print said was nonrefundable) but didn't get the loan. Good brokers won't waste their time with you if they don't think they can get you the loan, so they're happy to take their fee out of the loan proceeds.

Once you have a specific property in mind, interview several mortgage brokers before selecting one to handle your business. Tell them you're looking for loans for investment properties and ask about their parameters; their lenders; what types of loans they have; what the interest rates, points, and origination fees are; and in general how the process works.

Hard Money Lender. Sometimes called an equity lender, this type of institution will finance an average of 65 percent of the equity in a property, often without any credit or other background check, relying solely on the property to guarantee the loan. Often their interest rates are higher than other lenders'. You'll find these lenders advertising in the "Money to Lend" category of the newspaper's real estate section, or you may be referred to one through a mortgage broker. In recent years, some hard money lenders have begun considering the borrower's credit rating. Remember that the world of finance is fluid and ever changing, and you need to pay attention to what's happening so you can respond appropriately.

Private Lender. This is a private entity—perhaps an individual or a partnership—that is willing to lend money to fund your deals. Many private lenders are savvy investors themselves. Others are people with self-directed retirement accounts who are looking for substantial returns and have figured out they can get them by funding good real estate deals. You probably know plenty of people who either are or have the potential to become private lenders; if you don't, you can find them by networking with other investors or through a good mortgage broker.

THE CLOUT OF COMPENSATING BALANCES

Compensating balance is a fancy phrase for "cash flow." It's not the amount of money you have, but the amount of cash you control. And if you control significant amounts of cash, you can have significant clout with a bank.

Let's say you started a property management company and picked up five contracts. The buildings have fifty units each with average rents of $800 a month. That means every month you collect $40,000 from each building, or $200,000, to be deposited in the bank. In a year, that's $2.4 million—and that makes you a million-dollar player. Even though it's not your money, you get credit as the person who places those funds in the institution. If you control where it goes, it doesn't matter if it's your money or not.

Of course, you're going to be paying out $170,000 to $180,000 every month to the property owners, but there will be a lag time between the deposits, when you write your check, and when that check is cleared. That lag time is called float, and it's a time when banks can use that money to make more money for the bank. Anytime money is in a bank more than twenty-four hours, the bank is earning money on it. So while those deposits may be little more than a bookkeeping chore to you, they are valuable to the banker. Even though electronic banking has reduced the float, it's still important to the bank.

Remember, deposits are the lifeblood of a bank. Deposits make the banker look good. Some bankers even get paid a commission or a bonus based on new deposits and new good loans they generate. And a million-dollar account makes a banker look very good, indeed. Bankers will do a lot of nice things to attract and maintain accounts of that size. They'll take you to dinner, they'll give you rebates on loan closing costs, they'll pay for having your taxes done—I've even seen banks pay for the lease on a car for a good customer. And if you happen to control a lot of money but have poor personal credit, you'll even find bankers willing to help you get loans. In short, when you have a large compensating balance, you have clout.

Property management is not the only business with the potential for significant compensating balances. A typical fast-food franchise unit, for example, may net only $150,000 a year, but it may gross $1.5 or even $2 million, and that money has to be cycled through a bank. Over the years I've owned or had an interest in a variety of companies with millions of dollars in compensating balances. Believe me, the bankers who benefited from those deposits appreciated that business—and they still do today.

You don't necessarily have to have money of your own if you have compensating balances. You just have to realize how much clout you have and use it to your advantage. Keep your eyes open to opportunities to control where other people put their money, and let the banker know when you do have that control.

HOW TO DOCUMENT YOURSELF FOR A LOAN

The specific contents of a loan package will, of course, vary depending on the type of loan you are seeking. What should be consistent is that you present yourself in a polished, professional manner each time you approach a lender. Your loan package is essentially a marketing piece for yourself and your project; it is a tool you can use to sell yourself to the banker. And since so few people ever take the time to put together a sharp loan package, yours will stand out.

Put your documents in a folder with clips on each side. Put your tax returns on one side and the rest of the information on the other. You can choose any arrangement you prefer, as long as there is a logical sequence to your documents. Be sure everything is typed or prepared on a computer and printed on good-quality paper. If you are including copies of a form you have filled out by hand, be sure your writing is neat and legible. Make sure photocopies are clear and easy to read. Remember, complete documentation will increase your chances of approval and speed up the loan process.

DOCUMENTS NECESSARY FOR ANY TYPE OF LOAN

Cover Letter About Yourself—This is basically a résumé in paragraph form. Don't address this letter to anyone specifically. Put your name and address at the top and describe yourself. Include what kind of work you do, what your general background is, why you are a stable and reliable person who can be trusted to repay this loan. If you are involved in any community activities, list them; you may find you have something in common with the banker, and remember, bankers like to loan money to people who are like themselves. Keep it brief and to the point, but make it a strong sales piece.

Your Financial Statement—A listing of your assets and liabilities, that is, what you own and what you owe. The difference between the two figures is your net worth.

Copies of Your Credit Report—If you have a recent copy of your credit report (and it's easy to get; we'll talk about that in chapter 17), include it. If there are any derogatory entries, explain them in a brief statement.

Copies of Your Federal Income Tax Returns for the Past Two Years—Copy the entire return, not just the front page.

DOCUMENTS NECESSARY FOR A REAL ESTATE PURCHASE LOAN

A Statement About the Project—Describe the details of the project, including the history of the property and what you plan to do with it. Make it clear you have given thought to all the aspects that may affect the property's profitability.

Rent Roll Statement—This should include current and projected figures for the property's gross monthly and yearly rents and expenses. Break out your projected net cash flow so the banker can clearly see the profit potential.

Your Accepted Offer—A copy of the offer the seller has accepted.

Contractors' Estimates—If you are applying for a home improvement or rehab/construction loan, include detailed contractors' estimates for the work you plan to do.

Legal Description and Any Other General Information About the Property—Any additional information you can provide about the property will demonstrate that you have researched it thoroughly.

Photos of the Property—Snapshots taken with a good 35 mm or digital camera are best. If you use a digital camera, be sure the images are at least 200 dpi and print them on a color printer that can generate photo-quality output.

Details on Other Properties You Own—If you have bought and fixed up other properties, include before and after photos along with details such as the figures on positive cash flow or, if the properties have been sold, your profits.

DOCUMENTS NECESSARY FOR A BUSINESS LOAN

Because the types of business loans vary greatly, it's impossible to state exactly what you need for a business loan. If you are looking for funding to purchase an existing business, you'll need all the documents related to that business. If you want to start a new business, you'll need your business plan with short- and long-term (at least five years) projections. If you need a loan for a specific purpose, such as a major equipment purchase, or expansion, provide the appropriate details. The key is to anticipate any questions you think the lender may have and answer them in your loan package.

BUZZWORDS THAT OPEN DOORS

One of the most important elements of success in any business is establishing a comfort level for yourself. That also applies to borrowing money. The fastest way to become comfortable with borrowing money is to learn the language of bankers and other lenders. It will help you understand them, and your knowledge will make them feel more confident about making loans to you.

Here are some basic loan terms you need to know.

Adjustable-rate mortgage (ARM). A mortgage rate that allows the interest rate to be changed over the life of the loan. Since their introduction about thirty years ago, ARMs have generally saved borrowers significant sums over fixed-rate loans. *Caution:* Be sure any ARM you accept has both annual and lifetime interest-rate caps; the most common is 2/6, which means the interest rate cannot increase more than 2 percent each year, with a maximum increase of 6 percent over the lifetime of the loan. Also check how long the current interest rate applies; most rates are for one year, but some are guaranteed for as little as three months, others for up to five or more years. Never accept payment caps instead of interest caps; a payment cap means your payment won't go up but your interest rate might, and the result could be negative amortization. For example, if you had a twenty-year $150,000 mortgage at 6 percent, your monthly payments would be $1,075. At 7 percent, the payments would be $1,163. If you took a 5.5 percent ARM with a payment cap of $1,100 but no interest cap, and the interest rate went up just 1 percent (monthly payments on a 6.5 percent $150,000 mortgage would be $1,118), you would be adding $18 to your principal amount each month.

Amortize. Amortization is the reduction of a debt through installment payments of both principal and interest. An amortization table or schedule (also referred to as a loan and mortgage payment table) is a chart that shows the monthly payments for loans at varied interest rates and time periods. You can also find various mortgage and loan calculators under "student tools" at www.russwhitney.com. Use this resource to calculate your monthly repayment amount before you apply for a loan.

Assumable mortgage loan. A mortgage loan that can be taken over by another person. Some assumable loans require no qualifying (some older VA and FHA loans may fall into this category); others require qualifications just as they would on a new loan. If interest rates have changed, the lender may elect to adjust the rate of the loan before allowing a new buyer to assume it.

Equity. The difference between the value of the property and the principal balance of the loan, or what you owe.

Fixed-rate mortgage (FRM). A mortgage loan for which the rate of interest stays the same throughout the life of the loan.

Home equity loan. Similar to a second mortgage in that the loan amount is based on the amount of equity in a home, with widely varying terms.

Home improvement loan. A loan for the specific purpose of financing home improvements. The lender may or may not require a mortgage or other collateral to secure the loan.

Junior mortgage. Any mortgage that provides a lien subsequent in priority to another mortgage. A second mortgage is a junior mortgage.

Lien. The term used when a lender has interest in rather than title to the property being used as collateral for a loan. Liens can also be attached to property to satisfy unpaid debts. Under those circumstances, the lien holder is paid before the owner receives any money.

Mortgage. A document providing written evidence of the right of a creditor to have property of a debtor sold upon default and foreclosure. Also used to describe the use of real estate as collateral for a loan.

Mortgagee. The lender or mortgage holder; the one to whom the property is pledged.

Mortgagor. The borrower; the one pledging the property as security for a debt.

Negative amortization. The situation that occurs when a loan payment is less than the interest alone. Even though the payments are made in the correct amount and on time, the amount the borrower owes increases.

Second mortgage. A mortgage using the equity of a property as collateral for a loan. Mortgages are generally recorded in the order of date placed, but an existing first mortgage holder can elect to take a second position if circumstances warrant. In this case, the term *second* is not necessarily a chronological reference; it means the position the mortgagee holds when collecting in the case of default and foreclosure. It is possible for properties to have multiple mortgages.

Seller financing. When the seller of a property agrees to hold the note and accept payments rather than one lump sum.

A FEW FINAL BANKING BASICS

A banking relationship is not a single event, it's an ongoing process. Banking has changed significantly in the last couple of decades, and it's going to keep on changing. You have to stay in tune with those changes and keep working the system to your advantage.

It used to be that most banks were community banks and the bankers were longtime members of the community. They knew just about everybody, and everybody knew them; documenting loans was more of a formality than anything else, and lending was pretty much an old boy network kind of thing. Today, with all the bank mergers, takeovers, and failures, it's all different. And, like a lot of other things in my life, I learned it the hard way.

When I first moved to Florida, I had all my money in one bank. I had a good relationship with the banker, I made large deposits, and I got all the loans I applied for. But then the bank was taken over by a bigger bank, and the rules changed. Suddenly, despite my excellent track record, I couldn't get a loan—and my banker couldn't do anything about it.

So I moved my accounts to another bank. I established a rapport with a loan officer and had received several loans when that bank was taken over—and again, the rules changed. This happened to me two more times. Then I went to a new community bank that was headed up by the banker I had originally worked with several years before. We had a good and mutually profitable relationship, and I learned a valuable lesson from the whole experience.

Here are some of the rules for dealing with bankers I've developed over the years:

Never deal with just one bank; establish relationships with several banks. When a bank can't provide what you need, whether it's because the timing is bad, it doesn't make the type of loan you want, or it has been taken over and the rules have changed, you need a backup lending source, and you'll usually need it quickly. So build several solid banking relationships by dividing up your deposits and your loans among different institutions.

Interview the banker—it's a privilege for him to loan you money. You need a banker you are comfortable and compatible with. Remember, bankers are human and they will discriminate, even if it's unconscious. Find a banker who believes in you and what you're doing. That's the banker who will go to bat for you.

Also, make sure the banker has real authority. Early in your relationship, ask him what his lending limits are. If he doesn't have the authority to make the kind of loans you'll need, find out who does. If you tell him what you want and he stalls, you're probably not dealing with the right person. Especially in large banks, it's common for people in the branches to have grand titles but little real authority. If the loan decisions are made downtown, you should be dealing with someone downtown, not with someone in the branch who can't help you.

Be professional. Though you may eventually become personal friends with your banker, your banking relationship is a business one. Your first meeting should always be done by appointment and, if possible, with a referral from a high-powered mutual acquaintance. Subsequent meetings also require appointments; it shows that you value both his time and your own. And use your selling skills (the ones you'll learn in chapter 18) in every contact. Yes, it's true that you're the customer, but you want the banker strongly on your side, and you're going to have to sell him to get him there.

Give your banker all the ammunition he needs to work with you. Put together complete, attractive loan packages. I always bind my loan applications in an attractive cover, and I try to anticipate any question the banker may have and include appropriate documentation so he doesn't have to ask. Bankers tell me repeatedly such a presentation has a positive impact, but fewer than one out of every hundred applications are prepared this way.

Let the banker buy lunch. The person who picks up the tab for lunch or dinner is usually the person who benefits from the relationship. Remember, the banker is benefiting from your business, so always let him buy lunch. If you feel comfortable with the banker paying the bill, you've learned what I'm trying to teach you. If you feel intimidated about putting the banker in a position to buy, read this chapter again and work on your industry knowledge and communication skills. Most of the time, if you've done your job right, the banker will reach for the check. Remember, too, that there are no absolutes in this world. There may be a time when your strategy involves giving yourself the psychological advantage of playing the big-money host. Just always remember how much the banker stands to gain by lending you the money you need to become wealthy.

BECOME YOUR BANKER'S ADVISOR

As you get to know your banker, you may find yourself assuming the role of advisor, providing him with information about your investment strategies or perhaps your thoughts on the potential for growth in the area and how best to take advantage of it. This probably won't happen if the banker is nearing retirement, but if he's still got a number of years of working ahead of him, he'll appreciate your advice. And whether he uses what you tell him or not, bankers are always intrigued with how financially independent people make money.

Years ago, I met a banker who didn't own any property at all. We were both involved in Little League, and we got to know each other personally. I showed him a few of my properties and explained why he shouldn't be renting. He saw the wisdom in my advice, and less than a month later he'd bought a foreclosure deal he found out about through another banker. It didn't take him long to buy a second property, and he's made real estate investing a profitable sideline business.

He's also been a tremendous help to me. Besides going the extra mile for me when it comes to my loans, he teaches at our three-day intensified real estate training, so our students learn the real story about banking from a banker. If you take the time to teach your banker what you know, it will come back to you many times over.

CHAPTER 14

How to Find Continuous Prosperity

Chance favors only those minds which are prepared.
—Louis Pasteur

I've made millions of dollars in a number of businesses, though my initial fortune was made in real estate. If you look at the portfolios of most other wealthy people, you'll see the same or even a higher degree of diversity. They find businesses that generate profits, then park that money in real estate and watch it grow. That's how the top 2 percent of income earners become wealthy. That's how wealthy people become wealthier. And it's also how plain, old, average folks like you and me can build our personal fortunes.

Use real estate to build a little capital and credibility, then think about the business you've always dreamed of, or the thing that you've always said you would do if you had the time and the money. You may already know what kind of business you ultimately want to be in, or you may still be searching. If you haven't yet chosen a business, there are plenty of books and magazines on the market that discuss various opportunities and that will give you at least some of the information you'll need to make a decision.

My advice to you on this topic is simple: be sure you choose something you will love doing; be sure it has the potential to generate the income you need to meet your financial goals; and be sure you're building a business, not just making a job for your-self.

By "something you will love doing," I mean that life is too short to spend the majority of your waking hours doing something you hate. Choose a business that will be fun, one that you can approach with the enthusiasm you give your favorite hobby.

By "the potential to generate the income you need," I mean you must seriously examine the profit potential of a business. Find out what kind of revenue similar businesses generate. Compare that with your financial goals, and be sure you have a match before you make a commitment.

By "building a business," I mean something that will generate cash flow whether you're working in it or not. This is an area of special caution for home-based businesses. Plenty of so-called experts out there will tell you how to start a graphic design service, or a child care service, or a disc jockey service, or any one of hundreds of other operations they call businesses, but in fact that are just teaching you how to create a job for yourself.

A job is something that, when you stop doing it, it stops making money.

A business is something you can design, establish, pay other people to work in, and make money from whether you participate in the day-to-day operation or not.

It's hard to get wealthy if all you have is a job; it's much easier and much more fun when you have a business that is making you money whether you work or not.

THE GOLD WATCH SYNDROME

It's certainly true that owning a business requires a significantly higher degree of commitment than having a job, but it doesn't mean you have to keep it, own it, and run it for the rest of your life. I have created or bought into a variety of different businesses; some I built up and sold, others I continue to own. And I'm always on the lookout for new opportunities.

Let's compare this philosophy with having a job. Just a generation or two ago, people were expected to get a job and stay with that company until they retired and collected the traditional gold watch. Today, the average employee will hold ten or more jobs in two or three different career fields over his or her lifetime. In fact, for people interested in climbing the corporate ladder, changing companies is an effective way to move up quickly. Having several different employers on your résumé is no longer a sign of instability; it's a sign of ambition and perseverance.

We've pretty much shed the gold watch mentality when it comes to jobs; now it's also time to take a new look at business ownership. There's absolutely no reason why you can't own several different businesses at the same time, and just because you buy or start a business doesn't mean you'll have to own it forever.

Let's say you enjoy real estate, but you also like working with animals. You could own some income-producing rental property, a property management company, a pet-grooming salon, and a boarding kennel. At any given point, you could sell off one of those businesses and invest the proceeds in something else. Even better, you could consider setting up the grooming salon or the boarding kennel as a franchise and earn royalties from other entrepreneurs who want to copy your methods.

My point is that business ownership gives you the opportunity to pursue not just one dream but all of your dreams. The only restrictions you'll have to deal with are the ones you place on yourself.

OPEN YOUR EYES TO OPPORTUNITY

Getting started with your first business, no matter how small it is, will give you the confidence you need to keep going and growing. You've heard the saying "No man is an island"; the same thing applies to businesses. They have suppliers, they have customers who need other products and services, they have competitors with ideas and needs of their own. These are all situations that can offer potential for you if you're paying attention. Always be on the lookout for opportunities because they're around us all the time.

Developing businesses can be a lot like free-association word games, where one person says a word and the other says the first thing that comes to mind. My first business, real estate investing, led me into publishing, public speaking, mail order, computers, and more. I became a millionaire by reading and following the advice in business self-help books and literature on developing a better attitude. But even though I was successful, I knew from experience that there was plenty the books didn't say, and a few things that I had learned how to do better through trial and error. That's when I decided to write my first book, which I told you about in chapter 5. That book got me into the public speaking business, which led to the creation of what would evolve into one of the world's leading financial education companies, Whitney Information Network, Inc.

Though I often poke fun at "mail order millions" when I talk about my initial search for a way to get wealthy, the reality is that you *can* make millions in the mail order business. I know, because I've done it. Of course, the mail order business, which is now known as direct marketing, has changed in recent years, thanks to credit cards, low-cost toll-free numbers, and the Internet. The days of mailing off a check or a money order in response to an ad and waiting four to six weeks or longer for your merchandise are for the most part gone. But plenty of business is being done and profits being made through transactions that happen outside the traditional brick-and-mortar retail store environment.

Just about anything you might imagine can be bought through direct marketing channels, including clothing, furniture, gadgets, food, entertainment, and even livestock. Since today's busy consumers never seem to have enough time for shopping, they welcome the opportunity to make purchases comfortably from home without the hassle of fighting the crowds at malls. The potential to make money in direct marketing has never been greater—but neither has the competition. The key is to find a unique product and develop an effective marketing strategy. If you currently have a business with products that are suitable for selling by mail, consider establishing a direct marketing or online division to broaden your customer base and increase your profits. If you don't have a business you can expand through this strategy, study the industry carefully before jumping in with a new idea or product. Before I established my first mail order business, I looked at how other information companies sold their products; I improved on their methods and was able to make millions of dollars in mail order. (Mail order millions, how ironic.)

Today, the training my company provides is delivered through a variety of methods—classroom, live online, on-demand, and home study courses—but my point in this discussion is that I took my personal desire to teach people how to become wealthy and turned it into a multimillion-dollar, publicly traded, international corporation. The real estate side of my business has continued to grow, too. I started with low- and middle-income rental properties; today, I invest in substantial residential and commercial development projects in the United States and abroad, and I have an ownership interest in a number of related companies. And it all started with refinancing my own home and using that money to invest in a duplex. Where will it start for you? You must get into the game somewhere to start opening up the doors to success and prosperity.

IT DOESN'T HAVE TO BE RELATED

Don't limit yourself to related businesses; let your imagination and personal preferences lead you to other opportunities. If you follow my advice to study and learn your market thoroughly, you'll get a sense of what needs in the market are not being met. If you can start a business that will meet those needs, you'll increase your wealth. Of course, you should always take the time to research the business thoroughly and be sure you completely understand what you'll require in terms of cash investment, financing, operating procedures and costs, and potential income.

I can't stress this enough: whenever you see a need not being adequately met or a changing consumer trend, you are seeing a business opportunity. Do some research, figure out how to take advantage of it, and let your powers of observation make you wealthy.

CUT YOUR MORTGAGE BY ONE-THIRD

One of the ancillary businesses I started years ago is Equity Corp. That company's primary service is the Mortgage Reduction System (MRS), also referred to as the Mortgage Payoff Acceleration Program (MPAP). Before I show you how you can become a part of this business and make money helping people reduce their mortgages, let me tell you how you can save money doing the same thing yourself.

If you have a typical thirty-year mortgage, depending on the interest rate, you'll pay more than double to as much as three times the purchase price of the house over the life of the loan. Here are a few examples:

Amount borrowed	Rate	Finance charge	Total repayment
$200,000	6%	$231,676.38	$431,676.38
250,000	7	348,772.25	598,772.25
300,000	8	492,465.74	792,465.74

I used a fixed rate for illustration, but this is also true if you have an adjustable rate; the actual numbers will change a little as the interest rates fluctuate, but the impact is still the same.

What's more, because of the way banks calculate interest on mortgage loans, you have to pay on the loan for eight or ten years before you begin making any significant reduction in the principal amount you owe. In the first year of repaying the $200,000 loan used as an example above with monthly payments of about $1,200, you'd reduce your principal by less than $2,500—just slightly more than 1 percent of the total amount you financed. Why? Because lenders force us to use the most ridiculous loan-repayment method in the world. We pay interest in arrears, we pay interest on the unpaid balance, we pay compounded interest, and to top it off, most of us believe the bankers who tell us that thirty years is the way we should pay back mortgage loans.

It's an absurd amount of interest to pay, especially when you consider that our house payment is the largest payment most of us make each month. However, there are ways to beat this system and save yourself substantial amounts of money.

One solution is a fifteen-year mortgage. You'll pay off your loan in half the time and reduce your finance charges by 50 or 60 percent. But the bad news is your monthly payments will be approximately 20 percent higher than they would be on a thirty-year mortgage.

A better solution is to pay biweekly rather than monthly—that is, make your payments every two weeks, or twenty-six times a year, rather than make twelve monthly payments. Because most people are paid on this schedule, it makes sense to set up your single largest expense on the same schedule. The bonus of biweekly payments is that you are actually paying the equivalent of 13 monthly payments every year, so you'll reduce your principal faster and pay less interest. As you can see from the comparison, the savings are tremendous.

COMPARISON OF TRADITIONAL 30-YEAR MORTGAGE PAID MONTHLY AND PAID ON A BIWEEKLY SCHEDULE

	Accelerated Payments	Monthly Payments
Mortgage amount	$175,000	$175,000
Interest rate	7%	7%
Payment	$582.14 accelerated biweekly	$1,164.28 monthly
Years to repay	23.7 years	30 years
Total interest	$183,831	$244,140
Interest savings	$60,309	

MORTGAGE PAYOFF SCHEDULE

Year	Accelerated Payments		Monthly Payments	
	Payments	Balance	Payments	Balance
		$175,000		$175,000
1	$15,136	172,015	$13,971	173,222
2	15,136	168,814	13,971	171,316
3	15,136	165,381	13,971	169,272
4	15,136	161,700	13,971	167,080
5	15,136	157,752	13,971	164,730
6	15,136	153,518	13,971	162,210
7	15,136	148,978	13,971	159,508
8	15,136	144,109	13,971	156,610
9	15,136	138,887	13,971	153,503
10	15,136	133,288	13,971	150,172
11	15,136	127,283	13,971	146,599
12	15,136	120,843	13,971	142,768
13	15,136	113,936	13,971	138,661
14	15,136	106,530	13,971	134,256
15	15,136	98,587	13,971	129,533
16	15,136	90,070	13,971	124,468
17	15,136	80,935	13,971	119,038
18	15,136	71,139	13,971	113,215
19	15,136	60,634	13,971	106,970
20	15,136	49,369	13,971	100,275
21	15,136	37,287	13,971	93,095
22	15,136	24,331	13,971	85,397
23	15,136	10,436	13,971	77,142
24	10,711	0	13,971	68,290
25	0	0	13,971	58,798
26	0	0	13,971	48,620
27	0	0	13,971	37,707
28	0	0	13,971	26,004
29	0	0	13,971	13,455
30	0	0	13,971	0

Read this section carefully, because even if you have an existing mortgage, this is a way you can still save money without refinancing. Does this mean you can give your bank a call and tell them you're going to go on a biweekly payment program? No. Few, if any, banks offer biweekly mortgages. Even if they do, they will not likely change your repayment terms if you already have a mortgage unless you refinance. That means taking out a whole new loan, and if you do that, you'll have to pay points (a point is 1 percent of the amount financed; banks charge varying numbers of points to originate a loan) and other closing costs. It could cost you several thousand dollars out of pocket to change your payment program if you work through your lender.

If you're wondering why more banks don't offer biweekly loans, the reason is simple. In most cases, when you take out a mortgage loan, the bank doesn't wait for the thirty years you'll be making payments to get its money back. A high percentage of first mortgage loans are sold on what is known as the secondary mortgage market, where the loans are traded as investments. Insurance companies, the Government National Mortgage Association (known as Ginnie Mae), quasi-federal agencies (such as the Federal Home Loan Mortgage Association, known as Freddie Mac), and private corporations (such as the Federal National Mortgage Association, known as Fannie Mae) purchase these loans and package them into investments known as mortgage-backed securities. When you invest in a government-insured, mortgage-backed security through your local investment broker, what you're buying are home loans just like your own.

Banks sell their loans because they don't have a bottomless well full of money to lend out, and this gives them a way to replenish deposits and lend more money. If your bank has sold your loan, it can't change your repayment schedule because it doesn't own your loan anymore. It may still be servicing your loan—that is, collecting your payments and forwarding them to Freddie Mac or Fannie Mae or whatever organization owns the loan and earning a fee for that service. This is why most people never realize their loans have been sold.

Another reason that banks won't switch you over to a bi-weekly payment schedule is that they are just not set up to handle the paperwork in that manner. That's why most banks don't offer a biweekly option at all—and if they do, they typically set it up to match the same amount of money they'd receive with traditional monthly payments, so you don't really save anything.

So how can you take advantage of the intelligent and simple loan repayment method of accelerated biweekly payments? Your best option is to contract with a company that is set up to simulate a biweekly mortgage. There are a few good ones that will do all of the work for you at a nominal charge. They will draft your checking account every two weeks for half of your regular mortgage payment to your mortgage holder as you normally would, but at the end of a year you will have accumulated an extra payment, which is then applied to reducing your principal—ultimately shortening the life of your loan by as much as one-third (depending on the interest rate and when you implement the bi-weekly payment structure). Be sure the biweekly mortgage service company you choose is insured and that the bank it uses is a trustee of the fund, so your money is safe.

Perhaps the biggest advantage of a biweekly payment plan over a standard fifteen-year mortgage is flexibility. With a fifteen-year mortgage, you are committed to the payment amount. With the biweekly plan, if you encounter financial difficulties or for any reason need to reduce your payment amount, you can go off the program and make the lower payment. When you're ready, you go back on the biweekly program.

A number of financial writers are vocal in their criticism of companies that provide biweekly mortgage services. Their argument is that you could do this yourself without having to pay any service fees. And though you could, you probably won't. I have been explaining this concept for more than twenty years and have found that less than 1 percent of the people will actually act on the information by making that extra payment on their own. What's more, the average person does not know how to check to verify that the additional monies are being applied to the principal. Many banks will apply extra payments to prepaid interest, which means all you've done is pay more interest sooner. Some apply extra payments to the back end of the mortgage, which means you get no benefit until you're close to paying off the loan. Without a professional helping you, you could waste a lot of time and money and not gain the benefit of principal reduction. The small fee a biweekly mortgage company will charge is pennies compared to what you'll save with the program.

A biweekly mortgage is the safest, most efficient way for you to maximize the benefits from probably the biggest investment you'll make in your lifetime: your home. But students have asked me, if the biweekly mortgage is so good, why don't they hear about it from their attorney, their accountant, or their real estate broker? It's simple. Your attorney, accountant, and real estate broker won't make any money by giving you this advice. They don't get paid to help you figure out the best way to repay your mortgage.

Another criticism leveled at biweekly mortgages is that their very positive results—that is, reducing the term of your loan and the amount of interest you'll have to pay—cause you to lose a tax shelter. Yes, a home mortgage is a tremendous tax shelter for the average American. But it's foolish to spend $60,000+ more than you have to over the life of your mortgage loan just so you can deduct it from your taxes. If you need write-offs, start a business. Give money to charity. But don't give up building equity in your home.

HELP OTHERS CUT THEIR MORTGAGES, TOO

When I first discovered the concept of biweekly mortgage payments, I was so enthusiastic that I created a company to administer such a program—the first company of its kind in the United States. We developed a system to help people all over the country save money and make money by sharing this technique with others. It's the system I just told you about—the Mortgage Reduction System offered through Equity Corp. Since it was introduced in 1986, thousands upon thousands of homeowners across the United States have realized tremendous savings in mortgage interest and are paying off their mortgages earlier.

Some people who chose to get involved in this company have earned hundreds of thousands of dollars just by showing others how it works. Our mortgage consultants earn a substantial fee each time they put a homeowner on the system. Some do this as a part-time way to generate extra income; others work it as a full-time business and hire other consultants to work for them. Some of the really creative and successful consultants also encourage their clients to use this system with other loans, such as for automobiles, boats, and home improvement. The Mortgage Payoff Acceleration Program works with any loan that has compound interest and is amortized over several years. Funds deposited into the MPAP account for disbursement to lenders are fully insured by the federal government and run through the Federal Reserve System, just as any typical electronic transfer is handled.

A number of companies offer biweekly mortgage payment programs and in doing so provide a tremendous moneymaking opportunity for consultants. The best in my opinion is, of course, Equity Corp. If you'd like more information about setting up your own mortgage on a biweekly program and/or becoming an MPAP consultant to provide this valuable and much needed service, visit Equity Corp. on the Web at www.equitycorp.com or call (800) 741-7877.

FINANCING YOUR DREAMS

Many of the people who dream of owning lucrative businesses will use the techniques in this book to find seed money and use real estate to fund their companies. But wealth is not always measured in dollars. Plenty of people don't particularly care about having huge bank accounts; they're looking for something to pay the bills while they pursue dreams that have nothing to do with business, such as acting, singing, painting, any other creative field, or various types of community service.

Unless you are one of the few people who achieve superstar status, working in the arts can mean an unpredictable income. I have met a number of performers over the years—some who have been my students—who use real estate investments to provide the financial freedom they need to pursue their entertainment careers. And I can't count the number of times I've heard students say that their reason for learning my techniques is not to buy luxuries for themselves but to gain the time and material resources to help other people.

Remember, if you can find something that will generate enough nonjob income to cover your basic expenses, you have financial independence, and you can do whatever you want to do. Start a business, do volunteer work, go back to school, join a theater company, run for public office, secure your future—the dream and the choice are yours. You can still live comfortably without millions of dollars once you've started to develop your personal fortune.

CHAPTER 15

STOCK MARKET SECRETS

People become really quite remarkable when they start thinking that they can do things. When they believe in themselves they have the first secret of success.
—NORMAN VINCENT PEALE

I made my first fortune in real estate and I still love this business. But I have discovered a number of other things that I enjoy doing as part of my wealth-building plan, and one of those things is stock trading. As part of a sound diversification strategy, you may want to invest some of your real estate profits in the stock market. Or you may want to use stock trading to generate cash to invest in real estate. We have students who have used both strategies with tremendous success.

Knowledge is absolutely critical to profitable stock trading. Knowledge is also extremely valuable, because when you know how to invest in the market, you can work for just a few hours a day and make more money than you'll ever be able to spend.

I'm going to give you some basic advice and strategies for stock trading, but if you're going to become a successful stock trader, you need to take your education beyond what's in this chapter. If you're not familiar with the stock market, just the terms alone will seem overwhelming. And if you have money invested in the market, you can benefit from developing the skills to maximize those investments. In fact, many of our stock trading students come to us after they've lost money in the market because they realize they need education to make profitable trades. The resource guide at the end of this book has more information about the specific courses our stock training division offers.

What can stop you from making money in the market? Fear and greed. When you are afraid or when you get greedy, you will do things that will cost you money. You won't buy when you should, you'll sell when you shouldn't, and you'll hang on to stocks too long. The markets are emotional; they react to natural disasters, fears, rumors, and successes because so many of the people who own stock make their buying and selling decisions based on their own emotional reaction to those same events. If you are not emotional, if instead of with a knee-jerk reaction you respond to market changes thoughtfully and professionally, you will be a successful trader.

There are six types of traders. The first is the long-term investor. This is the person who buys and holds typically for five years or longer. The second is the position trader, who gives a stock weeks or months to perform as expected, then sells. The third is the swing trader, who operates on a shorter time frame—generally days or weeks—than a position trader. Fourth is the day trader, who buys and sells the same stock in the same day. Day trading is time-intensive. Fifth is the scalper, who trades on the variations between one exchange and another for small gains typically on the same day. The sixth is the floor trader, who is a stock exchange member who generally trades for his own account or accounts he controls.

While all types of traders can make—and lose—money, our students are generally position and swing traders. When done correctly, this type of trading can generate steady profits.

Let me stress one important thing: you will not make money on every single trade. At times a stock will not perform as you expect and you can lose money. Of course, there will also be times when a stock performs better than you expected and you make more than you thought you would. The key is to win often and never lose big.

ANALYZE STOCKS BEFORE YOU BUY

It is possible to make money in stock trading whether the stocks go up, go down, or stay the same. But to do that, you need to be able to identify the outlook on a stock so you can decide what strategy to use.

The five major areas of stock analysis are:

Fundamentals. Fundamental information is related to the earnings prospects of a company. The primary fundamental you'll consider is earnings per share (EPS). This is the bottom-line driving force for the stock and the market. To calculate EPS, divide the net income of the company by the number of shares outstanding. Monitor the earnings trend to see the direction and expectation of the company's future. When you purchase a stock, you own a piece of the company, and your concern should be not only the current status but also the future potential. This is why trends are important.

Another fundamental to consider is the PE ratio, or price-to-earnings ratio. To get this figure, divide the price of the stock by the earnings per share. The PE ratio benchmark is measured within similar industries. For example, the PE ratio for the drug sector will tend to be much higher than the utility sector. This is due to the fact that the drug sector has a higher growth potential, therefore the PE ratio is higher. Use the PE ratio to see how the stock compares to other stocks in the same sector as well as to itself.

The best indicator to help you determine what should happen next with a particular stock is the PEG ratio, or price-to-earnings-growth ratio. To calculate, divide the PE ratio by the projected EPS growth rate expressed as a whole number. For example, if the PE ratio is 25 and the growth rate is 10 percent, the formula would be: $25 \div 10 = 2.5$. If the PEG ratio is 2 or higher, the stock is overvalued. If it's 1.5–2, the stock is priced to perfection. If it's 1–1.5, the stock is fairly valued. If it's .5–1, the stock is undervalued. If the PEG ratio is under .5, figure out why. It could be that it's a cheap stock (or penny stock), or that the company has great earnings, great projected earnings, or great expectations.

Other key fundamental data to watch include revenue and revenue growth, market capitalization (the price of the stock times the total number of outstanding shares), company management, future potential and current product lines, and competitive analysis.

Technical Analysis. This is a method of evaluating stocks by analyzing statistics generated by market activity, including the opening and closing prices, the high and low of the day, and the volume. You're not trying to measure the stock's intrinsic value but rather identifying patterns that can suggest future activity.

With technical analysis, you'll want to consider the support line, which is the price the stock tends not to drop below. Essentially it's the base where the stock becomes an attractive buy. Support lines are great to use to identify entry and exit points.

You'll also want to consider the resistance line, which is the price the stock tends not to close above. Resistance lines are a great way to identify sell points. If a stock breaks through its resistance level, this may be a bullish indicator; check other indicators for confirmation before making a buy decision.

Another part of technical analysis is examining trends. In our training, we say, "The trend is your friend." That means you should look for the trend in the price chart and follow it—assuming, of course, that you get confirmation signals from other tools.

In your technical analysis, you'll also use a tool known as the moving average. This is the average price constructed in a period as short as a few days or as long as several years showing trends for the latest interval. As each new variable is included in calculating the average, the last variable of the series is deleted. Moving averages often act as support and resistance. Your technical analysis will also consider other issues, such as volume, moving average convergence and divergence (MACD), and the stochastic oscillator. Take the time to learn how these tools work so you can apply them effectively.

Sentiment. This is the general feeling of investors about the state of the market and particular stocks. It includes analyst ratings, which are generally categorized as strong buy, moderate buy, hold, moderate sell, and strong sell; institutional holdings, which is the amount of stock held by institutions such as insurance companies, depository institutions, pension funds, investment companies, mutual funds, and endowment funds rather than retail traders; insider trading, which identifies what insiders such as corporate officers, board members, and key employees are doing with the stock and can provide a clue to what the people on the inside expect of the company; and consensus trends, which is the average of many analysts' forecasts for a company.

News. When it comes to news, you have good news, bad news, and what we call data dump news, which is essentially public relations. News, especially bad news, triggers emotions, and remember I've already told you that the markets are emotional. You'll want to consider both historical news and pending news (such as upcoming earnings reports, pending FDA approval dates, court dates, pending mergers, pending stock splits, various economic reports, and Federal Reserve meetings). Learn to sift through the news and figure out what's important and what's not, and avoid getting emotional.

Economy. The overall state of the economy will affect your stock trading decisions. You'll want to pay attention to employment reports, which are released on the first Friday of the month; the consumer price index (CPI), which measures the average price of a set list of goods and services used by consumers for day-to-day living and is released monthly by the Bureau of Labor Statistics in the Department of Labor; and other economic reports, including the consumer confidence index, retail sales, new home sales, sector economics, and global economics.

YOU NEED A PLAN

I've already stressed how important it is to have a plan for wealth building and a plan for any business you may be involved with. If you are going to be a stock trader, you need a plan. Traders without a specific written plan that outlines their goals and the specific rules by which they trade are much more likely to lose capital. You can't predict the future, but you can prepare for its opportunities—and you do that with a trading plan.

Your trading plan needs to consider your personal reward-to-risk ratio, your acceptable win probability, and your risk limits. I also recommend that you put together a core group of stocks—perhaps twenty or so—and become intimately involved with those stocks. Know everything there is to know about those companies. Then trade that same group of stocks over and over, making money as the price of the stock moves up and down.

Here's a simple example of how that can work: You buy a stock for $20. It goes up to $26 and starts to decline. You sell at $25. It goes down to $22 and starts to climb again. You buy at $22.50. It goes up to $28 and holds steady. You sell. You've just made a total of $10.50 on a single share of that stock. And because you know the company and you know how to read the indicators, you know when to buy and sell the stock with the least amount of risk.

YOU HAVE OPTIONS

As an alternative to trading actual stocks, you may also want to consider trading options. With stocks, you can only buy and sell. With options, you have additional instruments (calls and puts) to work with. Understand that there is risk to trading options, so take the time to understand the process and learn how to reduce your risk through spread trading. If you know how to use options correctly, they can be safe.

An option is a contract between a buyer (the option holder) and a seller (the option writer) that gives the buyer the right, but not the obligation, to buy (call) or to sell (put) a specific stock at a specific price (the strike price) on or before a specific date (expiration date) in exchange for a market premium (what you paid for the option). Options are not traded in shares, they are traded in contracts, and typically one contract controls one hundred shares of stock. When options are quoted, they are quoted on a per-share basis, but if you want to control two thousand shares of stock, you would have to buy twenty option contracts.

Not all stocks have options available, but in addition to the stock itself, options are also available on various indices such as the S&P, Dow, Russell 2000, or individual industry sectors. The premium for options is standardized and set by the strike price.

When you trade options rather than actual stock, you limit your risk by controlling the stock without owning it. This is essentially the same technique I teach with real estate options, and it positions you to take advantage of an increase in market value but keeps your risk to the amount you paid for the option. Keep in mind that when you own stock, you can sell options on that stock. If you do that, you may realize a gain from the sale of the stock, or, if the option is not exercised, you'll keep the premium and still own the stock.

WHERE *NOT* TO GET YOUR STOCK ADVICE

There are plenty of resources with good information for stock traders, but you should ignore those unsolicited "hot stock tips" that land in your e-mailbox. Some of those pitches are well-done and you may wonder if you're missing out on a great investment. You're not. Legitimate brokers and analysts don't send out spam e-mails urging strangers to buy stock. The scammers who do send out these e-mails are doing something called pump and dump, and it's the most common type of investing scam.

It works like this: The scammers buy shares of a thinly traded (meaning an infrequently traded) stock at a low price. They praise the stock via e-mail, on investment message boards, and in chat rooms, often claiming that they have some special or secret information and they are going to share it only with you (and with anybody else they can rip off). When people believe the "tip" and buy the stock, the price is artificially pumped up. The scammers then dump their shares, which drives the stock price back down, usually well below what the victims paid for it.

The Securities and Exchange Commission has caught some of these scammers. Unfortunately, even when the scammers are caught and prosecuted, it is virtually impossible for the victims to receive restitution.

If you're still tempted to buy a stock promoted in a spam e-mail, check out www.spamstocktracker.com. The owner of this site decided to track paper trades of one thousand shares of every stock for which he received a hot stock tip via spam e-mail. He thought he'd get some short-term windfalls and then see big losses. He was surprised when he didn't even get the short-term windfalls—most of the stocks went up a few cents and then dropped dramatically. He tracks the stocks real time on his site. As I write this, if he had actually purchased these stocks, he would have lost about 50 percent of his investment.

Make your stock trading decisions based on sound, verifiable information that you understand and know how to analyze. You *can* make a lot of money with a relatively small investment in the stock market if you know what you're doing, but you have to take the time to learn how to do it—and that in itself is an investment that will pay handsomely.

CHAPTER 16

The Government Will Help You Become Wealthy

You don't get to choose how you're going to die, or when. You can only decide how you're going to live. Now!
—Joan Baez

Some of the best-kept secrets in our country are how government agencies help people in various businesses become wealthy. Even when those secrets get out, many Americans believe they can't take advantage of the programs that have been put in place to help them. Our view of the government is usually shaped by what we see and hear in the news: scandals, mistakes, and mismanagement by bureaucrats, and fraud by welfare and other entitlement recipients. And when we must have contact with government agencies ourselves, it's usually standing in line at a licensing agency or dealing with the Internal Revenue Service, which is never fun.

But this is truly just the tip of the iceberg when it comes to what the government does and how it works. In fact, the government wants you to take advantage of its programs to establish your business, because businesses create jobs and economic prosperity—two things that are important to politicians who want to stay in office. When all was said and done after the presidential election of 1992, the reason George Bush lost to Bill Clinton was summed up in one political slogan: *It's the economy, stupid.* And your congressional representatives will be happy to see you take advantage of government programs because then they can point out how much federal money they brought home to the district when they're campaigning for reelection.

Setting politics aside, there's another aspect to letting the government help you build wealth. During the early days of the westward expansion in the United States, land grants helped our country and its people grow and prosper. The modern version of those land grants is financial assistance in the form of loans and grants to entrepreneurs to help them build healthy businesses. These programs are generously funded—regardless of who is in the White House or which party is controlling Congress.

Donald Trump built a portion of his empire on government programs designed to encourage and reward the rehabilitation of run-down property. (No matter what people may think of Trump personally, and in spite of his many problems over the years, most of his real estate ventures have been successful.) When Lee Iacocca took over Chrysler, the first thing he did was get the government to guarantee $1.5 billion in loans to save the troubled automaker. EDS, the business that Ross Perot sold to General Motors for billions, made its profits largely from government contracts. Even success stories such as Federal Express, Apple Computer, Ben & Jerry's, and America Online were financed in part through programs funded by government money.

But don't think that only the already wealthy can get their hands on government money. Hundreds of thousands of people just like you and me across the country have received anywhere from a few thousand to hundreds of thousands of dollars in grants and loans from the government to start or expand businesses in just about every category. Years ago I helped my area's chamber of commerce develop a marketing seminar to educate the local business community on the various government programs that are available to them. I have been using government loans and grants since my early days of investing, and even I was surprised at the tremendous scope of the programs that are available.

WHAT THE SBA CAN DO FOR YOU

The Small Business Administration (SBA) is one of the most underused resources in the United States. The SBA has only a few grant programs, but they have a variety of short- and long-term guaranteed-loan programs that can be used for just about any legitimate business purpose. Note that the SBA is rarely the actual lender; rather, it guarantees repayment of loans made through private lenders.

SBA loans require the same documentation as any other business loan. The lender and the SBA want to be sure you know what you're doing and that you'll be able to pay the money back. To help you through the application process, the SBA has set up agencies in all metropolitan areas; contact the SBA in Washington, D.C., for a referral to the one closest to you. If you do the paperwork correctly, your loan can be processed quickly—sometimes in a matter of days, rarely longer than two or three weeks. Loans of up to $2 million are available for all types of business needs.

In addition to serving as a funding resource, the SBA can help with various aspects of building your business. Contact the SBA at (800) 827-5722 or visit www.sba.gov.

THE GOVERNMENT WILL HELP YOU
BUY REAL ESTATE

Government loans and grants for real estate are amazingly simple and easy to get. The reason is that the government, in its curious wisdom, doesn't consider real estate a business. If you apply for a business loan or a grant, you have to provide documentation on your business idea, the marketing you plan to do, your own experience, how much capital you have from other sources, and more. Real estate loans and grants are very different. Most are administered locally, so they are easier to process. In many cases, you don't even have to qualify for the funds; it's the property or your planned use for it that qualifies, and you may not even have to submit a financial statement.

Years ago, a partner and I bought two fourplexes in Pompano Beach, Florida. We went to the people at the local Department of Economic and Community Development and asked about the availability of grant money for fixing up low-income properties. They had more money than they had applicants. Without requiring a financial statement or a credit check, they allocated $36,000 per property in grant monies to rehabilitate the buildings. We didn't have to qualify for the money; the properties qualified because of their location. And it was a grant—meaning that we didn't have to pay it back. The only thing we had to do was commit to putting low-income tenants in the units. After we finished the rehab, the value of those two buildings quadrupled, and they were throwing off a steady positive cash flow.

You don't have to be rich, famous, or even particularly well connected to take advantage of government loans and grants. You don't have to be a business whiz, belong to a minority group, or have great credit. You just have to be willing to go after the money.

DEALING WITH BUREAUCRATS

The most important thing to remember about bureaucrats is that they are people, and they respond the same way other people do. In other words, be friendly, professional, and courteous, and you'll probably get all the help you need. Be abrupt, impatient, or condescending, and you won't get anywhere.

Call the government agency responsible for the loan or the grant you want to pursue and ask what the application procedure is. To find that agency, contact your local economic or community development organization or the local housing department, explain that you are a real estate investor and you want information on what government programs are available in the area, and you'll find out what agency has the money and whom you need to contact.

Be prepared to describe what you are planning to do and what you want. Also, don't become discouraged if you are shuffled around to a number of different people before you get to the person who can help you. Remember, the phone will be answered by a clerk, but you want to talk to the person in charge of loans or grants, and you may have to be filtered through a few people before you get to the one you need. This can happen in any large organization, either public or private. So treat it like a game: if you can get to the right person, you win—and the prize is wealth and security for the future.

TIPS ON APPLYING FOR MONEY

If you do your homework, you'll usually find that you are eligible for several different loan and grant programs. Apply for all of them! Simply applying for government money does not mean automatic approval, but by seeking assistance from different agencies you'll increase your chances of getting all the money you need—and maybe even a little more.

You'll find government money is available in the following forms:

Loans—money lent by a government agency for a specific period of time with an expectation of repayment. Loans may or may not require payment of interest; often the interest rate is below the general market rate.

Loan guarantees—programs in which a private lender makes the loan to the borrower, but the government agency agrees to pay back all or part of the loan if the borrower defaults.

Grants—money given by a government agency that does not have to be repaid. Some grants are paid in one lump sum; others are paid over time.

Direct payments—funds given to individuals, private firms, and institutions by government agencies. The funds may be for a specific purpose or for unrestricted use.

Before you fill out the application, take the time to contact a program official to go over the form. It's best to do this in person; many agencies have field offices all over the country to assist you. If a face-to-face meeting isn't possible, then do it by phone. Whatever you do, don't skip this important step. This discussion will help you gain valuable insight into what the government's expectations are for the program and what the officials who will be evaluating your application want to see.

Then give the government the exact information asked for— no more, no less, and even if it seems silly. It's the government's game. Play by the rules and you can win. If your proposal is rejected, find out why and try again. Sometimes the reason will be minor and may even seem petty. Do what you can to correct it and resubmit your application.

There may be times when, despite your best efforts and all your selling skills, you're not getting what you want. When you need help dealing with a federal agency, you can always call your congressional representative for assistance. Check the government section of your telephone directory for his or her local office listing. It's highly unlikely that you'll talk directly to the member of Congress; you'll probably deal with someone on the staff who's been designated to handle constituent problems. Tell that person whom you've called and what has happened, so that he is adequately prepared when he approaches the agency's officials. He can make a few phone calls on your behalf and help you cut through the clutter and red tape. Though this technique can be effective, use it as a last resort; don't abuse the service.

THERE'S MORE THAN ONE GOVERNMENT, AND MORE THAN ONE TYPE OF ASSISTANCE

Though I've used the term *government* in a generic way, remember that there are several layers of government—federal, state, and local—all with programs you can apply for. Don't overlook any resource; do your homework thoroughly to identify every opportunity.

For example, years ago in my own community of Cape Coral, Florida, the city and local banks formed a partnership to give low- and moderate-income people the opportunity to buy a home. This city identified abandoned homes, many of which were left vacant or partially completed by developers. The properties were condemned, refurbished, and then sold under a special loan program. The banks offered low-down-payment, low-interest, no-point loans in part to meet the standards of the federal 1977 Community Reinvestment Act, which requires banks to invest a percentage of their profits (referred to as CRA funds) back into the community.

Keep this in mind when talking to bankers. Ask them if they have CRA funds and what kind of properties or vehicles they are looking to invest those monies in. These questions will establish you as a knowledgeable investor and help you get the information you want about how much money is available and for what purposes. Cities and towns across the country have developed programs like the one in Cape Coral, which happens to be winding down because of the lack of "affordable" housing in the city. But circumstances may be different where you live. All you have to do is a little bit of research to find out what programs are available and how you can participate.

Government agencies usually apply a "use it or lose it" mentality to their grant money, which means that if they don't use all the money designated for a certain function this year, they won't get as much next year. What's more, the purpose behind the programs is to improve something—the economy, the labor market, housing availability, etc. In fact, federal, state, and local governments have always allocated monies for the renovation and rehabilitation of low- and moderate-income housing. Virtually every city and town in the United States has some sort of grant and loan programs available for housing. Housing improvement funds are the easiest and quickest money you'll ever find, with some of the best interest rates and most liberal borrowing terms. You can build your own wealth as you provide a decent place to live for people who need a hand. Clearly, it's in everyone's best interest to see that these monies are used.

Most local governments, at either the city or county level, have someone whose job it is to make sure that all the government money is used. This person is highly motivated to give away money; his job depends on it. Chances are the mayor, city council, or county commission is pressuring him to give away as much money as possible so they can apply for more the next year. I have seen situations where the person in charge of government grant and loan programs in a particular city didn't give away enough money and was fired because future allocations were cut back. Believe me, his replacement was hustling to find recipients for government loans and grants.

Think about what a great position this puts you in. How do you take advantage of it? Simple: most communities have an organization that focuses on community development—a resource I've already mentioned. It will be named the Economic Development Commission, the Department of Economic and Community Development, or something similar. It may be a government agency, a private group, or a public-private partnership; that doesn't matter, the function is the same. Call and set up an appointment to meet with the director of this agency; tell him or her you're an investor, you've got some property, and you want to know what's available in the way of funds and support from the government. Especially if you're willing to provide safe, sanitary, and decent low-income housing, you'll find yourself welcomed with open arms.

Once you have determined your own wealth-building strategy, apply for governments funds at the local, state, and federal levels. Put your tax dollars to work for you.

GUARANTEE YOUR RENT PAYMENTS

When you own rental property, one of the easiest ways to keep your units occupied and your rent payments coming in on time is through the federal government's Lower Income Housing Assistance Program Section 8, often referred to as Section 8 rental subsidies. The program is designed to assist low-income families in affording decent housing by paying a portion of their rent directly to the property owner. If it becomes necessary to evict a Section 8 tenant, your subsidy payments continue through the eviction process.

To be eligible for Section 8 direct rent payments, you must provide safe, sanitary, secure housing. You don't have to do anything more than keep your units clean, painted, and in good overall shape. A government representative will inspect your units to verify that all health, safety, and security standards are met and to determine a fair market rent rate. You have the right to screen tenants as you normally would, and you'll receive tenant referrals from the program, which can keep your vacancy rate at virtually zero.

Many property owners are afraid of Section 8 tenants because they believe low income means low quality. This is not true! Section 8 tenants can be the best tenants you'll get. They receive counseling in the proper care of apartments and facilities. What's more, if the tenant damages the dwelling or does not live up to the lease, you have the right to terminate the tenancy—and the government will assist you with the process. But Section 8 tenants know such action will jeopardize their ability to receive future rent subsidies, and they don't want that to happen.

Many cities have waiting lists for Section 8 rent subsidies because there is not enough eligible housing, not because there is not enough federal money. The vouchers are there; all you have to do is apply for the program. To get details on what's available in your area and to begin qualification, contact your local HUD office.

GETTING YOUR SHARE ALLOWS YOU TO DO MORE THAN YOUR SHARE

Every year the government gives billions of dollars to cities and towns across America to pay for building and maintaining roads, bridges, sewers, and other infrastructure projects; to revitalize disadvantaged areas; to provide housing for low- and moderate-income people; and for a variety of other reasons. I have seen some of my students become specialists in government grant and loan programs and provide a vital service to their communities with the renovation and rehabilitation of low- and moderate-income housing. Believe me, there is no more satisfying way to build your own wealth than by helping others—in this case by providing safe, decent housing to people who might not otherwise have a place to live. And doing this lets you do more for people who need help than you could probably do by just having a job and doing a little volunteer work for a charity in your spare time.

Let the government help you become wealthy while you use government programs to help your community. This is absolutely the best example of a win-win situation I have ever seen.

CHAPTER 17

CREDIT: BUILD IT, REPAIR IT, USE IT TO BECOME WEALTHY

It had long since come to my attention that people of accomplishment rarely sat back and let things happen to them. They went out and happened to things.
—ELINOR SMITH

In the United States and in many parts of the world, conventional credit is not absolutely essential for you to start acquiring assets. However, it can definitely help. So let's take a look at how to establish credit, clean up bad credit, and play the credit game in general.

Though credit can be a component of wealth, it's also what keeps many people in poverty. An estimated 70 percent of American households live paycheck to paycheck, and the average middle-income American spends more than he or she earns, creating a staggering level of consumer debt. You already know my view on borrowing: it's good when whatever you're borrowing for will appreciate in value and ultimately make you more money than the amount you borrowed; it's bad when used for consumable items or depreciating assets.

A financial reality is that the economy of the United States and many other countries is based on the extension of credit. If credit was eliminated, the result would probably be an immediate and prolonged recession. In most financial situations, whether you're a simple household or a giant corporation, having credit available can be helpful. But it can also be disastrous if you don't use it properly. The key is to make credit work *for* you rather than *against* you.

HOW KNOWING THE RULES OF THE CREDIT GAME CAN HELP YOU BECOME WEALTHY

Good credit means that over the years you have borrowed money for various things and always repaid it on time, and that makes you a good credit risk. You might believe that bad credit means just the opposite, but that's not necessarily so. Many people have late payments, judgments, and even bankruptcies on their credit histories, and they can still get credit because they know how to play the game. There are many degrees of so-called bad credit, and as you learned in chapter 13, plenty of factors other than your payment history will influence a lender who is considering your loan application.

You can begin applying your wealth-building strategies even though you may have limited or poor credit, but a decent credit rating will definitely be helpful if you are to achieve long-term success. Even if you currently have established credit, understanding how the credit system works will make it easier for you to maintain and improve positive relationships with current and future creditors.

Let's begin with a look at basic credit terms and what they mean.

Credit bureau. A credit bureau is a private, for-profit business that collects and distributes credit information on consumers. The three national credit bureaus are Equifax, Experian, and TransUnion. In addition, many smaller firms serve specific local markets. Lenders who subscribe to specific credit bureaus provide information about consumers that is then disseminated to other subscribers.

Not all lenders report credit data to a bureau, and not all subscribers are lenders. Typically, institutions or lenders that report to credit bureaus include:

- ❖ major banks
- ❖ travel and entertainment credit cards
- ❖ bank credit cards
- ❖ major savings and loan associations
- ❖ major department stores
- ❖ finance and consumer loan companies
- ❖ collection agencies

Institutions or lenders that are not likely to (but may) report to credit bureaus include:

- ❖ some small banks and S&Ls
- ❖ individuals who hold seller financing
- ❖ utility companies
- ❖ oil companies
- ❖ insurance companies
- ❖ small- and medium-size credit unions
- ❖ medical care providers
- ❖ apartment building owners and other residential landlords
- ❖ small mortgage companies

Credit bureaus also acquire information such as bankruptcies, judgments, liens, wage garnishments, and the like from public records. Employers may subscribe to a credit bureau to get credit reports in evaluating prospective employees.

Credit report. This is the document issued by a credit bureau that contains a consumer's credit information; it is your basic financial history.

Credit rating. Prior to the development of popular credit-scoring systems, the term *credit rating* was used to describe your creditworthiness. Credit bureaus did not assign ratings; instead, lenders made their own determination about your creditworthiness based on their own standards, the amount and purpose of the credit requested, the information you provided as part of your application, and the credit report.

Credit score. Your credit score is a mathematical summary derived from the information in your credit report. It's a number lenders use to decide if they will lend you money, and if so, at what interest rate. The most well-known credit-scoring system is known as FICO (Fair Isaac Corporation). Scores range from 300 to 850; the higher, the better. We'll talk more about credit scores later in this chapter.

Credit correction agencies. These organizations help consumers with credit problems. The largest nonprofit group is the National Foundation for Credit Counseling (NFCC), a network of agencies that offer low- and no-cost services to help people get their debts under control. Private, for-profit agencies charge consumers for assistance. Both the NFCC and for-profit agencies review and correct credit reports, work out budgets and debt repayment plans, and make payments for clients; in general they serve as go-betweens for consumers and creditors. The for-profit agencies are sometimes referred to as credit-repair consultants.

KNOW THE SIX C'S OF CREDIT

Lenders, especially bankers, use a formula known as the six C's of credit when evaluating a credit application. Understanding them will help you make your applications as attractive as possible.

Character. This is essentially a summary of the individual. Creditors look for people who appear to be trustworthy and reliable, and who are willing and able to meet their financial obligations.

Capacity. This is the individual's ability to repay the loan; it is based on present and anticipated earnings balanced against existing debts.

Collateral. The item pledged by the borrower as security for the loan, which may be real estate, stocks, savings, a mortgage, etc.

Conditions. Both regulatory and economic conditions are considered. Regulatory conditions apply to the lender's individual circumstances; for example, when banks are not lending in specific areas. Economic conditions determine the lender's general policy toward loans. Both are affected by the current economic cycle.

Credit. This is the individual's credit history.

Capital. This is the net worth of an individual as indicated by a personal financial statement.

Take a moment to notice how far down on the list credit is. It's fifth—the next-to-last consideration. Notice where character is. It's first. Any banker will tell you that character—his or her personal judgment and assessment of you—is a key part of the loan decision. Remember, bankers are human, and their personal assessment of you is going to have a great influence on their decision about your loan.

Most people think that if they have a good credit report, a reasonably high credit score, and a good job, they can get a loan. The reality is that if you do not have a positive rapport with the banker, he or she may go to the loan committee with your request and say, "I know this person has credit, I know he has a job, but I just don't feel good about him. There's something I don't like." If that's the way the banker presents your loan, do you think the loan committee is going to approve it? Highly unlikely.

However, you could have marginal credit and some late payments, and that loan officer can go to the loan committee and say, "I know this person has had some late pays, but she's solid in the community, I have a good feeling about her, and I think the bank would be doing her an injustice by not giving her a hand." If that happens, in many cases, you will get the loan even though your credit history isn't great.

The point to remember is that credit does not carry the weight most people think it does, especially when it comes to commercial lending. Projecting an image of good character, trustworthiness, and professionalism is a much more important part of the loan application process.

A FEW FACTS ABOUT CREDIT REPORTS

The previous section notwithstanding, credit is still important, especially when you're looking for conventional financing. Let's take a look at your credit report and what it includes:

Identification. Consumers are identified by complete name, address, telephone number, previous addresses, Social Security number, and date of birth. Some credit bureaus include employment information and salary history.

Credit inquiries. When a report is requested on a consumer, a note of the inquiry is made in the file and retained for up to two years.

Public records. Credit-related information, such as bankruptcies, judgments, and liens, that is gathered from courthouse documents that are public record.

Collection accounts. Information reported by collection agencies.

Credit history. Entries from each reporting subscriber that generally contain the date an account was opened, original balance, credit limit, terms, monthly payment amount, payment history, the date of the last subscriber input, and any other important or unusual information about a consumer's account. The subscriber may indicate details such as an account being in dispute, having a cosigner, being secured by collateral, being written off as a loss, or that the consumer has cosigned other debts.

Consumer statement. A hundred-word statement from consumers regarding any item on their reports that they wish to dispute or clarify.

The format and presentation of a credit report may vary with the reporting agency; when a copy of the report is sent to consumers or subscribers, most agencies will include instructions on how to read the report and an explanation of the abbreviations used.

Only individuals and businesses with a "permissible purpose" (as defined in the Fair Credit Reporting Act) can access your credit report. Examples of permissible purpose include for a credit transaction, in determining eligibility for a license or government benefit, for insurance underwriting, or for a business transaction you initiate. Employers may view a modified version (account numbers are omitted) of your credit report for employment purposes, but they must have your written consent to do so.

If you notice credit inquires being made by companies you don't recognize, you can and should challenge them. Call or write the reporting agency and request the full contact name and address of the company that made the inquiry. Then send a letter to that company, advising that you know it made an unauthorized check of your credit report and ask why it did so. You may want to remind the company that unauthorized inquiries are against the law; if you are not satisfied with its response, consider filing a complaint with the Federal Trade Commission.

Remember that a company checking your credit this month will know who checked your credit last month because it will appear on your report. Too many inquiries may cause a lender to wonder why you are seeking so much credit and thus to suspect a hidden risk. Too many inquiries without a corresponding opened line of credit or account may cause a lender to think others have turned you down, and that he or she should also deny your credit application.

After a specified time, negative credit items must be removed from your report. For most items, it's seven years; for bankruptcies, it's ten years from the date you filed. Most credit bureaus automatically do this, but if you are coming up on the anniversary date of a negative entry, follow up to be sure. You are entitled to a free copy of your credit report from each of the three major credit bureaus once each year. To order yours, go to www.annualcreditreport.com or call (877) 322-8228.

Keep in mind that some lenders have their own more lenient

standards for considering negative items. For example, it might be an internal policy for a lender to consider a bankruptcy only if it occurred within the past four years, even though the entry remains on your credit report for ten. This is one reason why, if you have negative entries on your credit report, some lenders will approve your loan and others won't.

It is not uncommon for individuals to have more than one file with the same credit bureau. These alternate credit reports are usually caused by clerical errors, and the credit bureaus will usually make every effort to correct them. The most common way an accidental alternate file is discovered is when a consumer is denied credit and begins researching to find out why. If you determine this has happened to you, notify the credit bureau in writing and ask to be advised in writing when the situation is corrected.

It's possible to manipulate the system and use alternate credit reports to cover up bad credit or even create a new identity. This is fraudulent and may be prosecuted under different state laws. If a credit-repair consultant suggests this, get out of his or her office as fast as you can. There are plenty of legal, ethical ways to build good credit and overcome bad credit, and I'll be sharing them with you. Don't be tempted to cheat. You can make your personal fortune legally and ethically. You can push and be aggressive, but there's never any reason to step over the line. Honesty, ethics, and good morals will always win in the end.

CORRECTING AN ERRONEOUS CREDIT REPORT

You can't correct an error you don't know about, so the first step in maintaining an accurate credit file is to check it regularly. As I've already told you, you can receive a copy of your credit report from each of the three major credit bureaus free once a year. You are also entitled to receive a free copy of your credit report if you've been denied credit in the previous thirty days or if you have been the victim of identity theft. Requesting these reports is quick and easy, so take advantage of them.

The number of credit bureaus is a major frustration in maintaining a positive credit report. One bureau may be reporting your information accurately; another may have errors that are causing you to be turned down for credit. That's why some people want to get their report from all three of the major credit bureaus at the same time so they can compare them; others request one report every four months so they can catch new and possibly erroneous information on the report faster.

Once you receive the report, study it carefully for accuracy. Make note of any item with which you disagree. The report should include instructions for filing a dispute; if it doesn't, send a letter to the credit bureau outlining the points you are disputing and why. Ask for the items to be investigated and for an updated copy of the report to be sent to you when the investigation is complete. Don't make threats or provide lengthy explanations, just ask the bureau to verify the information it has. Keep copies of all correspondence, whether by regular mail or e-mail. In your file, note all telephone contacts with the time and date of the call, the person you spoke with, and the result of your conversation.

The credit bureau is required to investigate and respond within thirty days. If after that time you have not received a response to your letter, follow up with another letter and then a phone call. Maintain a professional, businesslike demeanor at all times—no foul language, no threats, and no shouting, and be sure your paperwork is presented in a neat, orderly fashion. Check the ink or toner cartridge of your printer and be sure your letter and any other documents are legible. Your name and address, along with the credit bureau's reference numbers, should appear on each page.

Remember that credit bureaus report only what they are told by subscribers, and they can change information in your file only if advised to do so by the creditor involved. In many cases, your initial request will succeed in having a disputed item removed from your file. If that doesn't work, request a reinvestigation. Do this in writing, and also ask for the name, address, and telephone number of the creditor the bureau is contacting. If your requests to the credit bureau don't produce the results you want, you can go directly to the creditor. Write a letter explaining as simply and briefly as possible why you are disputing the entry and asking the creditor to advise the credit bureau to change or remove the information. Again, a calm, businesslike presentation is important. Use the communication skills you'll learn in chapter 18 to persuade the creditor to help you. Allow a reasonable length of time for the action to be processed and follow up with the credit bureau to make sure your file is changed.

WHAT TO DO WHEN THE NEGATIVE REPORTS ARE TRUE

Though mistakes account for a significant portion of the negative entries in credit files, all too often the reports are accurate. Your credit file may indicate a period of late payments, and you know that you were then unemployed, going through a divorce, facing a medical emergency, or had any number of other legitimate reasons that can cause a financial bind. This happens to a lot of people and lenders know it, so you can overcome this situation fairly easily. If you've declared bankruptcy, it's going to be more difficult, but there are still ways you can gain credit.

Begin by making sure all of your bills are paid on time, so your current record is good. Then tackle the history. You *can* erase bad credit records from your file—even though they may be true. Remember that credit bureaus must be able to verify everything in your file, or they have to take it out—no matter what it is, even a bankruptcy. You don't need a reason to ask for verification.

A technique the so-called credit-repair consultants often use is to simply challenge every negative entry and hope that at least some of them will get dropped because they cannot be verified. Credit bureaus and creditors know this and will probably recognize what you're trying to do if you decide to take this approach. This technique worked years ago when many companies maintained paper rather than electronic files; these days, it's much easier for a creditor to verify its own records.

If a creditor verifies a negative report and refuses to change its position, it's time for a personal meeting—face-to-face, if possible, or via telephone. Assuming the item involves a poor payment history, explain the circumstances to the credit manager. If you are still a customer, point out that you are interested in maintaining a positive relationship for the future. If there is an unpaid amount, make arrangements to handle it. Sometimes creditors will accept a partial cash payment as payment in full, in much the same way that a mortgage holder will accept a discount. Be sure you negotiate the removal of the negative item in your credit file as part of your payment agreement, and get it in writing.

If you are unable to get the unfavorable reports removed, balance them with as many positive reports as possible. If you have good credit with a company that does not subscribe to the credit bureau, ask the bureau to include that record in your file; there may be an administrative fee involved, but it's worth the effort. Also, get statements concerning your payment habits from these companies so you can use them with credit applications to balance any negative information provided by the credit bureau. Cleaning up a bad credit report isn't difficult if you are systematic and follow up carefully, but it does take some time and effort.

RESPOND IF YOU MUST

You are entitled to include a hundred-word explanation of any unfavorable report in your credit file, and any inquiry must be provided with your statement. Include the details of what happened and how you attempted to correct it. If you feel the creditor was uncooperative, say so, but do it in a calm, unemotional manner. Finally, ask the bureau for an updated copy of your credit report once the statement has been added so you can verify its accuracy.

Having said that, let me add that I never bother with this, and

I don't recommend it. You'll never find any moneyed businessperson whining to the credit bureau about his or her misfortunes or mistreatment by a lender. A better way to deal with negative credit reports is to provide your own professional explanation at the time you apply for your loan.

When you put together a loan package, include a copy of your credit report and an explanation of anything that might raise a question. For example, years ago I was applying for a real estate loan and at the time had a judgment against me that was listed in my credit file. However, the judgment was in litigation, and I believed it would ultimately be removed. (It was.) I explained this in a brief letter and directed the lender's attention back to all the positive information I was providing. As a result, I was able to borrow the money I needed. This is the best way to minimize any negative information in your credit file.

Rather than adding an explanation to your credit report, you may want to flag the questionable entry with a statement that reads, "There is a dispute on this entry. Please see application and personal financial statement for explanation." This will help prevent a lender from making a snap judgment based on either a negative entry or a short written explanation that may not tell the entire story.

CONTACTING THE CREDIT BUREAUS

Here is the contact information for the three major credit bureaus:

Equifax
Equifax Credit Information Services, Inc.
P.O. Box 740241
Atlanta, GA 30374
888-766-0008
www.equifax.com

Experian (formerly TRW)
National Consumer Assistance Center
P.O. Box 2002
Allen, TX 75013
888-397-3742
www.experian.com

TransUnion LLC
Consumer Disclosure Center
P.O. Box 1000
Chester, PA 19022
800-888-4213
www.tuc.com

To request your free annual credit report from one or all of these bureaus, contact:

Annual Credit Report Request Service
P.O. Box 105281
Atlanta, GA 30348-5281
877-322-8228
www.annualcreditreport.com

UNDERSTANDING CREDIT SCORES

Your credit score is a number that lenders use to evaluate your credit risk. It's based on what's in your credit file and is essentially a numeric snapshot of your credit report at a particular point. The most widely used scoring system is known as FICO, and you'll often hear people refer to their credit score as a FICO score.

This number is used by lenders to assist in determining whether to extend credit, and if they do, what interest rate and other terms to offer. Your credit score is not the only factor that lenders consider; they also look at your income, your current debts, your employment history, and your credit history. Based on their own policies, they might extend credit even though your credit score is low—or they might decline your application even though your score is high.

It's possible for your credit score to change whenever your credit report changes, although it usually won't change much from month to month unless something dramatic happens. Your score will drop quickly if you file for bankruptcy or suddenly start making payments late; driving your score in the other direction usually takes more time.

For a credit score to be calculated, your credit report must contain enough recent information on which to base the score. Generally, if you have at least one account that has been open for six months or longer and at least one account that has reported to the credit bureau within the last six months, the bureau can calculate a credit score.

Your score is calculated based on five categories of information contained in your credit report: payment history, amounts owed, length of credit history, types of credit in use, and new credit. For tips on raising your credit score, go to www.myfico.com.

As this book was going to press, the three major credit bureaus introduced VantageScore, a new credit scoring system designed to compete with the FICO score. Previously the credit bureaus used different scoring systems; with VantageScore, they will all be using the same system. However, even with this added consistency among the credit bureaus, most lenders use the FICO score and it's hard to say at this point whether or not they will make the change to the new system. You can find out more about VantageScore at www.vantagescore.com and more about FICO scores at www.myfico.com.

ESTABLISHING CREDIT FOR THE FIRST TIME

The importance of establishing credit at an early age cannot be stressed too strongly. Consumers over twenty-six years old without a credit history are viewed with great suspicion by lenders. If you do not have credit right now with at least four different sources, no matter how old you are, begin building that credit immediately.

Your first step is to open individual checking and savings accounts in your own name. Over time, your record of deposits, withdrawals, and transfers will demonstrate that you can handle money responsibly.

If you are in college, you may be eligible for a credit card even though you have no credit history—and no job! Banks issuing Visa and MasterCard, as well as American Express and Discover, have special programs to encourage students to apply for their cards. It's a great deal for them, because initial credit lines are relatively low, which means a limited risk, and the earlier they gain a customer, the more money they will make over that person's lifetime. (Remember, credit card companies make money both from the interest cardholders pay and the fees merchants pay.) If you're not in school and have limited or marginal credit, consider enrolling in an inexpensive night school class to take advantage of this easy credit source. The credit card applications are usually available on campus just about anywhere students gather, from the bookstore to the registrar's office.

If you apply for and receive one or more of these cards, exercise care and discipline to charge only what you can pay in full each month, and never let the lure of instant gratification and easy credit tempt you to build a debt you could spend years paying off.

You might also consider a secured credit card, which means you secure the amount of your credit limit by placing that much on account with the card issuer. After making payments promptly for a while, ask that your security deposit be released. If it is not released, try another credit source, because now you've established a payment history other card issuers will respect.

Another option is to apply for department store and gasoline credit cards. They are generally easier to obtain than major credit cards and allow you to create a payment history for your credit file. You must use these accounts for them to have a positive impact on your credit, but be sure to avoid accumulating debt you cannot afford to repay.

You can also apply for a loan with the bank where you have your checking and/or savings account. You can secure the loan by the funds you have on deposit or by items you own, such as a car. Just remember that loans require the payment of interest, so just borrow enough so you can get a positive entry in your credit file.

Several of the major automobile finance companies offer special first-time-buyer loans, and independent companies are often willing to work with people who do not have a strong credit history. Once you receive a car loan, be sure your payment record is reported to the credit bureau.

Once you have established a payment history, consider closing some of the accounts you don't use. Too many open accounts, even with zero balances, can be a red flag to prospective lenders. They think that if you have access to a lot of credit, you might be tempted to get in over your head. It's an insulting attitude, but it's there, and fighting it will get you nowhere. On the other hand, you do want to have some amount of available credit you're not using, because your credit score will drop if you have maxed out all your credit sources. Also, when deciding what accounts to close, it's a good idea to keep the oldest ones open. Creditors and the credit scoring systems like to see accounts that you've had for a long time. Ideally, you should have two bank credit cards, an American Express card, and lines of credit for times when plastic isn't appropriate.

Whenever you are turned down for credit, call the credit manager and find out why—even though you should receive a letter stating the reason. Let him know you want to do business with his company, and ask if there's anything you can do to change the negative decision. A tactic that works well is to ask what he would do if he were in your position, then consider following his advice.

Remember that building credit takes time. Lenders want to be able to see that you have a pattern of paying your bills on time.

They look for other indicators of stability and responsibility, such as how long you've lived at your current address, how often you move, and how you present yourself. Look at yourself through the eyes of a lender and work on becoming someone you would loan money to.

GET RID OF CONSUMER DEBT

The best thing you can do for your credit rating and your overall financial health is to clear up your consumer debt. I can hear what you're thinking—that paying off your debts is easier said than done. But if you follow the steps I'm sharing with you, getting out of debt is easier than you think. More important, getting out from under a mountain of useless consumer debt is an essential step toward becoming wealthy.

The approach you take will be determined by your level of debt, so begin by doing a financial statement. List your assets, liabilities, income, and expenses. Don't rely on your memory— *write it down!* You'll probably be shocked when you total the numbers and realize how much you owe on depreciating assets. Once you know where you stand, set up a budget and begin paying off your bills. Here are a few budgeting tips to keep in mind:

Be realistic. Don't create a budget so tight you won't be able to stick to it. Remember to include small items that add up, such as tolls, parking, newspaper and magazine subscriptions, haircuts, and so on.

Allow for entertainment and recreation. It's okay to go to a movie or have dinner in a restaurant once in a while. Don't eliminate everything you enjoy doing or you will associate "getting out of debt" with "pain," when in fact it should be a pleasurable goal.

Don't go into additional debt for consumables. It's okay to continue using credit cards for convenience, but pay off the current charges in full every month.

Understand the terms of all your credit cards, loans, and

other debt. Know what the interest rate is, when payments are due, and when late charges and penalties kick in. For credit cards, know how the minimum payment is calculated. If you receive a "change of terms" notice from a creditor, read it carefully and be sure you understand it—and if you don't like the terms, close the account.

Remember the rule of compounding. As you begin implementing your wealth-building strategies, reinvest your returns into additional appreciating assets.

Have a purpose for each investment. If you are deeply in debt, you will want to use some of your returns to pay off bills. One strategy is to designate a specific investment for a particular purpose, either to pay off a certain bill or to fund a particular expense. For example, if you have young children, consider buying each of them a house; let the mortgages be paid off by the rent revenue, enjoy whatever positive cash flow they produce, and let the houses appreciate in value. By the time your kids are old enough for college, there will be enough equity in those houses to finance a major portion, if not all, of their education. Or designate the positive cash flow from a particular property to pay a specific debt; you'll eventually get rid of the debt and have the asset that your tenants have paid for. Just be sure to reinvest enough of your earnings to maintain your financial growth.

Consider negotiating with lenders to reduce debt. Some creditors may be willing to take a smaller amount than your balance due in order to cancel your debt. Do this only if it will not cause a negative report in your credit file and if the lender will release you in writing from any future obligation. Generally you'll have more success taking this approach with smaller, private lenders, though you may find a conventional lender who will negotiate with you if the account is in danger of being turned over to a collection agency. This also works with business debt to independent vendors—and sometimes the vendor will come to you for a deal. For example, we had a balance of $70,000 with one of our vendors and were paying it according to the original terms of our agreement. But when he got into a cash crunch and needed money, he asked me for $50,000 cash to cancel the debt. I offered $40,000 and he accepted; the debt was settled at a discount of $30,000. If the lender won't reduce the amount due, ask for a lower interest rate to help you get the principal paid off faster.

Let your creditors know what you're doing. Especially if you're finding it difficult to make payments, tell your creditors what is happening *before* your accounts get in arrears. Many will lower your monthly payment or interest rate to avoid a problem account on their books. Remember, bankers in particular can suffer serious career consequences if they have made too many bad loans, so they're motivated to work with you to keep a loan from going bad. Even if they don't make any concessions, creditors will be less likely to take aggressive collection action if they know you are working to pay off their bill. Remember, creditors don't want to reposses whatever property you put up for collateral, and they don't want to take you to court—they just want their money. They may try to bluff you at first, but if you communicate with them and work with them, they will usually work with you until you get over your tight spot. If the person you're dealing with is uncooperative, ask for a supervisor. Creditors live in the same world you do, and they have a lot more flexibility than you might imagine.

LIVE LIKE A MILLIONAIRE

Don't confuse lifestyle with wealth. People who live glamorous, big-spending lifestyles may have big incomes but may not necessarily have a significant net worth. There are plenty of people who earn $200,000 a year and owe $205,000. One lost paycheck could cripple them economically. One unexpected bill would bankrupt them. By contrast, many millionaires live below their means because they would rather invest their money in wealth-building vehicles than in depreciating assets. Most millionaires do not have significant credit card debt; in fact, they would rather do without than charge.

Just as aspiring actors study the methods of great performing artists and medical students learn the techniques of established physicians and surgeons, if you are going to become a millionaire, you must copy the behavior of other millionaires. And as I have said before, millionaires may have thousands of dollars' worth of debt, but they have gone into debt only to acquire assets that will eventually add to their millions.

CHAPTER 18

COMMUNICATION SKILLS THAT WILL MAKE YOU A MILLIONAIRE

Many receive advice, few profit by it.
—PUBLILIUS SYRUS
(FIRST CENTURY BC)

If you take a look at people who have made a lot of money— regardless of the circumstances or the vehicle they used—you'll find they have at least one trait in common: they have learned and developed top-notch selling skills. Lee Iacocca may be a talented automobile designer, but he was able to turn Chrysler around a quarter century ago by selling people on the company's cars— and he's trying to do it again. Federal Express is one of the largest start-ups ever funded by venture capital, but only because Fred Smith was able to sell investors on his idea of an overnight delivery service. The individual most identified with Apple Computer is Steven Jobs, who did the selling; Stephen Wozniak was responsible for the initial technology, but you rarely hear about him. When the late Dave Thomas went on television to sell Wendy's hamburgers, profits rebounded and more than doubled in two years. I was doing okay in my real estate business and approaching my early goal of $1 million net worth when I discovered the value of sales skills; when I started using them, my income and my assets soared. It didn't take me long to realize these skills could be applied to any situation: buying and selling businesses, real estate, or products.

Look around at the successful people you know. Their job titles may or may not include the word *sales*, but they know how to sell, and using their sales skills is reflexive. Shortly after Bill Clinton's first State of the Union address, *Newsweek* magazine referred to the President as the First Salesman—and an important part of his job was to sell the American people on his programs, as it is any President.

A solid understanding of sales techniques is essential if you're going to achieve financial independence—and sales is the ingredient that's missing from most wealth-building programs. Don't be alarmed; I'm not suggesting that you hit the street with a vacuum cleaner or a water treatment system, knocking on every door until you make a sale. It's unfortunate, but too many people have preconceived notions of selling that are just plain wrong. Selling is not a slick, fast-talking presentation, nor is it tricking people into buying things they don't want, won't use, and can't afford. Selling does not have to be a pressure business, and the top salespeople rarely use pressure to complete a sale. Selling is simply helping someone do what he or she *should* do in a situation that can benefit you both. A great salesperson provides the positive leadership people need and want.

Think about all the things you do in the normal course of your life that would be easier with sales training. Think about all the new ideas you're getting for wealth building and how much easier those will be to accomplish if you apply selling skills. Buying a house for no money down involves selling. Getting a loan at a bank involves selling. Convincing your boss to give you a raise involves selling. In most successful businesses, the leaders have mastered the art of selling. In fact, I can't think of any personal or professional situation that wouldn't be enhanced by the understanding and application of sales techniques, right down to convincing an energetic toddler that he really does want to go to bed at bedtime.

Anytime you try to persuade people to do what you want

them to do, you're selling. The use of sales techniques gets people on your side; it makes them want to help you. A product doesn't have to change hands for selling to occur, and a successful sale isn't always a financial transaction. Just about any successful interaction between you and another human being requires sales skills.

YOU DON'T NEED SALES SKILLS—IF YOU WANT TO REMAIN BROKE, THAT IS

When the topic of sales comes up in my classes, there's always someone in the crowd who says something like "I'm not a salesperson. I couldn't sell a winter coat to an Eskimo."

That's usually a poor person talking. And it's a person who may end up poor not only financially but also in his or her personal and professional relationships.

Or sometimes I hear, "It takes someone special to be a salesperson, and I can't do that."

That's just plain not true. Anyone can learn and develop the techniques of positive communication. The only reason to think you can't is apathy. If you don't want to learn, if you're too lazy to practice, if you're not willing to do the work necessary to improve yourself and your status, then you *won't* develop the selling skills that will enhance all aspects of your life. It's not a question of *can't*. Anyone *can,* but only a few *will.*

Selling requires communicating and understanding, and people who do this enrich their lives in ways far beyond their bank accounts. That good salespeople rank among the top 2 percent of income producers is not an accident, and it's also only one of the many benefits their skills provide them. Top salespeople earn more than brain surgeons; they earn more than the President of the United States.

Think about it. Brain surgeons spend at least twelve years in school at a mind-boggling cost before they can begin to practice their profession. Then it's several more years before they reach their income potential, because it takes time for them to build up their business. (Would you want someone fresh out of school cutting open your skull? I didn't think so.)

Salespeople, on the other hand, can learn the fundamental skills they need in a matter of days or weeks. By applying and fine-tuning those skills, they can reach the top of their profession in two years, with the potential to outearn any medical expert.

Brain surgeons also need some very expensive tools to perform their work. But as the surgeon operates with a scalpel, the salesperson operates with his or her tongue. And the skill with which each of these tools is used determines the outcome of the process.

HOW TO TELL IF YOU'RE A BORN SALESPERSON

It's simple—you're not.

Of the estimated 6.6 billion people living on our planet today, not one was born a salesperson. Women give birth every day to sons and daughters, not to salespeople. Selling is a communications skill that you learn and develop, and it's something that all of us can learn and use in every aspect of our lives.

Though you're going to get the basics in this chapter, there are plenty of books and audio programs about sales on the market, and I recommend that you add a number of them to your Mindfeed library. Consider attending a few live seminars; they have a totally different flavor from written or recorded material, and you'll learn something new from every sales trainer. The easiest way to teach and apply sales techniques is in a business context, but as you learn them and make them a part of your everyday habits, you'll find yourself applying them virtually all the time in all aspects of your life to enrich all of your relationships.

WHY DO PEOPLE BUY?

People buy based on emotion, then look for logic and reason to justify their actions. It's up to you, the seller, to provide the excitement they need to make the buying decision *and* the logic and reason they'll need afterward to feel completely satisfied.

People will buy when the following circumstances exist:

* They like you.
* They respect you.
* They can find some logic and reason to help them justify their decision.

If any one of these elements is missing, your chances for a successful sale are reduced by far more than one-third. But when someone likes you and respects you, and your presentation has logic and reason, you'll have a distinct advantage. The result, if you're prepared, is that you'll make the sale, and both of you will win.

It sounds simple enough, but how do you do it? With a great presentation.

WINNING PRESENTATIONS

An effective sales presentation has four basic parts. Though we'll be discussing them separately, when you actually use them, you'll find they often blend and overlap. What's important is that you understand each step and how it's designed to lead to a successful conclusion.

Introduction Period. This is the time you get to know your prospect, identifying common interests and building rapport. This is also your opportunity to create the "like" that is necessary for a sale.

Begin by expressing a genuine interest in your prospects that is outside of your business purpose. Find out who they are and what they like to do by asking questions. If you're on their territory—either in their home or office—look around for clues to potential topics of discussion. Are there any trophies or plaques on display? Any models or collections? Books or magazines on specific topics? If you're in your office, on neutral territory, or on the telephone, just ask questions. Where are they from? How long have they lived where they live now? Do they have children? How do they spend their spare time?

People love to talk about themselves and their hobbies. It's critical, though, that you listen to them carefully and respond appropriately. In other words, your interest must be genuine, not artificial. If you're busy thinking about what you're going to say next instead of listening to them, they'll know it—and they'll know you're not being sincere. So be honestly interested, because it will show if you're not.

Another word of caution: Don't make the introduction period seem like a test, with you firing off one question after another and the prospect providing the answers. Make it a conversation, not an exam. This is not only the time for you to get to know them, it's also the time for them to get to know you. Tell them things about yourself that will make them feel comfortable about doing business with you.

Presentation. Once you've established a mutual comfort level, you can move into a discussion of your product or service. This is the time to explain the benefits the prospect will receive by agreeing to your proposal. Don't bore him with a list of features; excite him by drawing a verbal picture of the specific advantages he'll receive from your product.

Your presentation should be thorough and answer as many questions as possible in advance. The formality will vary based on the situation, but keep it as conversational as possible and maintain a high energy level. Involve the prospect as much as you can. If you have a tangible product, let him touch it, feel it, try it out. If you're renting or selling a piece of property, walk the prospect through each room and say things that will help him imagine living there. If you're trying to buy a piece of property, explain your offer and use words to vividly describe the advantages of accepting the offer. If the prospect expresses a strong interest in a specific aspect of your presentation, capitalize on it.

You help the prospect like you during the introduction stage, and you build respect during the presentation. This is when you demonstrate your product and your knowledge of the business or market. It's also the time to subtly feed in the logic and reason that will be necessary for the buyer to justify his decision.

Progress Checks. Ask committing questions throughout your presentation as you go along to gauge your effectiveness so you can make adjustments if necessary. Committing questions are designed to make sure the prospect is following your presentation, agrees with what you're saying, and is preparing to make a commitment. When I do a presentation, whether it's to one, five, or a thousand people, I involve them by asking questions and encouraging responses.

Committing questions are phrased to get yes answers; they are actually mini-closes so that when you get to the end of your presentation, the close itself is simply the final yes. Committing questions lead the prospect into agreement with you and let you know if there's a problem.

Examples of simple committing questions are:

* ❖ Would you agree?
* ❖ Does this make sense?
* ❖ Is that a fair statement?
* ❖ Do you like this part?

Pay attention to the subtle structure of a committing question. It's a closed question—that is, it's designed to draw a single response, either yes or no, and not a lengthy answer. Don't say, "How do you feel about this?" Instead say, "Does this sound good to you?" When the prospect says yes to a committing question, you can move on to the next part of your presentation. If he says no, then you can take the time to find out just where the sticking point is and deal with it.

The idea of committing questions is not to get your prospect's head nodding like a bobble-head doll; it's to be sure he understands and agrees with you. Don't make the question so basic that only an idiot would answer in the negative. For example, questions such as "Is quality important to you?" and "Do you want to deal with people you can trust?" are not effective committing questions and just make you appear to be attempting to manipulate the prospect. Your goal is not manipulation, it's clear communication.

Close. The close is the process of concluding your presentation by making the sale. The close shouldn't be a frightening experience, but it's where most salespeople fail, and it's usually because of the fear of rejection. If you don't close, you not only walk away without a sale, you're never sure why. But if you have checked your progress along the way, the close should be a natural and logical conclusion to the presentation.

Part of conquering the fear of rejection is learning how to deal with rejection. The first step is to understand that rejection is normal; it's not personal and you shouldn't take it personally. Just because a prospect can't afford to buy your product or turned down the offer you made to buy his property doesn't make you any less of a person. The prospect is rejecting a business deal, not you as an individual.

Having said that, let me add that closing is almost always a scary process. Especially when what you're selling is a bid on a property or a loan request, you're not only risking rejection, you're also risking not getting something that you want. And no matter how textbook perfect your presentation is, at times you won't make the sale. But keep in mind that the only way to make money and finalize deals is by closing.

Your success ratio will significantly increase when you develop strong closing skills. The two basic techniques you'll use are the yes-or-no close and the assumptive/alternative-choice close.

As the name implies, the *yes-or-no close* is a question asked in a way in which the answer must be a yes or a no. It's similar to the committing questions that you ask during your presentation, but it's stronger and more definitive. After you ask the question, be quiet and give the prospect time to answer. He may need some time to think; don't distract him by starting to talk. Just wait confidently for the answer. A good example of this type of close is to ask, "Shall we get the paperwork handled?" A yes answer means you've closed the deal; a no means you still have issues to address.

The *assumptive/alternative-choice close* is more subtle. You ask a question or offer the prospect a choice that assumes the deal is concluded. Some examples of this type of close are:

❖ Which color did you want, blue or red?
❖ Where will I be shipping this?
❖ Would you prefer to schedule the closing for the third or the fifth?
❖ How many did you want to order?

Positive answers—such as "I'll take it in blue" or "The fifth is a better day for me"—are clear indicators that you've got a deal. Vague or negative answers—such as "I'll have to think about that"—tell you that you need to find out where the problem is and handle it.

THE PSYCHOLOGY OF EFFECTIVE SELLING

I've said this already, but it's worth saying again: people buy based on emotion, then look for logic and reason to justify their purchase. Your job is to provide both the emotion and the justification.

Excitement sells. Excitement is the primary emotion that prompts people to buy. It's up to you to generate the excitement that will lead to a sale.

Keep your voice up and the tone varied. Don't shout, of course, but make sure your prospect doesn't have to strain to hear you. Changing your tone increases the interest the prospect has in what you're saying. Think about how you react when someone talks to you in a dull monotone; don't do the same thing. Another way to generate excitement is to tell stories. Share examples of how other people have benefited from doing business with you. Use vivid, visual words so your prospect can see himself doing the same. That's what I do when I teach and what I've done in this book. In telling stories about myself, my family, and my students, I'm helping you see what *you* can do if you follow my methods. When you're face-to-face with a prospect, support your words with hand gestures and other body language that help keep the level of enthusiasm up.

When your prospect is excited, *then* provide the logic and reason he needs for buying.

ESSENTIAL BASIC SKILLS

Just as the brain surgeon's primary tool is a scalpel, yours is your ability to communicate. You don't need an extraordinary vocabulary, but you do need a strong command of the language. Your grammar doesn't have to be letter-perfect, but it should be correct most of the time. Most important, your speech should be clear and your pronunciation accurate. If you have a strong regional accent or if English is not your first language, work on your diction so that you can be easily understood.

Practice your presentation into a tape recorder and give yourself a ruthless critique. You've got to eliminate any mumbling or slurring; if people can't understand you, they won't be able to get the information necessary to make a purchase. Using consistently poor grammar and mispronouncing words cast a strong shadow on your credibility.

Use Mindfeed to help in this area if you need it. There are plenty of adult-oriented vocabulary-building courses on the market that you can purchase and use at your own pace. This won't be the most exciting part of your wealth-building program, but it will be a valuable one because it will increase your self-confidence and your success ratio.

Another important tool is product and business knowledge. You need to know everything you can about your product and about the competition. If a prospect does ask a question you can't answer, never try to fake it; tell him he's raised an interesting point and you'll have to check on it and get back to him. Then make a note and do it.

Read trade publications, check out the competition's products, go to conventions and trade shows, and study everything you can get your hands on about your own business. The payoff is more than worth it.

OBJECTIONS ARE JUST QUESTIONS THAT LEAD TO MONEY

The term *objection* is sales-training jargon. It doesn't necessarily mean the prospect is objecting to something; usually it just means that he needs more information. Objections generally come in the form of questions, but sometimes they will be statements. Objections offer the greatest opportunities in sales because they are the steps that lead you closer to a deal. They are the signal that tells you that your prospect is looking for the logic and reason that will justify a buying decision. Ideally you want to answer all of your prospect's questions before he can ask them; in reality, rarely will you go through an entire presentation without at least one objection, so don't let this frighten you. Sometimes your committing questions will lead to objections, and that's fine, because it gives you the chance to handle the issue and get it out of the way early. When you hear an objection during your presentation, apply the following steps:

Restate and clarify the objection; if appropriate, determine why the issue is being raised. Rephrase what the prospect has said to make sure you understand it. Sometimes that simple step will eliminate the objection. At other times, you'll find that what the prospect said isn't what he really meant and you won't waste time dealing with an objection that doesn't really exist. Just say, "So if I understand you correctly, you're saying that . . ." and then repeat the objection. Wait for him to either agree that you're accurate or to correct you. There will always be times when our brains and tongues don't quite seem to connect, and what comes out isn't what we meant to say at all. It happens to you, and it happens to prospects, too.

It's always a good idea to find out why the prospect has made the objection; that will help you determine the best response. For example, if you're making an offer on a property and you want the seller to hold the financing, he may say, "One of the problems with holding a mortgage is that it takes such a long time to foreclose." Is he implying that he thinks you may be risky? You need to find out. So say, "Are you concerned that you might have to foreclose on this mortgage?" He might be; then again, he might just be making a general comment about the foreclosure laws in your state.

Finding out why a prospect is asking a particular question is especially important if the answer to the question would be negative or reveal a potential shortcoming in your proposal. For example, a prospect may ask if you provide twenty-four-hour service, but you don't. Don't say, "I'm sorry, we don't." Instead, ask, "How often do you need twenty-four-hour service?" You'll be relieved if he says, "Oh, I've never needed service past six o'clock. I was just curious." And if he does actually need twenty-four-hour service, you've bought yourself a little time to think about how to meet his needs within your parameters. You have to stay razor-sharp and be able to think on your feet.

Give the objection value. Let the prospect know you respect his concerns. Even if you think what he just said was the silliest thing you've ever heard, don't let it show. Try saying something such as "That's a good point, and I'm glad you brought it up because it gives me a chance to tell you about . . ." or "I understand why that would be important to you. Let me show you how this could work."

Resolve the objection. Answer the question, make the explanation, or negotiate more if you have to. "Does the product come in red?" Either it does or it doesn't. "How does that work?" Show them. "Can you make the terms better?" Look for places where you can compromise.

This approach should be used primarily for objections that come during your presentation. Remember, objections during a presentation are a good sign; they mean the prospect is listening, is interested, and is looking for the information he needs to make a decision. The more objections you can handle during the presentation, the fewer you'll have to deal with at the close, and the more likely you'll make a sale.

When you hear an objection during your close, consider a slightly different approach. My favorite is to question the objection, and I do this by repeating what was said as a question. I don't change the words, I just repeat them with a different inflection in my voice. For example, if I'm making a low-money-down offer on a property and the owner says, "I need more cash," I say, "You need more cash?" That forces him to justify his objection, and often he starts to sell *himself* on my offer. The key is never to challenge the objection, but to turn it into a hot potato and toss it back in the tone of a question. Your prospect won't want to hold on to it, and by refusing to keep it yourself, you're forcing him to answer his own objection.

When you're closing, you must also isolate the objection to make sure it's the only one your prospect has. I don't want to negotiate on the down payment and then find out he's still not happy with my offer or the interest rate. You isolate the objection with a simple question; just ask, "If we can solve this issue, is there anything else that would keep us from doing business today?" If the prospect says no, then you simply resolve the objection and close the deal. If the prospect says yes, then find out what the other objections are and what you'll have to do to deal with them, one at a time.

LEARN TO SPOT SMOKE SCREENS

Often an objection the prospect may verbalize is not what is really bothering him. Pay close attention to what he doesn't say so you can spot smoke screens. Most smoke screens come in the form of price objections. In many cases, if the prospect says, "I can't afford it," he is really asking you to justify the price. Or he may be saying, "Solve my money problem and I'll buy," which means you may need to help with financing issues.

At other times, a prospect may voice a variety of objections because he really doesn't have the money but doesn't want to admit it. When you've offered a reasonable resolution that he won't accept, or he starts to repeat objections, there's an excellent chance the real issue is money. If you think this might be the situation, tackle it head-on. Be gentle and tactful; say something such as "George, it's been my experience that when people say the kinds of things you've said, what they're really trying to tell me is that they feel they may not have the funds for this kind of an investment. Very often I'm able to help them, but I can do it only if I understand their true feelings and circumstances. So, George, if you had the funds in ready cash, would you place your order today?"

If your product is good and your deal is fair, but the prospect continues to make objections, it's always the money—no matter what else he says. And when he doesn't have the money and there's no way you can help him with financing or guide him to a lending source, there's nothing else you can do. Don't blame yourself; just move on.

Other smoke screens are phrases such as "I want to think about it" or "I never make a decision the same day." When you hear statements like this, dig for the real objection. Try saying something such as "I understand that this is an important decision, and you don't want to make it hastily. Is there any point in particular that you need to think about?" Then treat that point like an objection, answer it, and close again.

NEGOTIATING WIN-WIN DEALS

All too often we view negotiating as a war: deal making between adversaries where if one wins, then the other must lose. But effective negotiating produces win-win situations, where everyone walks away satisfied. True negotiations are built on persuasion, not power. And when you think about it, win-win negotiations do more than just make everyone feel good; they are tremendously practical. When people come away from a deal with you feeling like winners, they'll be back for more. If at the same time you've managed to get what you wanted, you'll be glad to see them again, instead of ducking them in shame.

Win-win negotiations begin and end with active listening. Pay careful attention to what your prospect is saying and repeat it if necessary. You might say, "So if I understand you, Sharon, you need delivery within five days of placing your order. Is that correct?" Or, "Let me make sure I have the numbers correct, Dave. You want $5,000 in cash and you're willing to consider holding a second mortgage. Is that right?"

Compare what they want with what you can do. If it matches, chances are you've got a deal. If it doesn't, you must begin the give-and-take of negotiating, adding a point here, taking away there, until you both have an agreement you're happy with. Remember, you can't beat your prospect into submission; persuade gently with questions that allow the answers (or the yes decision) to be his or her idea.

THE ONE TIME IT PAYS TO BE NEGATIVE

One of the most dynamic and powerful sales tools is called negative selling or reverse selling. Essentially, it's when you dare the prospect not to buy, and it can take you from closing one deal out of ten to five deals out of ten.

The way I demonstrate this technique is to offer to sell a $25 gold pen to a student for $3. The student accepts the deal, I hold the pen out, but as soon as he reaches for it, I pull it back. He'll reach farther until he realizes what I've done. Then I say, "I'm not sure I want to sell this to you, after all." I spend a few seconds in apparent thought, then hold the pen out again. He reaches again and I pull back again. Repeating the routine proves my point, which is that people want what they can't have. They're reaching for the pen because I'm pulling it away. Try this yourself to see how it works. You don't even have to include the selling part; just ask someone to hold a pen and withdraw it when he reaches for it. He'll keep reaching as you pull back.

When you apply this technique to a true sales situation, you must use it in a subtle and sophisticated manner. If you botch it, you'll appear clumsy and manipulative, so practice extensively before you use it with a real prospect.

Negative selling builds a sense of urgency because of the implication that the prospect may not be allowed to purchase what you have to offer. Remember the banking paradox—bankers only want to lend money to people who don't need it. When you use negative selling, what you're projecting is that you don't *need* the sale; you would certainly enjoy doing business with the prospect, but it's no big deal if you don't. Negative selling is always maintaining a positive posture, never begging for the business. You don't need them, and you don't need their deal. Act as if you have plenty of other deals in the works—and if you've been following my advice, that will be true.

In fact, negative selling is an ideal technique to use when you're applying for a loan. I let the banker know I'm shopping and get him to sell me on using his bank. I say something such as "I was referred to you because you offer certain types of loans [I name them], and I wanted to see what types of interest rates and terms you have. I've put together a package that I've showed to a few lenders, and before I make a final decision, I'd like to see what you can do."

If I've made an offer on a property and the owner wants to stall for time, I use negative selling this way: "I understand that this is a big decision for you. By the same token, I'm sure you understand that I'm an investor and businessperson. I have a number of offers in right now, and there are two that have been accepted that I'm very interested in. There are some benefits your deal has that the others don't, but there are also some advantages the other deals have that yours doesn't. I would definitely like to move forward on this, but I have to make a decision in the next couple of days on where I'm going to allocate my money. When will you be in a position to make a decision?"

ADD A NEW WORD
TO YOUR VOCABULARY: SINALOA

SINALOA is an acronym for "safety in numbers and the law of averages," which are two important aspects of selling. Sales is a numbers game, and you must have noes to get to the yeses. It works like this: Let's say a ten-year-old boy is selling plastic combs door-to-door for $1 each. What's going to happen? Some people won't be home, some won't be interested, some will have enough combs—and some will buy. If that boy knocks on enough doors and says, "Would you like to buy a comb for a dollar?" he'll sell some combs. And if he applies some sales techniques, such as a bright smile, an energetic tone, and a presentation that includes some benefits, he'll sell more. It's a matter of making enough presentations (safety in numbers) to find enough people who will buy (the law of averages).

If I showed you ten envelopes and told you eight of them were empty, but one had $50 in it and one had $1,000, and to get that $1,000 you just had to keep picking envelopes until you picked the right one, would you do it? Of course you would. It's the same with sales.

The law of averages is something a lot of people don't understand, and it has caused many an investor, business owner, or salesperson to quit before he reached his goal. If your presentation is good and your offer fair, and if there is logic and reason to what you're doing, the law of averages says you'll make sales. If you're not making sales, take a critical look at your presentation or your offer and see if there's something that needs changing. Keep working on your technique until you find something that is successful. If you keep trying, the law of averages says you will achieve success.

Once that happens, you'll develop a ratio of results. You'll know how many sales calls it takes to get a sale. You'll know how many offers you need to put in on properties to have one accepted. You won't make the mistake so many people do of quitting when you're almost there.

In baseball, a batting average of .300 is great. It could earn a player a multimillion-dollar contract and a place in the Hall of Fame. But do you understand what it means? It means that the player gets a hit only three times out of ten when he's up at bat. It means that 70 percent of the time, he's out. There's a story about Babe Ruth that I like. It seems that each time he struck out, he headed back to the dugout with a big smile on his face. Why was he so happy? Because with each strikeout, he knew he was that much closer to his next home run.

The best of the best understand the law of averages. They know it's a numbers game. We don't expect professional athletes to win every game, and you shouldn't expect that as a professional salesperson you'll make every sale. Just remember that each time you strike out, you're that much closer to your next home run. So keep playing.

PRESENTING AN OFFER TO A SELLER

Because I feel so strongly about real estate being a part of your wealth-building program, I want to specifically address how to use sales skills when buying property. Remember, people expect to negotiate on real estate deals, and there are plenty of angles to consider: the price, the points, closing costs, financing, down payment, and so on.

I begin by establishing my own credibility during the introduction period. I get to know the owners, and I let them get to know me. I want them to like me because when people like you, they are more likely to listen to your entire presentation. When I get ready to present my offer, I want the owners to consider the complete offer before making a decision—and they can only do that if they've listened to everything I've said.

After we've gone through the introduction period and I've inspected the property, I set up an appointment to make my offer, which is, of course, a sales presentation. I put my entire offer and any support documentation (such as estimates for improvements) in writing. If I'm dealing with a couple, I make a complete copy of the offer for each of them. By the way, I always talk to both the husband and the wife, never just one or the other.

When I make a presentation to a couple, I always try to seat the wife between me and the husband so she is included in the conversation. Don't assume the man makes the decision. In most cases, he really doesn't—or he doesn't do it alone. The wife may not say anything during the presentation, but she'll have plenty to say after you leave. And if you ignore her, you won't have a deal. On the other hand, if you focus on her and ignore him, you probably won't have a deal, either. Always arrange the seating so you can comfortably talk to both members of a couple and involve both of them in the discussion.

I hand them the offer and explain it step-by-step. If I'm asking them to hold all or part of the mortgage, I tell them how much money they'll receive over the life of the loan so they can see how much they'll really make. For example, if I want them to hold a $30,000 second mortgage for fifteen years at 8 percent, I tell them they'll receive a monthly payment of $286.70, which totals $51,605.21—or $21,605.21 more than the amount they would have received in cash. (Note: this is the exact opposite of the approach you take when you're offering to discount a mortgage.)

If my offer price is lower than their asking price, I explain why. I rarely, if ever, lowball for the sake of lowballing. If the property needs work, or if comparable properties in the neigh-borhood are appraised at a lower amount, I tell them. I point out that as an investor, it makes sense for me to buy the property only if I can make a profit on it, and that I've done my best to come up with a deal that will be advantageous to us both.

Once I explain the details of the offer, I shut up. I give them time to digest the deal and to think of any questions they may have—and they usually have at least one or two. Once they start asking questions, then I start closing.

COMMUNICATING: THE MORE THINGS CHANGE, THE MORE THEY STAY THE SAME

The foundation of effective communications and salesmanship is the ability to listen and understand the other person, and to con-vey your message in a way that is understood. This is the way it's always been and will always be—no matter how many new high-tech communication gadgets we have.

When I started investing in real estate, we didn't have laptop computers, e-mail, the Internet, or cell phones. Those tools have made the process a little easier, but they have not and will never replace the need for mutual understanding as a critical element of a successful transaction. In fact, if you're not careful, these so-called productivity tools can actually work against you.

While a cell phone is a wonderful tool for confirming ap-pointments, getting directions, and utilizing the hours spent in the car, waiting for meetings, and so on, there is one place this de-vice doesn't belong: a sales presentation. When you're in a sales presentation, turn your cell phone off. Even if you don't answer a call, the fact that one came in will distract both you and your prospect, so turn the phone completely off. If you excuse yourself in the middle of your presentation to take a call, you're telling your prospects that something else is more important than they are. Give your prospects your total attention—they deserve nothing less. The only exception to this rule is if you are waiting for a call from someone with information directly relating to the transaction at hand.

E-mail is another double-edged sword. It's great for fast communication, but it can also be misused and abused, and it can waste your time. I like a good joke as well as anyone, but I don't want to get hundreds of them by e-mail. I've made that clear to people, and they know not to send me junk. I also discourage people from copying me on e-mails just because they think I might want to see what's being written to someone else.

While you should respond to e-mail promptly, you don't have to do it immediately. Don't stop what you're doing when an e-mail pops in. In fact, set two or three times during the day when you read and respond to e-mail; the rest of the time, focus on your business.

Remember that anything you put in an e-mail is not private. If you wouldn't want to see it on the front page of the newspaper, don't write it in an e-mail.

Though e-mail is generally a more casual method of communication than paper letters, it's a good idea to spell-check and proofread everything you send out. Include a subject line that clearly indicates the content of the message. And before you click on Send, be sure you're sending it to the right person. It's too easy to click Reply when you meant to click Forward, or to hit the wrong name in your address book. The results of such a mistake can at the least be embarrassing and at the worst, expensive.

Technology will never change human nature. I've always said that money doesn't change people, it just makes them more of what they are. Technology is similar—it doesn't change you, but it gives you the tools to be more of what you naturally are. If you're efficient, productive, thoughtful, and courteous, technology will help you be more so. If you're easily distracted, careless, and self-centered, technology can make those unfavorable characteristics even stronger.

Use technology to improve and enhance your communications and sales skills. Just remember that you're in charge—don't be a slave to your cell phone or computer; make these devices work for you.

PRACTICE, PRACTICE, PRACTICE

Like any skill worth having, sales skills aren't something you can learn once and then forget about. Just as performers and athletes practice every day to stay in peak condition, you must practice your selling skills.

Visualize each selling situation in advance. Walk it through in your mind, anticipating what the prospect will say, what the objections might be, and how you'll handle them. See yourself making the close and walking away with a successful deal. This will give you an edge few salespeople bother to take.

Some people worry that if they practice too much, they won't sound natural in the presentation. Actually, just the opposite is true. If you practice and know your material, you'll sound comfortable, confident, and knowledgeable—and the more you practice, the more natural your presentation will be. Can you imagine a Broadway actor telling the director that he doesn't want to rehearse because he's afraid his performance won't be natural if he does? That would never happen because actors know that the more they rehearse, the better the real performance will be.

At the end of each presentation, regardless of its outcome, do a "curbside" critique. As soon as you leave the prospect, go over the presentation in your mind. What worked, what didn't? If you made the sale, what clinched it for you? If you didn't, why not? Do this with every presentation so you know what you're doing right and what you need to improve.

Keep your Mindfeed going and battle that old programming. You *can* be a super salesperson; you *can* be one of the top 2 percent of income earners.

CHAPTER 19

BENEFITS OF BUSINESS

Shallow men believe in luck, believe in circumstances: it was somebody's name, or he happened to be there at the time, or it was so then, and another day it would have been otherwise. Strong men believe in cause and effect.

—RALPH WALDO EMERSON

Though money is the most tangible benefit of being in business for yourself, and it's the one we tend to focus on the most, there are many others. We saw clearly during the 1980s what happens to people who are driven by greed. If your only reason for getting into business is to make money and get rich, you may well find everything working against you. If, on the other hand, you're getting into business because you like what you're going to do and you feel good about it, and if you focus on doing the business right, the money will come automatically.

In many areas across the country, there is a serious shortage of low- and moderate-income housing. This type of housing has always been in short supply. So it naturally follows that low- and moderate-income housing has the lowest vacancy ratio of any type of property, which is a strong indicator that you can make money investing in low- and moderate-income rental property. But if you're going to be truly successful as a real estate investor, you've got to get into the business because you care about people, not just because you can make plenty of money. You've got to get into the business because you want to provide safe, decent, sanitary housing for people who can't afford higher-priced neighborhoods. If you do that, and if you focus on the challenge of being the best property owner you can be and apply the formulas for positive cash flow I've shared with you, the money will happen.

The same principle applies to any type of business. Choose one that has the potential to make money, then forget about the money and concentrate on doing the business right. If you get too wrapped up in counting pennies, you'll never get to the dollars. And you'll never have the opportunity to appreciate the many other reasons for getting into business.

WHY PEOPLE ARE STARTING THEIR OWN BUSINESSES

The only way you will achieve financial independence is to stop being dependent on someone else for a paycheck. The easiest, fastest, and most popular method for accomplishing this is to go into business for yourself, which is a primary reason we have seen an explosion in the start up of small businesses in the United States and around the world. In the United States alone, there are more than 24 million small businesses (defined as having fewer than five hundred employees), and those operations employ more than 56 million people—about half of the country's workforce.

But there are reasons for starting businesses other than financial independence. Among my students, I see people driven to become entrepreneurs by a variety of forces. One is that the baby boomers are maturing, which means a greater number of older, more experienced workers as well as young retirees. These people have the knowledge and ability to start successful businesses, and they are doing so in steadily increasing numbers. A related reason is the streamlining of large corporations. After big companies eliminated the unnecessary layers of workers accumulated during the 1980s, large numbers of middle managers found themselves unemployed with no job prospects at all. The go-getters took the skills they'd learned in the corporate world and used them to start their own businesses. After all, looking for a job is hard work. Why not invest that effort in a business of your own instead of someone else's?

Another strong group of entrepreneurs is made up of women who, instead of fighting discrimination in the corporate world, invest their efforts in creating their own companies, where there is no limit to what they can accomplish and earn. And the group that appeals to me most is the workers of all ages who go into business for themselves because they're tired of the corporate rat race and the demands that come with it. They see their own company as an opportunity to build a lifestyle of their choice.

Even more exciting these days is that small-business successes are producing more millionaires than ever before in our history— millionaires who are creating jobs and contributing to their communities in a variety of ways.

Starting your own business is definitely hard work, but it's never been easier. You can begin from scratch, buy an existing company, or take advantage of a wide variety of franchise opportunities with an equally wide variety of terms. You don't necessarily have to have a lot of capital. Technological advances have made it possible for more people than ever before to start and build highly successful companies, often in a spare room in their home with a relatively small investment. A telephone and a computer are all you need to operate on a global scale these days; add a little creativity and your options are virtually unlimited.

One reality you can't ignore is that it takes time to build profitability in a company. But you can start part-time while you continue to work at a regular job that pays the bills. Once your business is off the ground and generating income, you can expand to a full-time operation and quit your job. Or you may want to work only part-time and spend the rest of your time doing something else; your own business lets you make that choice. And if you don't want to work at all, just build your business to the point where the employees run it for you—then sit back, relax, and enjoy the profits.

When you own your own business, you're not locked into someone else's schedule. You set the hours you're going to work and decide when you're going to take off. Do you want to come in late on Monday and leave early on Friday? No problem, it's your decision. Want to take a few days off and go on a cruise with your spouse? Again, no problem, it's your choice. On the other hand, if you want to get an edge on the competition or make more money by working longer hours, you can do that, too. And when you work longer hours in your own business, you get to keep all the profits—not just the pittance of a time-and-a-half overtime rate.

I often travel on weekends to participate in conferences and manage my investments, which means I frequently work seven days a week. But when I'm home during the week, I have the freedom to leave the office early to play tennis or golf, or even take a whole day off to do something with my wife or kids. Also, I take a family vacation every Christmas, another in the summer, and at least four or five shorter breaks during the year. This is the advantage of having businesses that generate income whether you're working or not, whether they are real estate or something else. My businesses make money for me whether I'm in the office or not.

Chances are you'll work longer and harder as a business owner than you ever did as an employee, but you'll do it on *your* terms. You'll make your own choices about when and where to invest time and energy and when and where to sacrifice. You'll be able to balance your life according to your own priorities instead of someone else's—and when you are working, you can run your business the way you want to, not the way someone else thinks you should.

For example, have you ever had a boss or known anyone who had a boss who did everything wrong? And have you ever been in a situation where you knew that if the top people in the company would just listen to you, you could give them dozens of ideas to make the operation run more smoothly and be more profitable?

It's happened to all of us. Even as an ignorant kid working in the slaughterhouse, I saw plenty of ways the company could improve, but no one in management would listen to me, and I didn't see much point in trying too hard to get my message across. I have learned from that experience, and today I encourage all my employees to participate in management decisions and to offer suggestions—but because it's my company, the final decision belongs to me.

Worldwide, creative workers are stifled by bosses and company structures that dictate how things will be done. But when you're the boss, you can move immediately to take advantage of opportunities as you see them and to correct problems quickly. When it's your business, you have the freedom to operate in the manner you know will be most effective and efficient. You have the freedom to make changes when necessary. And you have the freedom to make as much money as you want.

FINANCIAL ADVANTAGES THAT GO BEYOND CASH

Whether it's part-time or full-time, your business will probably provide you with tremendous tax advantages. The way the U.S. Congress (and remember, it's Congress, not the IRS, that creates the rules) has written the tax code has been a tremendous benefit to accountants, publishing houses, and software developers. The laws are so complicated that average people can't understand them and must turn to professionals to prepare their tax returns. And the laws change often enough that most tax-advice manuals are out-of-date shortly after they are written. Tax preparation software must be updated every year. Even so, the tax advantages of being in your own business are significant and will likely remain so. A lot of the details may change, but one thing the government has never done (and won't do as long as income is taxed) is to take away the right of a businessperson to deduct the cost of doing business.

As a business owner, you are entitled to a host of tax deductions generally unavailable to nonbusiness owners. Just a few examples are your automobile and the fuel to run it; your office, or, if you work from your home, the cost of the mortgage or the rent, utilities, furnishings, and maintenance of the portion of your house you use for business; your VCR or DVD player if it's used to show training or other business-related films; magazines and books (like this one); dinners and other forms of entertainment with partners and customers (business must be discussed at these events); and all or part of the cost of your vacations if you arrange to conduct some business either along the way or at your destination.

If you come up with more deductions than income from your business, you can use those deductions to reduce your tax liability on income from other sources—such as your job. Even part-time businesses qualify for tax deductions, and you do not have to make a large up-front investment to deduct your operating expenses. All you have to do is keep careful records. It's also a good idea to establish a relationship with a qualified accountant who can guide your tax strategy in accordance with current and changing tax laws.

Remember, just one rental property, even a single-family home, constitutes owning a business. The same applies to a network marketing distributorship or any of hundreds of other profit-making activities you might do in your spare time. When you become a business owner, you are qualified for all the same tax deductions any Fortune 500 company is entitled to take.

Your own business also provides a built-in hedge against inflation. During inflationary periods, employees are helpless to do anything but watch their purchasing power erode; they don't have the authority to give themselves a raise. As a business owner, when your costs go up, you can increase prices to maintain profitability levels. Of course, you shouldn't just arbitrarily raise prices; you have to consider your overall market, what your competition is doing, and how your customers will react, but the decision will be made *by* you, not *for* you.

Another benefit of your own business is the opportunity to give back to your community. You have the resources to make in-kind (either merchandise or services) or cash donations to deserving organizations whose missions you support.

IF YOU COULD LIVE ANYWHERE,
WHERE WOULD IT BE?

I realized fairly soon after getting into business for myself that I had a level of freedom employees don't have. Besides being able to establish my own working hours, I realized I didn't have to live in upstate New York and endure that region's bitter cold winters. My dream location was Florida, and because I had my own business, I was able to move there.

Maybe your dream location isn't where you are right now. Maybe you'd like to live in the tropics and enjoy year-round sunshine, beaches, and warm temperatures. Maybe you prefer the mountains with winter sports and summer hiking, the charm of a New England village, or even the excitement of a big city. When you own your own business, you can choose to live anywhere in the world you want. The key is to start a business now that you can move to your ideal spot in the near future. Or consider the idea of multiple locations, so you can move among them. All you have to do is stay alert to the opportunities that will cross your path every day.

ARE YOU DRIVING A CAR
OR A HORSE AND BUGGY?

That's a figurative question to get you thinking about the tools you use in your business. If you're going to get around efficiently in our modern world, you need modern transportation. If you're going to run a profitable business, you need the most up-to-date tools available. And the bare minimum in the way of tools is a computer.

Even if you are only investing in real estate, a computer gives you access to online information such as public records and tax rolls and will let you automate your records. That means you'll spend less time doing research and keeping records and have a higher rate of accuracy in both areas. You can take advantage of programs, such as my Real Estate Success Software™, that will help you analyze property and produce financial statements in minutes. Business paperwork that is professionally prepared labels you a serious investor, and a computer makes it easy to create this image.

A computer also opens the door to literally hundreds of other businesses, such as the Mortgage Reduction System I told you about in chapter 14. Many are home-based and can be started in your spare time. Just be sure you choose a business that is a business, not one that is a job.

As a business, you want to be sure your telephone (whether landline or cell phone) is always answered—by a human if at all possible and definitely by an answering system if no one is available. You should also learn about and get comfortable using devices such as PDAs (personal digital assistants) and handheld devices that provide wireless phone and e-mail services and even Internet access. Telecommunications technology is advancing rapidly, and the choices are far greater than they've ever been, so take the time to consult with several service providers to decide on a system that will work for your operation.

WHAT DO YOU REALLY WANT TO DO?

What would you do if money weren't an issue? How would you spend your time if you didn't have to concern yourself with paying bills?

I don't mean what you'd like to do on your vacation—I like to snow ski in the winter, but I wouldn't want to do it all the time—but what would you do with the majority of your waking hours if you didn't have to earn a living? Whatever it is, look for a business idea related to it.

Test your idea for feasibility and profitability by creating a business plan. I know many people think a trip to the dentist is more fun than writing a business plan, but this basic step is critical to your success. Before you start, you need a vision of what your business is going to look like:

* Are you going to buy an existing business or a franchise or start a totally new company?
* Who is your market?
* How will you communicate with your market?
* Will your product or service be affordable in that market?
* Will your product or service sell in that market?
* What is your profit margin?
* How much start-up capital do you need?
* Who will be your suppliers?
* What sort of licenses/permits do you need?
* Who are your competitors, and how are they likely to react to your entry into the market?
* Do you have an adequate labor pool?
* What are your short- and long-term income and expense projections?
* What is the growth potential?
* What is your estimated return on investment?

Writing a business plan lets you evaluate your business idea in much the same way that you would evaluate a property by inspecting it and then calculating the rents and expenses. If you put together a realistic business plan and show a return on your invested cash of 20 to 30 percent or higher, you've got the potential for a successful company. If the profitability potential isn't there, look for ways to adjust your plan, or look for a different business. There are plenty of them out there.

ONCE YOU'RE UP AND RUNNING, GET OUT OF THE WAY OF GROWTH

One of the biggest challenges any entrepreneur faces is knowing when and how to get out of the way of the company's growth.

Building a $1 million company can actually be easier than taking that same company from, say, $20 million to $40 million.

I didn't start any of my businesses with the idea that I would take them to a certain size and stop growing them or deliberately allow them to decline. When I start a company, I do it with the goal of growing it to the point that it can operate independently of me, and that when it reaches that point, it will continue to grow, create jobs, and satisfy customers whether I'm directly involved or not.

When our education company was smaller, I was involved in every aspect. We didn't have a comprehensive long-range plan, we didn't have systems and processes, and we didn't have a plan to evaluate individual performance. But I knew if we were going to grow, we needed those things. I had been studying other successful companies, and I figured out what I had to do. If the company was going to grow, if it was going to reach its full potential, I had to get out of the way. So I went outside our company and hired senior managers who had experience running Fortune 500 companies. It was a tough decision, and it was not easy for me to let go of having total control, but it was the right decision and it produced immediate results.

MANAGE BY P&L

I manage by P&L. I look at the profit-and-loss statements of every business unit every month. If the numbers look good, I'll give the manager a call, congratulate him or her, ask if there is anything I can do to help, and then get out of the way. If the numbers are off, we might have a conversation to figure out what the problem is and what needs to be done to get back on track—and again, I get out of the way. We have some of the finest executive and managerial talent in the world on our staff, and I'm not going to stifle them by interfering. They were hired because they knew how to get the job done—not because they needed me to tell them how to get the job done.

It's really a matter of two things: First, you have to believe that there are people out there who can do things better than you. Second, you have to have the guts to hire them. So you bring them in, tell them what you expect and what you want them to do, then get out of their way and let them grow your company. It really is as simple as that.

KEEP AN EYE ON THE CASH

Watching your cash flow is one of the most important things you have to do. If something is going wrong and you're losing money, you need to know *now*. If it takes you a few months to notice, you may not be able to survive.

Learn to read financial statements and look at them often. Once a week, I get a report that shows me every bank account and how much we have in it. I also get a printout of every check we cut—who it's payable to and how much it's for. I know some CEOs insist on signing checks. I don't—I think it's a waste of my time. But I know what we're spending, and if I see anything I'm not familiar with or that looks odd, I make a note on the report and send it back to accounting for an explanation. I also review the balance sheet and profit-and-loss statements monthly.

We have a lot of checks and balances to protect the company and our employees. We have procedures that make it difficult to commit fraud, and procedures that make sure employees are never put in a position that might be suspicious. For example, if we need to send a wire transfer, one person does the paperwork and another actually sends the wire. When we get cash at events, it's always counted by two people. This isn't rocket science, it's just good business.

We don't do this because we don't trust our employees. Quite the contrary: I wouldn't have anyone working for me whom I didn't trust. But if there ever is a problem, I don't want anyone's integrity to be called into question unfairly.

STRUCTURES AND SYSTEMS

When I started investing in real estate and then moved into my first few businesses, the operations were built around me. That's typical of entrepreneurs. We're the ones with the ideas and the energy, and we're out there making things happen. But as your organization grows, and as you build your wealth, you begin to realize that it isn't wise for you to be the center of things. What you need are structures and systems that will continue to work whether you are there or not.

Right now, I don't see myself ever retiring. But I do know that one day I'll die. I hope that's a long time into the future, but it will happen to all of us. I want the companies I have worked so hard to build to go on when I'm no longer here. I want to leave a legacy not only to my children and eventual grandchildren but to my customers and students, my community, and the world. To do that, I've worked to create companies that are strong and healthy and independent of me.

Though I expect to be active in my companies for many more years, I also appreciate that I can go on vacation for a week or two or longer and know that when I return, all will be well. If I decide to surprise my wife with a romantic getaway, no one is going to freak out because we're not in the office for a few days. That's because we have structures and systems in place that are not dependent on any particular individual. We value every single member of our team, but no one is indispensable—not even me.

THE BOTTOM LINE

Have you ever worried about losing your job through no fault of your own? The reality is, there is no such thing as job security for employees anymore. But there is security for people with an entrepreneurial spirit and the determination to create their own financial security. No paycheck is more secure than the one you write to yourself. Whether you start a new business, buy an existing operation, or purchase a franchise, one of the quickest paths to financial independence is through owning a business.

CHAPTER 20

ILLUMINATE YOUR FEARS

Obstacles are the scary things you see when you take your eyes off your goals.
—RUSS WHITNEY

Let me guess how you feel now. There's a part of you that's fired up with excitement because you can truly see a future of adventure and financial freedom. You know you don't have all the answers yet, but you have plenty of ideas and you can't wait to start putting some of them into action. Then there's the part of you that's afraid. It's a fear that may be in the form of skepticism about your ability to put your ideas into action. So let's address those fears and see how to get them out of the way so you can move toward your financial goals.

The methods I'm sharing with you *work*. I've used every single one of them, over and over, and I know they work consistently. I've taught thousands of people to do the same thing, and they've been successful, too. Many of these techniques are not new; people have been using them for decades. But you don't have to be a Wall Street broker or a financial whiz kid to apply these same principles and build your own wealth.

Remember, different circumstances require different techniques, and you must be able to evaluate many situations and make the right decisions about how to handle them. Sometimes deals will fall through for reasons beyond your control; when that happens, you just go on to the next one. But if you use my methods, and you use them consistently, you will build wealth and make steady headway toward your goals.

What about your ability? Believe me, you *do* have it. My tech-niques and strategies are not difficult, nor do they take any special degree of intelligence to apply. However, they do require commit-ment, and you are demonstrating the foundation of your commit-ment right now by educating yourself on how to build wealth. Continue that commitment with more education and action.

Wealth building is a lot like cooking: just about anybody can do it. If you can read and follow instructions in a recipe, you can cook. You may not ever be the greatest chef in the world, but you can prepare meals that taste good. If you follow the strategies ex-plained in this book, you will build wealth. Your net worth may not surpass J. Paul Getty's, H. Ross Perot's, or Warren Buffett's, but you *can* become a millionaire and enjoy financial security and independence.

A student of mine who lives in Troy, Michigan, began using my methods in 1985. In seven years, he had purchased eighteen income-producing properties (eleven single-family homes, four duplexes, a triplex, a six-unit, and an eight-unit) with a total mar-ket value exceeding $1.5 million and an annual positive cash flow of more than $60,000.

The first property one of my Atlanta students purchased was a foreclosed house. The only cash he needed was for closing costs; he immediately leased the house at a monthly profit of $300, then sold it to the tenant for $10,000 more than he paid.

Another student moved to Florida from Norway in search of both a pleasant climate and economic opportunity. He bought a restaurant that failed. He tried several businesses and jobs— including selling vacuum cleaners door-to-door—before he read one of my books on real estate investing. A year later, he owned thirty-six apartments, four houses, an office building, and some lots; those properties have given him a net worth of well over $1 million and produce enough cash flow to support him and his family in comfort.

After taking our Millionaire U course, a couple from Colo-rado went home and made more than $41,000 on their first deal, a distressed property they fixed up and sold. Then they bought another property and walked away from the closing with $5,900. A Wisconsin student used my techniques to purchase a commercial building for no money down that generates $1,700 a month in positive cash flow. That same student bought a vacant lot, sold it an hour later, and made $5,500. He says, "This is so much fun." A twenty-year-old student from Kansas City bought thirteen units with no money down and walked away from the closing with $40,000 cash and more than $100,000 in equity.

I could go on, but my point is this: every day, people all over the country—indeed, all over the world—are using my techniques to build wealth and financial security. The only special thing about these people is that they have taken the time to learn how to do it and are willing to put in the effort to make their success happen. You can do it, too.

ILLUMINATE THE FEAR
BY TURNING THE LIGHT ON

When you were a child and imagined horrible monsters under the bed or in the closet, your parents helped you deal with your fear by turning the light on and showing you that the monsters didn't actually exist. What they did was illuminate your fear. Many adults are being held back by fears that are no more real than imaginary monsters—fears that would go away if a light was turned on.

One of the scariest things I've done in my life was buy my first piece of rental property. My wife and I both had knots in our stomachs about the deal. But we knew that if we were ever going to get anywhere in life, we had to make the decision. We had to try.

We made the decision and it worked.

But what was even more scary than the first property was the second and the third. The first one worked, but what if the second one didn't? Were we getting greedy? Were we making a mistake that would wipe out everything we'd gained on the first property? In spite of our fears, we made the decision. It worked. And we didn't have to face the fear of failure again—until we had to make our first half-million-dollar decision.

We looked at the numbers, and all those same fears and doubts came rushing back. But we knew that if we didn't make a decision, we couldn't move forward. We would never make any more financial progress. So we made the decision and it worked. We had overcome the fear of failure one more time. And we didn't have to face it again until our first million-dollar decision.

My point is that these fears will crop up, no matter who you are or what you're doing. They are natural and normal, but you can't let them cripple you. If you're going to get somewhere in life, you have to make decisions, and you make decisions by evaluating the logic and reason of the situation.

When we began buying rental property, my father-in-law would ask me things such as "What are you going to do if all the tenants move out? What are you going to do if all the furnaces break down?" Sure, those are scary ideas, but when I thought it through, I realized they were no more than the adult equivalent of a child's imaginary monsters. People have been renting properties in America for more than two hundred years. Just because I buy one, does that mean all the tenants will move out? Of course not, that's ridiculous.

The same thing applies to businesses. Maybe you've been thinking about buying a retail or convenience store that's been operating successfully for years. Will the customers stop coming in just because you bought it? Of course not. If you're worried that they will, you need to realize you're experiencing the natural fear of failure. Understand it, overcome it, and know that good things come only to those who seek them out. Or what about the fear you might feel when you first invest in the stock market? Are you afraid that the market will crash just because you've bought some stock? Trust me, you're not that important. The reality is that you will always be a little afraid when you step out into new territory. That's okay. Just don't let the fear stop you from moving forward and taking action.

One of my students told me she really liked the rooming house idea and could see where the need existed in her community. She could handle purchasing the property and arranging any necessary rehabilitation. What was stopping her, she said, was concern about management and maintenance. Who would mop the floors? Who would clean the bathrooms? And how would the rents be collected?

In chapter 8 I explained the mechanics of running a rooming house, so you have those answers. I could have done that with this particular student; I could just have answered her questions. But in talking with her, I wanted to help her realize that these were silly fears, not real ones. So I asked her if she inherited a rooming house today, if all of a sudden it was hers with no effort at all on her part to acquire it, and if she knew it would make her $1,500 a month on a part-time basis, would she figure out the details of running it? Would she figure out what to do if a window broke and how to keep the common areas clean? Would she manage to collect the rents?

Of course she would. She was a little embarrassed when she looked at the picture from that perspective and realized that maybe she was using her fear as an excuse to avoid action and maybe even sabotaging herself without realizing it.

When you see an opportunity but feel the fear of failure creeping up on you, you must ask yourself better questions. If you focus on the negatives, you'll stay trapped in the negatives. Don't worry about what will happen if all the tenants move out; instead, develop a plan to advertise and show your units to keep your occupancy rate as close to 100 percent as possible. Don't look at cleaning apartments between tenants or maintaining the common areas of a rooming house as oversized obstacles; just figure out a way to get the necessary work done.

Much of our fear comes from the conditioning we received as kids. Most of us had too many role models telling us that it was okay not to achieve anything significant with our lives—or, worse, telling us that we probably wouldn't be able to do it if we tried.

Most parents would be shocked to realize they were doing this. Here's how it usually happens: A child brings home a bad grade, and the parent, in an effort to be comforting, says, "It's okay, we really didn't expect you to do any better than this. We're not disappointed and we know you tried." The parent will usually add, "You'll do better next time," but do you think the child hears that part? Of course not. He's too busy processing that *underachieving is acceptable.* Conversely, when that same child does something exceptional, the parent will say, "Don't get a swelled head from it." The parent may be trying to help the child avoid becoming conceited, but the result is a message that says achievements aren't anything to strive for or be proud of.

Naturally we carry this negative conditioning into our adult lives, and when we are introduced to the abundant financial opportunities that are available, there is a major collision in our brains. We get a mixed message that results in a huge lack of confidence. We're afraid we're going to fail, so we may never even try. We literally self-sabotage. Believe you can become wealthy by putting my techniques and strategies into action and see how fast that belief becomes a reality.

I encourage you to take a close look at yourself. Study your feelings about wealth and about your present situation. Deep down, are you afraid of success? Are you afraid of becoming wealthy? If you are, use the knowledge you're gaining, your newfound confidence and common sense, and my faith in you to turn the light on your fears. Once you do, your life will become more manageable and less stressful, because you'll start to control your life instead of it controlling you.

DEVELOP MONEYMAKING, PROBLEM-SOLVING SKILLS

Dealing with your fears doesn't mean you won't have problems. Though sometimes the simple process of illuminating a fear will eliminate it, at times you will have to handle a problem. Problems are a part of life. We have big problems and little problems. We have problems that matter and problems that don't. We have problems that are easy to handle and problems that are more difficult. And that's why you need problem-solving skills.

Occasionally you're going to run into problems on your way to becoming wealthy. That's okay, because once you solve them, you'll get paid—and that can be some pretty healthy motivation. The key is not to allow problems to overwhelm you. Don't try to swallow the elephant whole; eat it bite by bite. When you think you have a problem, apply these simple steps:

Illuminate the Problem—Focus directly on the source of the problem, and make sure it truly is a problem and not simply a groundless fear. Then decide how important it really is and how much attention it requires. Too many people get all wrapped up in the little things and never get around to handling the truly important things. Don't do that. Refuse to invest your valuable time "majoring in minors." Attack the major things first.

Define the Problem—Make sure you have a clear understanding of what the problem really is. Many times the real problem is hiding behind a variety of symptoms. For example, our cancellation ratio for advanced training—that is, people who sign up for advanced courses in real estate investing or stock trading and then change their minds about attending—is fairly consistent, but occasionally we'll see a spike. We expect an occasional cancellation, but we get concerned when the number goes beyond the expected and understood amount. We also understand that the problem isn't the cancellations themselves, but *why* the students are canceling.

Identify the Cause—Once you understand the problem, track down the root cause. Examine all the possibilities until you find the real reason. When we see an increase in cancellations, we know it's not because of the quality of the education we provide. We study the reasons the students give when they cancel; sometimes we will call students and talk to them to get a better understanding of why they changed their minds about our programs. You may have to do some serious digging and research to get to the real cause of a problem, but you have to do it or you will never be able to fix the problem.

Determine How to Correct the Cause—In many cases, simply understanding the cause will highlight the solution; other cases may take some additional study and thought. Either way, the next step is to decide how best to correct the problem. We have implemented some simple but critical programs that include training for our enrollment counselors, as well as follow-up telephone calls and letters designed to address any questions or concerns the students may have.

Develop a Strategy for the Correction—Plan how you will accomplish the correction. If different people will be involved, make sure each person knows what he is responsible for and when he must do it. It's a good idea to put this strategy in writing so there are no misunderstandings.

Take Action—You know what you're going to do; now, do it.

Follow Up to Make Sure the Problem Has Been Corrected— Check back after an appropriate time to make sure your correction has the desired effect. If you have figured out the root cause and come up with a sound solution, you should see positive results. If you don't, go back to defining the problem and identifying the cause to be sure you aren't trying to fix something that isn't broken. Then consider what other changes or corrective actions you can take to get the outcome you want.

I once bought an apartment building that had what I considered excessive water consumption. The tenants weren't unusually clean, but the building did have a number of leaky faucets. New washers in the faucet fixtures solved the problem. The problem-solving process looked like this:

Define the problem: Excessive water consumption resulting in high utility costs.

Identify the cause: Leaky faucets in several apartments.

Determine how to correct the cause: Replace washers in leaking faucets.

Develop a strategy for the correction: Maintenance worker will purchase necessary parts and replace washers within two working days.

Take action: Work is done.

Follow up: Review of the next utility bill indicates water consumption has dropped to an acceptable level.

Let me emphasize to you that when I saw the high water bill, I didn't get overwhelmed and say things such as "Oh, boy, I knew this rental property would be a hassle." I just identified the problem, took it a bite at a time, got it corrected, and made money. And fixing those drippy faucets in an income-producing property I owned was a lot easier than struggling to pay bills on the low hourly wage I earned at the slaughterhouse.

After you have consciously applied the problem-solving process a few times, you'll be so comfortable with it that it will become automatic. With a systematic approach to problems, you'll never be overwhelmed, no matter how complicated they may appear on the surface.

GO ON THE OFFENSIVE

The best way to deal with problems is to avoid them in the first place by adopting offensive rather than defensive strategies. One of the areas where this is absolutely critical is asset protection.

By asset protection, I mean protecting what you've worked so hard to acquire from attack by frivolous lawsuits and fraudulent claims. Asset protection also involves taking advantage of every possible legitimate tax-reduction strategy and making sure that your estate is structured in a way that reduces the tax burden on your heirs. If you have a legitimate debt, pay it. If somebody is injured on your property and you're responsible, step up and do the right thing—if you're properly insured, this shouldn't be a problem. But don't let the government or anyone else take anything from you that they're not entitled to.

I discuss asset protection in detail in my books *Millionaire*

Real Estate Mentor and *The Millionaire Real Estate Mindset.* We also offer three-day comprehensive training in asset protection through Wealth Intelligence Academy™ (see "Resources" for more information), which will teach you how to set up your business and explain the various forms of ownership for your assets. I highly recommend that you learn the principles of asset management early on in your wealth-building journey.

DON'T SWEAT THE SMALL STUFF

If it isn't important, don't worry about it.

THE BENEFITS OF MAKING WRONG DECISIONS

I could quote you a whole string of cute and catchy clichés about the concept of failure, but you've probably heard them all already. Notice I use the word *concept,* because that's all failure is. Failure is a state of mind. It's not real; it's just an attitude and a way of thinking that you have the power either to accept or reject.

Now, I'm not going to guarantee that you will never have a brief setback on your way to wealth; in fact, I can almost guarantee that you will. But learning from your mistakes will make you stronger, more capable, and eventually wealthier.

A bad decision is better than no decision at all. Indecision is the greatest thief of opportunity. Indecision will rob your bank account and your peace of mind. Indecision will steal from you daily.

Think about this: You may be worrying about making the right decision on a wealth-building strategy, but what will it cost you if you do nothing at all? You'll stay where you are, worrying about paying bills and getting deeper in debt. No matter what kinds of problems you have, they'll be easier to manage with money in the bank. I know that wealth is not a cure-all, but it will remove some of the stress from your life and give you the freedom to handle your nonfinancial issues.

While you sit on the fence not making a decision, the clock keeps ticking. Another second of your life is used up with every tick of the clock. Don't sit on that fence wondering what will happen if you get off on the wrong side—just get off! If you find you've chosen the wrong side, you can always climb back over the fence. Remember this: wrong decisions give you the experience you need to make better decisions the next time.

CHAPTER 21

Get Started Building Your Personal Fortune

Reach high, for stars lie hidden in your soul. Dream deep, for every dream precedes a goal.
—Pamela Vaull Starr

Now that you're at the beginning of your own path to financial freedom and wealth, you're excited, you're motivated, and you can't wait to get started. You have learned how to find seed money and grow it into serious capital. You know how to make money in real estate and how to watch for and benefit from other business opportunities. You know, too, that you've probably been the victim of bad programming. Most, if not all, of the people in your life up until now have told you that you can't be wealthy. Your parents, teachers, other role models, and even your peers have sent you the message that wealth is beyond you, that financial success is for others, that whatever you try to do to break out of your mediocre mold won't work.

It's not true! You *can* be wealthy, you *can* be successful, and you *can* make a difference in the world.

You can reverse the negative programming you've received over the years with Mindfeed. You're already off to a good start, but you must prepare now if you are to maintain the momentum you've built. Remember, it's not the how-to or even the want-to that will get you wealthy—it's the will-do. And the will-do is the most challenging part of wealth building, because it is easily sabotaged by negativity.

Fight back by setting aside time every day for Mindfeed. Reread this book and look for positive messages. Collect books and audio programs by people who have something worthwhile to share. Study wealthy people. Learn their habits and techniques, and make those habits and techniques your own. Reject negativity. Wealthy people don't have time to be negative. The winners of this world consciously look for the good and avoid the bad, and Mindfeed is the tool you can use to make yourself a winner.

MAKE YOURSELF UNCOMFORTABLE

When I'm teaching or speaking to groups and I ask for a show of hands from the people who want to be successful, every single hand in the room is waving. But when I ask how many people are willing to do what it takes to be successful, at least half of the hands go down. Those people don't have the mind-set for wealth.

What is a wealth mind-set? It's the ability and willingness to identify, focus on, and take action on a wealth-building vehicle. It's staying open to new ideas and new opportunities. It's flexibility and creativity. It's doing what it takes so you can enjoy the rewards.

The single thing that prevents more people from becoming wealthy is their comfort zone. If you're comfortable, if you're getting by, if your house is okay, your car runs, and you're earning enough to pay your bills every month, it may be hard for you to find the motivation to develop the wealth mind-set.

Human beings are, for the most part, creatures of habit. Are you comfortable with your habits of getting up, going to work every day, coming home, and watching television every evening, maybe fitting in a little hobby or community work on the side? If you are, you may feel you have no reason to change. As long as you are satisfied with your life, your life will never be anything different from what it is.

But let's say you lost your job, or your spouse or one of your parents became seriously ill, and you needed money. Would that make you uncomfortable enough to change your habits? Would you be uncomfortable enough to develop a wealth-building mind-set?

Here's something else to think about. You may be comfortable today, with heat in the winter, air-conditioning in the summer, and plenty to eat, but what's going to happen when you retire? According to a variety of different studies, the majority of Americans expect a significant decline in their standard of living when they retire. A report by the Economic Policy Institute said that more than 40 percent of households headed by someone between the ages of forty-seven and sixty-four will not be able to replace even half of their income once the person stops working—and nearly 20 percent will have incomes below the poverty level. Believe me, *that's not comfortable*! And as our expected life spans increase, that means more years of poverty and penny-pinching and working menial jobs to make ends meet because we spent our earlier years being comfortable instead of building financial security.

Getting uncomfortable may be easier for people who are truly miserable, people who are like I was at the age of twenty, with little education, a dead-end job, and a family to support. But you must have at least a small sense of discomfort if, deep down, you know that you can have more material things, that your bank balance can be larger, that you can build a future that is truly secure and not based on the economy or the whims of the market.

Let's build on that feeling of being uncomfortable, because that's the feeling that will drive you out of your present rut and propel you toward wealth and financial independence. And you know where to start. You have to get disgusted. You have to make a decision to change. You have to visualize that change becoming a reality. And you must take the action necessary to make it happen.

TRY SOMETHING

Once you're feeling uncomfortable, you must do something. Don't wait until you've read ten or twenty or even two hundred more books, or gone to ten or twenty seminars, or listened to more audio programs. If you wait, you'll end up with all the information you need, you'll be smart, but you'll still be broke. You must keep reading, listening, and learning, but you must take action at the same time. Action will build your personal fortune one step at a time. Then all of a sudden one day you'll look up and be stunned by the magnitude of what all those little actions have done for you.

If I said to you that you must go out and buy an income-producing property with a positive cash flow within sixty days or you would die, do you think you could do it? Of course you could. And if you could do one within sixty days, do you think you could do a second one within the following thirty days? The answer, again, is yes.

Of course, the motivation in this example is extreme, but if you read this book and don't do anything to change your financial circumstances, I believe that a small part of you, deep inside, will die. One little bit at a time, your dreams will wither and die because you never did anything to keep them alive.

The time between this moment, right now, and your first action is critical. Anticipation builds anxiety, and anxiety builds fear. Think about it. When you're at the doctor's office and you find out you need a shot, the anticipation of the needle going in is usually much worse than the injection itself. The longer you wait to take action, the more boogeymen your mind will conjure up.

Action overcomes anxiety and fear. Action gives you the opportunity to see what you can really do, to see if you really have what it takes to make your dreams and wishes come true. Action will make you wealthy.

So try something—anything. And if the first thing you try doesn't work, try something else.

From there it's just a matter of duplication. If you can do it once, you've got what it takes to be rich. Because if you can do it once, you can do it again, and again, until you build your personal fortune.

UPGRADE OR QUIT

Once you've had a taste of success, once you've made some money in business or real estate, then you can decide if you want more. Did you enjoy yourself, does it feel good, is this something you want to do again? Or did you hate it, did it make you think that living from paycheck to paycheck and retiring in poverty is okay?

We know that money makes money and success breeds success. I believe that if you have just one financial achievement under your belt, you'll want more, and you'll get more.

If you inherited a business, would you learn how to run it? If you won a million dollars in a lottery, would you learn how to manage that money? If you were given a rental property, would you learn how to maintain it and keep it producing positive cash flow? I believe you would. And you know you would. And since we both know that you can do what it takes, what's stopping you?

The only possible thing it could be is fear. One way to take care of that fear is to give yourself permission to quit. The catch is that you can't quit until you have one success.

Think about it: one success, and then you can quit.

Or you can keep going, which is what I believe you will do. Because that one success will prove what I've been telling you, and it will give you the confidence to keep going.

So just do one small deal. One little duplex. One part-time, home-based business. Do it right, according to the formulas I've given you. Savor the taste of success. Revel in the freedom to control your own life. And make your own decisions about your future.

FIND A NICHE

Finding a niche allows you to focus your energies on one or two profitable ideas. It gives you the chance to learn all you need to know about them and to sharpen your skills in those areas so you can maximize your opportunities.

In real estate, for example, you'll find that certain techniques work better in some parts of the country than others. I've seen many students become specialists in government grants and rehabilitating low-income housing. You'll find that the older, larger cities have more government grant monies than rural areas or new communities.

Along the same lines, both college towns and inner cities are usually excellent opportunities for rooming houses. Remember, one or two rooming houses can mean financial independence for you. The experience you'll gain by making those one or two investments will make the rest easy, because you'll have all your renovation and management systems in place.

In urban areas, you may concentrate on apartment houses. In the suburbs, your focus may be on single-family homes. You may do particularly well in the area of foreclosures, or you may have a talent for putting together lease-option deals. Just find a niche that you're comfortable with, that you can become an expert at, and make it work for you.

In other businesses, the same strategy applies. Find a well-defined area where you can become an expert. Identify a need that isn't being met and figure out a way to meet it. Then create an operation that can run with or without you.

When you see an opportunity, latch onto it and work it for all it's worth. It could be the tidal wave you ride to success and wealth.

COURAGE AND GUTS

Courage is the ability to face the unknown, to take something you don't know about, figure it out, and get it done. We draw courage both from within ourselves and from outside sources.

When you've made your plans and started to put them into action, and things don't go quite as you thought they would, it takes guts to keep going. It's much easier to admit your failure and go back to nestle in the comfort of the ordinary masses. They'll take you back, too, because quitting makes you one of them. They'll pat you on the shoulder, give you a few "I told you so"'s, and reaffirm their own conviction that wealth is beyond them.

It takes guts to face the rejection and torment you'll get from the 95 Percenters in your life. It takes guts to keep going after you've encountered a few setbacks. It takes guts to be different, to become wealthy.

You might be full of great plans right now and get shot down on your first few telephone calls. Or you might start out with a few great successes and hit a dry spell just when you think you're on a roll. And you might think that the whole thing won't work, that you can't get wealthy. You might think that going to work and drawing a paycheck is a whole lot easier than this get-rich business.

But if you have guts, you'll get over that and get back on track.

JERK YOURSELF OUT OF THE ROUTINE

Your first step to building wealth is to change your routine right now. Jerk yourself out of your comfortable rut, the humdrum pattern you've gotten used to. Get up an hour earlier. If you usually get up at six o'clock, set your alarm for five. Go to bed a little earlier if necessary. You don't need to watch the late-night news;

there's nothing on that broadcast that you won't hear or read about tomorrow. If you eat meals at a certain time, eat at a different time. Do something different!

Set up an area in your home to serve as your office. If you have a spare room, great; if you don't, set aside a corner when you can put a desk, a chair, and a telephone. Make this designated area a place where you do business and nothing else. The kids don't play there, you don't watch television there. This is your space for serious time, serious thinking, and serious action.

In your office, begin building your Mindfeed library. Arrange your business reference material so you have easy access to it. Put this book in a prominent spot so you can refer back to it. And if you didn't use a marker to highlight what you thought were important points as you read, go back through this book and do it now—and do it with every Mindfeed book you read from now on.

Spend time at your desk early every morning before you have to head off to your job. Get the newspaper and start reading the classified ads. Make some phone calls to prospect on property or other business opportunities. You don't have to commit yourself, but do something different and learn how wealth-building activities feel. Call a few real estate agents. Tell them you're looking for cosmetically distressed low- and moderate-income properties with owner financing and that you have money to put down. Let them get to work for you finding properties you can use to build your wealth. Then go take a look; get used to inspecting real estate. You don't have to commit to anything, you don't have to buy. But if you take this action enough times, you just might find a great deal, so be prepared for that.

WAKE 'EM UP EARLY AND MAKE 'EM SAY THANKS

Start making your calls early, as early as 7:00 a.m. You may think calling people at this time of the morning will upset them or make them angry. But think about this. If you're spending good money to run an ad to sell a piece of property or a business and someone calls you at seven in the morning because he or she might want to buy it, are you going to be upset? Of course not. You'd welcome the call—and you might even feel just a little bit guilty or embarrassed that you weren't up earlier so you could answer the phone in a sharp, crisp voice. Making calls early in the morning puts you at an advantage, not a disadvantage.

When you make calls this early, you won't reach a lot of answering machines or voice-mail boxes. But if you do get an answering machine or for some reason you can't reach the right person, set aside a time in the evening when you know you'll be home to take calls; when you leave your message, let the seller know when to call you back. That lets you concentrate your business into designated hours so you'll be more productive.

Plan the rest of your day and evening to get the most out of the time you have. Turn off the television; successful people don't spend much time in front of the TV. Take charge of your life. Break up your old routine at all costs; that was the routine of mediocrity. You now want to establish a routine of wealth.

SET PERSONAL FORTUNE GOALS

You hear about goals all the time, and I've even mentioned the importance of goals several times in this book. What's interesting about goals is that most people think they have them. They want to be rich, or they want to own a fancy car or a big house. They think about it, they fantasize about it, and they might even tell a few people about it—and so they think they have goals. But those aren't goals, they're dreams.

When you just think and wish and talk, it's a dream.

But when you write it down and commit to it, it's a goal.

That's right, you commit by writing your goals down, giving them deadlines, and figuring out a plan to achieve them.

And it isn't easy. So once you've got your office set up, make goal setting a priority. You need goals to give you direction, to help you plan each day to bring you closer to your personal fortune, to make your life richer both personally and professionally.

As you set financial goals, it's also important to remember that money is a result, not a cause. If your cause is right and if you do your business correctly, you will make money. Set action goals—that is, things that you can do that will produce the financial results you want. For example, if you buy income-producing property, and you do it with the formulas I've given you, you'll make money. If you buy a business, and if you research it thoroughly and run it wisely, you'll make money.

So make your goals things you can literally do and check off when they're complete. Not "I want to be rich," but "I want to own ten income-producing properties" or "I want to start my own business by a specific date, and I will take the following actions every day [list them] to achieve this goal."

Your goals must have a life of their own. When you see the words you've written, you need to see more than just ink and paper. You need to be able to see that goal coming to pass; you need to be able to see a future that is far better than today.

Develop both short- and long-term goals. Where do you want to be in five years? In three? In one? What will your bank account and investment portfolio look like? What will your business look like? Most important, what will *you* look like? Set your goals high enough so you have to stretch to reach them, but not so high that they are unattainable.

In my early days of investing, I set a goal of buying one hundred rental units in one year. That sounds like a lot, especially if you've never invested in real estate or don't have much cash, but it's realistic and attainable. I know today that it was a realistic goal, because I did it. And I've had more students than I can count do the same.

Now, I understand why the phrase "buy one hundred rental units in one year" can seem overwhelming to most people. If I had set that goal and done nothing else, it would probably have been overwhelming to me, too. But after I decided that my one-year goal was one hundred units, I asked myself what I had to do in the first six months. To do one hundred units a year, I only had to buy fifty in six months. That's still a large number. So I broke it down to three months, and I only had to buy twenty-five units. That's just eight units a month, or one little duplex a week.

Just one duplex a week means you can meet a goal of one hundred units in a year. Just one eight-unit rooming house means you've met your monthly goal. A twenty-four-unit apartment building means you've almost met your three-month goal. It doesn't sound so difficult when you look at it from that point of view.

The year I set this goal, I ended up with 123 units. At times I went weeks without buying any property, but then I'd find a property ideal for a ten-unit rooming house conversion or a great eight-unit apartment building. At the end of the year, I'd met my goals—and the money was rolling in.

Once you have your goals clearly spelled out and broken down into manageable increments, you must then decide what you have to do to accomplish them. Those are your daily tasks, and they, too, need to be written down, given a deadline, and checked off when they're completed. For example, your daily tasks might look like this:

1. Get up at 5:30 a.m.
2. Make as many calls from the classified ads as possible (at least ten).
3. Have flyers printed.
4. Tell at least five people that I am investing in real estate and looking for properties.
5. Talk to at least two real estate agents.

A fundamental part of goal setting is maximizing your available time. Time is what puts everyone on a level playing field. It's a nonrenewable resource; when it's gone, it's gone, and you can't get it back. I have twenty-four hours in my day—no more and no less than you do in yours. It's what you choose to do during those hours that will keep you broke or make you wealthy.

DAY PLANNING

If you don't have a good day-planner, you need to get one. Use it to write down your daily tasks and appointments, then check things off as you accomplish them. Take it with you everywhere, and use it for both personal and business items. Your daughter's music recital is just as important as inspecting a piece of property, and you want to be sure you don't let those events overlap. Keeping more than one calendar is cause for confusion, so don't do it. And if you have your day-planner with you all the time, you'll never forget something because it didn't get logged in the right place.

You can spend a lot of money on a paper or electronic calendar system, or you can keep track of your appointments and tasks in a spiral-bound notebook. The method doesn't matter; the key is to use a system that works easily for you. Many of the traditional time-management systems are too complicated to be truly effective. What's important in a day-planner, whether it's paper or electronic, is that you have a place to record appointments, things you need to do, and follow-up notes. The nice thing about electronic systems is that you can program them to remind you of upcoming events with an alarm, and you can transfer information from your handheld unit to someone else's unit. Shop around and ask people who are organized and successful what system they use, then decide what will work best for you.

Every year, I set aside time in December to plan my goals for the coming year. I write them down, then break them into monthly and weekly goals. Then I note what I need to do day by day in my planner. I encourage you to do the same. Start with long-range goals, then break them down into manageable monthly and daily goals. Write them down in your day-planner; put the yearly goals in the back if you're using a paper system or in a separate file if you're using an electronic system, then note the monthly and daily items throughout the calendar where they belong.

Writing down goals and making to-do lists is only part of effective goal setting. I also use my planner to record notes about what I've accomplished so I can make adjustments if necessary. In effect, you have to keep score; if you don't, how will you know where you stand? You wouldn't go into a championship basketball game without keeping score, and you couldn't hold a successful charity fund-raiser without tracking how much money you collect.

So set goals and keep score. Know whether you're winning or losing the game of life.

KEEP YOUR EYES OPEN

You must put your goals in writing, but they should never be written in stone. You can adjust them up or down, or in a different direction entirely. Once you get going on your wealth-building plan, more things are going to come your way than you ever thought about, and you need to be prepared to take advantage of them.

You might run into someone selling a small apartment building who is also selling a business you could be interested in. You might meet a contractor who knows about a new government grant program you can take advantage of if you change your strategy just a little. When you're playing the wealth game, opportunities will happen to you, so don't be surprised when the source is unexpected. Keep your eyes open and be prepared to take advantage of anything that comes along.

Pay particular attention to the cycles of the economy we discussed in chapter 6. Remember, when the economy is slow and prices are down, it's a good time to buy and arrange seller financing. When the economy picks up, go back to those sellers and arrange for discounts on their mortgages. Consider selling the property or the business when you can get top dollar for them.

You don't need a degree in economics to watch for economic cycles. Pay attention to the news, but keep your guard up against too much negativity. Track property prices. Listen to your instincts. You'll know when the time is right to buy and to sell.

THE FUEL FOR WEALTH

Energy is the fuel for wealth, so develop productive habits that keep you energized. That means talking in an enthusiastic tone, standing up straight, and smiling. It means staying in shape with proper diet and exercise. You don't have to jog thirty miles or lose fifty pounds by next week, but you should set some goals to improve your physical condition to increase your energy level.

If you maintain a positive energy level, you never have to be depressed. Have you ever seen an energetic depressed person? Of course not. That doesn't mean you won't ever have problems; some days will always be better than others. But why is it that when some people get depressed, they stay down for an hour, and others stay down for three months?

How long you are depressed is your decision. It's up to you. When you get tired of it, you'll do something to get out of it. So take a walk. Eat a nutritious meal. Get some fresh air. Laugh out loud. Do whatever it takes to keep your energy level up, because energy beats depression. Energy gives you hope to visualize your dreams. And energy is your fuel for wealth.

WHAT TO DO SATURDAY NIGHT
OR SUNDAY MORNING

Most of us associate Monday morning with going back to work, back to the grind, back to the salt mines. We talk about the Monday-morning blahs. You might find it hard to begin your wealth-building program on a day that has such a bad reputation. But don't wait to start getting wealthy—do it now! Whatever time or day it is right now, make your plan and put it into action. Get out of your rut. Make every day a great day because now you're working for yourself and your financial future. You're going to do the things that the 95 Percenters can't or won't do. You're an achiever, so get excited about it.

Go back through this book and focus on the one or two wealth-building techniques you're going to try first. Though I have used every technique explained in this book, I didn't apply them all at once. That would have been impossible, and I wouldn't be where I am today if I had tried. You shouldn't try to do it all at once, either. Just choose one or two ideas and make some plans to accomplish those things. Put your plans into motion, make them work, and then go on to something else. If you take a systematic approach, you will see results—and you'll see them quickly.

COME BACK FOR YOUR WEALTH WORKOUT

A man who runs a health club gave me a statistic I think is ridiculous. He said that 40 percent of the people who join health clubs never come back for their first workout. Think about that! These people pay hundreds of dollars and never get any benefit at all from their investment. They don't even try it and decide they don't like it. They don't do anything at all!

Reading this book through the first time is the equivalent of signing up at a health club. To really get any benefit from your investment of time and money, you must come back for your workout. Because this is the workout of wealth.

RESOURCE GUIDE

⎯⎯⎯◦⧉◦⎯⎯⎯

Investment training resources available through:

Wealth Intelligence Academy
1612 East Cape Coral Parkway
Cape Coral, FL 33904
(800) 737-9533
www.wiacademy.com

REAL ESTATE INVESTING

Millionaire U™: a three-day, hands-on program that teaches how to find investment properties, how to talk to sellers, how to finance purchases, how to build a professional support team (a Power Team), as well as a field trip where students visit properties that are actually on the market to learn how to evaluate those units and formulate real-world offers.

Wholesale Buying: students learn to locate, evaluate, and negotiate for wholesale properties; how to find owners of vacant properties; how to assign contracts and set up double closings; and how to develop profitable exit strategies.

Foreclosure Training: during this intense three-day program, students learn foreclosure basics and strategies, how to find foreclosures and make contact with owners, how to determine values and create a profitable deal, how to buy at auction, short sales, and more.

Lease Option: these solid, proven strategies show students how to control property without buying it, how to buy with little or no money down, and how to maximize cash flow with a variety of creative techniques; students learn a variety of techniques and strategies, including how to get paid multiple times from a single deal.

Property Management and Cash Flow: a three-day comprehensive course in property management that includes how to acquire property, legal issues, evictions, risk management, tenant and landlord rights and responsibilities, taxes, rental subsidies, and more.

Commercial Real Estate Investing: students learn how to locate and determine the value of commercial properties, the ins and outs of commercial leases, and how to profitably manage commercial real estate.

Keys to Creative Real Estate Financing: this three-day training program shows students how to structure financing with bad credit or no credit, prepare and present a powerful financial statement, work with a mortgage broker, work with bank lenders, work with hard money lenders, create a mortgage, and more.

Manufactured/Mobile Homes & RV Parks: students learn how to develop and operate a manufactured/mobile home or RV park; how to buy, sell, and rent existing manufactured/mobile homes; how to get bargains through foreclosures and repossessions; how to line up regular and unconventional financing; and more.

Rehabbing for Profit: a real-life training that teaches students how to plan the job; create a cost estimate and time line; streamline the permitting process; understand codes, zoning, insurance, and risk; when to do it yourself and when to hire someone; and more.

Asset Protection and Tax Relief: students learn to develop a personal step-by-step plan to protect both business and personal assets, reduce income taxes, and eliminate estate taxes.

Discount Notes & Mortgages: students learn how the cash flow industry in general and the discount notes and mortgages business in particular can help build wealth and enhance real estate investing.

Land Investing and Development—Domestic: students learn

seven strategies to profit from the ground up; how to invest in vacant land, create value, make a market, control value, and create pricing.

Land Investing and Development—International: at a luxurious resort in Costa Rica, students learn how to invest in foreign real estate; how to build an offshore Power Team; how to develop multijurisdictional strategies for true asset protection; as well as having the opportunity to network with some of the world's best international finance and investment planners and practitioners.

STOCK MARKET INVESTING

Master Trader: students receive a complete foundation of practical advanced technical analysis; learn ideal trends and topping/bottoming characteristics; swing and position trading; exiting guidelines and a refined stop adjustment strategy; and more.

Trading P.I.T.: this three-day program shows students how to master bi-directional trading and profit whether the stock goes up or down; how to successfully hedge trades; increase profit potential through the power of online resources; enter and exit a trade with strategies used by professionals; and more.

Advanced P.I.T.: building on the Trading P.I.T. course, this program teaches students nine advanced spread strategies; how to lock in on winning trades and adjust underperforming ones; how to flip from bullish to bearish and vice versa on open positions; and more.

H.I.T.S. (Hedging and Institutional Tactics and Strategies): this program covers revolutionary new tools, including single stock futures, indices, and ETFs, and keeps students "in the know" with the latest trading developments.

The Trading Room: in this unique program, trading principles are taught and applied to live market scenarios as a group or individually, depending on the student's risk parameters.

Advanced Covered Calls: students learn to generate reliable, predictable, consistent monthly cash flow by writing calls and puts while building a highly profitable stock portfolio.

Home-study programs available through www.russwhitney .com.

Building Wealth Home Study Course: the home-study version of Russ Whitney's Millionaire U Advanced Training; package includes manuals, software, videotapes, and CDs taken from the heart of Russ's live training.

One in a Million 90 Day Challenge: the plan and tools necessary to break the chains that have held you back so that you can achieve your goals, win at the game of life, and build your own personal fortune.

Overcoming the Hurdles & Pitfalls of Real Estate Investing: Russ Whitney's first book, outlining his early days as a real estate investor and how he went from being a laborer to one of America's youngest self-made millionaires.

Millionaire Real Estate Mentor by Russ Whitney: the bestselling book that helps you identify the real estate investments that are right for your talents, temperament, interests, and circumstances, and shows you how you can create a net worth of $1 million or more in a year or less—even if you have nothing now.

The Millionaire Real Estate Mindset by Russ Whitney: the groundbreaking bestseller that answers the question, "Why aren't you rich?" and provides a specific plan for mastering the mental skills to build your fortune in real estate.

INDEX

Free
Real Estate Workshop
Certificate

As a thank you for purchasing *Building Wealth*,
Russ Whitney cordially invites **you and a guest** to attend a local
FREE Real Estate Workshop.

Designed to keep you on track, moving towards your next
important step - this motivational event will help you focus
on your success goals.

At this workshop, a member of Russ' own Wealth Team
will expand on the valuable insights provided in this
book by discussing:

- Investing strategies that work in *your* market
- How to buy real estate at 30%-40% below market value
- How to establish an unsecured line of credit
- How to get cash back at every closing
- Preparing yourself for the really BIG deals
- How *you* can invest in and develop raw land
- New international real estate investing options
- How to live debt-free and achieve your dreams

"Keep your eye on where you are going, not where you have been."
– Russ Whitney

To register for a FREE workshop in your area go to
www.russwhitney.com/buildingwealth/workshop
Or call **1-877-296-4700**

BW051006